READING THE NEW TESTAMENT

Also by Patrick Grant

THE TRANSFORMATION OF SIN: STUDIES IN DONNE, HERBERT,
    VAUGHAN AND TRAHERNE
*IMAGES AND IDEAS IN LITERATURE OF THE ENGLISH
    RENAISSANCE
*SIX MODERN AUTHORS AND PROBLEMS OF BELIEF
*LITERATURE OF MYSTICISM IN WESTERN TRADITION.
A DAZZLING DARKNESS: AN ANTHOLOGY OF WESTERN
    MYSTICISM
*LITERATURE AND THE DISCOVERY OF METHOD IN THE
    ENGLISH RENAISSANCE

*Also published by Macmillan

Reading the
New Testament

PATRICK GRANT
Professor of English
University of Victoria, British Columbia

MACMILLAN
PRESS

First published 1989

Published by
THE MACMILLAN PRESS LTD
Houndmills, Basingstoke, Hampshire RG21 2XS
and London
Companies and representatives
throughout the world

Typeset by Mid-County Press, London, S.W.15, England
Printed in China

British Library Cataloguing in Publication Data
Grant, Patrick, 1941–
Reading the New Testament.
1. Bible. N.T.—Commentaries
I. Title
225.7   BS2341.2
ISBN 0–333–43618–0

For My Parents
Anne and Desmond Grant

Contents

Contents

Preface

The worst bad men, C. S. Lewis says, are religious bad men, and I am a great suspector of religious faith in case it turns out to be the bad sort. The present study suggests that a literary reading of the New Testament reveals that the documents are deeply insightful about the perilous nature of faith, and about how uneasily it can stand in relation to our sense of reason, justice and freedom. I do not imply that the New Testament somehow 'really' attacks the faith it so imperatively recommends; only that it presents the problems of religious belief imaginatively and in a strong form, so that the full challenge of faith is brought home to us.

I would like to thank James P. Mackey, who encouraged me in this undertaking from the start, and whose advice has been of inestimable help throughout, as has the example especially of his book, *Jesus, the Man and the Myth*. I thank Larry Hurtado and Ian McDonald for sharing their expertise as New Testament specialists, and for great kidness in reading my typescript. As ever, Charles Doyle, Laurence Lerner and A. D. Nuttall have provided astute criticism and helpful advice without which the inadequacies of this book would be considerably more pronounced.

Quotations throughout are from the Revised Standard Version.

1

Introduction: the New Testament and the Literary Reader

It is difficult to say exactly what sort of book the New Testament is. It consists of twenty seven documents, broadly classifiable as gospels, letters, acts and apocalypse. Of these main kinds, the gospel is peculiarly Christian; the other three were familiar property in the ancient world, adapted by the New Testament authors to their special purposes. Yet it is not clear how much the gospel is indebted to other sorts of writing to which it seems closely related, such as memoirs or the 'lives of famous men'. Moreover, the word 'gospel' (*euaggelion*) in the New Testament always applies to speech and dialogue rather than writing, and was not therefore originally used to describe a book.[1] Likewise, Paul's use of letters for preaching purposes has left scholars uneasily conscious of how different is the result from ordinary letters in the ancient world. And although the title 'Acts' (*praxeis*) was conventionally used to describe narratives of heroic deeds, the author of the book we now call *The Acts of the Apostles* does not use the word at all. The canonical title was added long after the book was composed. Finally, although John's Revelation draws on examples of apocalyptic writing from the intertestamental period, it differs from them by not being pseudonymous, and by its strong emphasis on prophecy.[2]

The language of the New Testament is also a mixture of elements. The actual texts are in *koine*, the popular Greek of the Hellenistic world. *Koine* was not a literary language, and seems not to have been Jesus' first language either, for he spoke Aramaic, a dialect akin to Hebrew but distinct from it. Yet Greek was widely used in Palestine, and Jesus might have been bilingual, as many Jews were. Certainly, the New Testament texts abound with echoes of Aramaic, as they do also with echoes of the Hebrew scriptures, though these frequently come through the Greek Septuagint. As Amos Wilder says, none of the New Testament writings would have been classified as 'literature' in the

Roman Empire.[3] The New Testament, in short, is an anomalous and peculiar set of documents without conventional literary pretensions.

Indeed, it is sometimes held that the New Testament is authoritative precisely because it is not literary in a conventional way. Critics such as C. S. Lewis and Helen Gardner make this point in order to highlight the overriding historical claim that Jesus, the chief character in the New Testament story, is in fact God.[4] Whatever else one might think about Jesus the crucified-and-risen-one (as the early church would have it), the claim that he was God has made history on a grand scale, and that is one clue to his identity. And from the centre of that identity comes a piercing utterance about the Reign of God, a declaration that salvation is available in the present moment and that judgement will come upon us. Jesus thus proclaims himself as the event which clarifies history, so that there can be no turning back, no avoidance of decision. 'I and my Father are one' (John 10:30), he says with breathtaking effrontery, and if we are to have eternal life, we must believe (John 3:36); otherwise, we stumble amidst the shadows of this world, to our own undoing and the undoing of others' good around us. Such claims might well be sustained by a fascinating set of narratives and letters, symbols and parables, but basically they are impatient of a merely fictive imagination.

The distinction which I am now beginning to draw between literature and history, however, can easily be over-simplified, and a great deal depends on how I have used the word 'conventional'. The New Testament might not fit accepted notions of literary excellence in the Roman Empire, but our decision about its historical claims is inextricably bound up with the vision of human experience which the story presents. In St. Paul's epistles, for example, we can feel on the one hand a theologian's mind at work, convinced that definitive truth has been revealed in Jesus and now must be understood. Paul's semi-technical terms – flesh, spirit, body, heart, law, grace, charity and so on – declare his conviction that Jesus is the Christ who introduces a new dispensation of grace and offers salvation to those who believe in redemption through his death and resurrection. Yet, on the other hand, Paul's special words are often used with shades of meaning appropriate for his different audiences, and reflect his own developing thought. Although he struggles to make clear the one, central fact of Jesus' saving significance, Paul's concepts are imbued with the suggestiveness of metaphor, presenting us with ideas richly fraught with emotion and the rhetoric of desire. The very fractiousness of his audiences, with their misunderstandings and enthusiasm, their resistance and evasions, causes Paul's writing to veer and swerve as would a dialogue (or, more accurately, one side of a dialogue), full of persuasive energy and careful solicitude, expressing a variety of moods from love and affection to exasperation and anger.

In a similar manner, Jesus' amazing clarity in the gospels is complicated by the fact that there are four of them. His message does not come to us univocally, but through a set of stories – or versions of the same story – each with different emphases and a different slant. The final redactors draw upon traditions of oral, written and liturgical materials which they are at pains to relate faithfully, but they also address particular problems in their communities, and their distinctive situations and aims are reflected in their writing.

Admittedly, each gospel relates the same main events: Jesus was proclaimed by John the Baptist, preached in Galilee where he performed miracles, proceeded to Jerusalem where he was tried, executed, and rose from the dead. This very consistency, however, makes the wide variety of other elements – in chronology, miracles, parables, details of the trial and so on – all the more provocative. Our impulse is to settle down and eke out from the different versions an account of what actually happened. And yet at every turn we are prevented, because there is no account in the New Testament of a historical Jesus distinct from the faith in him held by those who composed the documents. Also, the Jesus of the gospels is surprisingly unconcerned about his autobiography apart from his mission to proclaim the Father.[5] In a way, the overpowering assertion that his message is supremely relevant is inversely proportionate to our sense of his individual, historical identity. Relevance and identity (as Jürgen Moltmann says)[6] are polar opposites. Thus, Jesus the individual remains deeply enigmatic because we do not really know him separately from the relevance of his preaching the Reign of his Father who sent him. This preaching is developed through parables, metaphors, symbols, and other literary devices which engage our desire for transcendent meaning. In short, the objective, historical claims that the gospels make about Jesus are not clearly separable from their imaginative expression.

Consequently, the New Testament is laden with indirection. This is the case with its language, generic peculiarities, its message and interpretation of events. Sorting out the innumerable difficulties raised by such issues is the labour of professional Biblical scholars, and debate about the various layers of traditional and other material, the interdependence of documents and reliability of texts is dauntingly sophisticated. Yet this very sophistication re-confirms the experience that even a casual reader might have, of being thrown into the midst of some complexly-layered experience which resists our efforts to get a firm hold of it, to see it steadily from an assured viewpoint. Indeed, the quality of literary indirection itself expresses the process theologians would later describe as incarnation. Eternal truths, that is, come to us in and through our contact with material things within certain circumstances, and it is important to grasp the pertinacity of this fact: we are not to flee the material world nor our own contingency, but to cherish these as the means by which the Reign of God can enter our human realm. The New Testament tells us that while we participate in such a process we live by faith, or partial sight, for we do not see God face to face. We know, that is, imperfectly because we are in the midst, and life does not offer us a resting place. Even our hopes of happiness and justice force us to acknowledge the negative power of all in the world impeding their realisation, and again Jesus offers us a hard example in his own death. There was no security for him either, going among the things of this world with his imperative blessing of love and forgiveness.

However, we should not forget that scholarship since the nineteenth century has striven carefully, and fruitfully, to pursue the kind of distinction with which I began this chapter, by attempting as far as possible to disentangle actual history in the New Testament from its mythic embellishments and imaginative indirection. To those nineteenth-century scholars who sought to conduct research on the life of Jesus and the evolution of New Testament documents in a manner fit to win respect from hard-headed positivists, imagination and myth seemed exactly the kind of words to condemn rather than extol.[7] Such language suggested fiction rather than fact, fanciful interpretation of reality rather than reality itself. Nor is this concern without substance, because it is indeed important for faith at some point to declare that the New Testament is not just fiction, but true: Jesus is God. However much our appreciation of symbol and metaphor in the primary documents might enable us to relate such a claim to the depths of experience, in the end unbelievers are bound to conclude that the New Testament is 'just a story', whereas believers will claim that it is much more.

The distinction between history and fiction on the question of faith is thus neither easily maintained nor easily dissolved. A good deal of nineteenth-century Biblical scholarship indeed made the distinction too sharp, thereby denigrating imagination which was felt rather to be the province of the secular arts. Yet some nineteenth-century theologians were affected by the Romantic interest in imagination as a restorer of those beauties and depths of experience smothered by excessive rationalism. The like of Schleiermacher, Renan, and the hard-pressed Kierkegaard are touched in their way by Romantic ideals of affective sensibility and the creativeness of solitary, misunderstood individuals. Still, the theory of literary imagination as developed by Wordsworth and Coleridge, with its emphasis on restorative and health-giving knowledge, has remained uncertainly related to theology and to New Testament criticism.[8] This uncertainty remains with us, as scholars such as Owen Barfield and Mary Warnock demonstrate while undertaking to bring Romanticism to age (to paraphrase a title of Barfield's)[9] by investigating with fresh energy the uneasy relationship between imagination and the truth claims of theology.[10]

Among secular literary critics, in turn, there has been surprisingly little interest in the sacred texts, as Frank Kermode points out.[11] This is partly explained by the fact that the texts are sacred, and a secular critic is inclined to feel they are not his province. Also, the technical sophistication of Biblical scholarship is sufficiently daunting to cause those untrained in it to feel a respectful diffidence. However, a whole new range of approaches is now being investigated, not only because of a renewed interest among Biblical scholars in imagination, but also because literary scholarship has been much engaged during the past fifteen years in shaking its own foundations.

The well-tried methods of practical criticism and the so-called New Criticism of a generation ago, taught readers to concentrate on analysis of texts with a view of disclosing patterns of metaphor, tensions, paradoxes and ambiguities which the work of art holds together in unity. Despite certain modifications, the broad influence of a Coleridgean theory of imagination is not hard to detect here. Coleridge had stressed the polar relationship between the whole and parts of a poem, and had proclaimed that a literary work carries within itself the reason why it is so and not otherwise.[12] A similar emphasis on 'the text itself' among New Critics (and here I can include the followers of F. R. Leavis) produced much fruitful interpretation, but also effectively separated literary criticism from philosophy. The doorway to a vigorous new concern about the philosophical bases and implications of critical procedure and indeed of 'writing' itself, opened first upon the hallways of linguistics and anthropology.[13]

The speculations of Ferdinand de Saussure on the structure of linguistic discourse as a system of differences has combined readily in modern literary theory with Claude Lévi-Strauss's investigations of the myths and social structures of so-called primitive cultures as complex relational systems expressed as metaphor and ritual. The joint influence of Saussurian linguistics and anthropology is further implicated in dizzying ways with phenomenology, Russian Formalism, Semiotics, Marxism and psychoanalysis, in a creative ferment which has its share, indeed, of smoke and mirrors, but also of brilliant illuminations and far-reaching challenges. The net result for the future of literary studies is not at all easy to predict. But certainly, the questions raised by the literary theorists are radical, concentrating on the fact that texts now seem less privileged and more a part of the network of other texts, dependent for meaning not only on the writer's culture and language, but also on those of the reader, who may be said partly to create the literary work in the act of reading it. Also, because writing is arbitrary it is a system of codes aiming to persuade, though this apparently is often not acknowledged even by great authors who covertly or tacitly assume transcendent values to stabilise their thinking.

Not surprisingly, the philosopher who most energetically has set about discovering the metaphors which give away key latent assumptions in the works of other philosophers, has appealed most to literary critics. Jacques Derrida's 'deconstruction' of philosophical texts sets out to show that philosophy is more like literature than philosophers assume. Like all writing, philosophy is rhetorical, and because it uses language (an endless network of signifiers the sense of which depends mainly on differences from other signifiers), it never manages to stabilise meaning, which is perpetually deferred. Derrida pushes his case to the very edge of (some think, beyond) self-defeating scepticism. How, we might ask, can he make such a case at all, if language is incapable of reliable meaning? The notion that philosophers (and other writers) always rely on metaphor understandably appeals to literary theorists because poets and critics usually have been quite open about the rhetorical nature of their discourse and the self-referencing element in imaginative writing. It is as if literary people have been onto the game all along, as the others are now coming to realise.

A great deal of discussion among literary humanists these days is therefore concerned with the nature and possibility of meaning itself. In short, modern literary theory is much given to hermeneutics, a discipline which had its origin in the study of Biblical texts. There, too, relationships between belief and meaning, texts and the spirit of interpretation, words and the stable, transcendent Reality which they indicate, are the core issues. Indeed, the latest trends in literary theory seem to have led critics back to the kinds of questions about meaning and belief originally engendered by study of the New Testament itself, just as recent developments in Biblical criticism have led to a renewed interest in myth and imagination. Significantly, the literary critic Northrop Frye acknowledges that he approaches the Bible by way of the hermeneutic theory of Paul Ricoeur and H. G. Gadamer.[14] Conversely, the New Testament scholar Daniel Patte's study of the Pauline Epistles draws on A. J. Greimas, and reads remarkably like a modern study of a literary text.[15] These are typical examples of what seems to be a widespread rapprochement, still in the making, between Biblical scholarship and secular literary criticism.[16]

All of this brings me back to my opening remarks on how difficult it is to say what kind of book the New Testament is. As we have seen, its very language depends heavily on translation, and the compelling story told in the gospels raises perplexing inter-textual issues through which the events are compounded enigmatically (indeed, irrecoverably) with myth and symbol, and the identity of the central figure is elusively conflated with the relevance of his message, which in turn depends on what we make of the stories and parables, signs and symbols with which the texts confront us. The gospels are full of stories within stories, signs referring to further signs, and just as the parables are ways of describing the kingdom, so Jesus himself is, in a sense, a parable.[17] There is no privileged perspective, and at every turn our desire for security, for the 'transcendental signified', is shaken and undermined by elaborate intertextual play. Yet this, I would suggest, is itself an expression of the vision of faith which the New Testament enjoins. For religion is concerned with the whole purpose of human life, with destiny and the experience of time and death, which we cannot hope to test objectively in our present condition as participants. Such questions of course are perennial in human experience, but we should notice that the very asking of them requires imagination which, as Mary Warnock says, enables us to think of absent things and to see one thing as signifying or symbolising another.[18] The imaginative process by which we order our everyday lives is thus inseparable from the process by which we raise questions about the overall meaning of those lives.

It is therefore entirely appropriate that the New Testament should so energetically deploy imagination, for by doing so it addresses our full condition as thinking and feeling creatures. It does not offer the kingdom of heaven as some kind of superadded special event, but as one that comes through normal human consciousness and experience, including our insecurities and doubts about the very possibility of such an event.[19] Jesus, after all, went among the things of this world, raising them to significance by his words and actions until he too was raised up, first on the cross and then in the resurrection, which we are invited to see as the true meaning of his death. He went among children and fishermen, women and foreigners, he touched the lame and the blind, fed people, allayed their fears and rebuked their indifference, he talked of water and wine, bread and life and death, marriage and birth, work, robbery and kindness, money and loss, labour and journeys and a host of the things that constitute our everyday, living contact with the world and with one another. He did all this by telling stories and giving signs, and by himself becoming a story after the fact yet without relinquishing the claim itself of the fact, so that our humanity in the fullest range of its experience should be engaged by his promises. And these at last (as with all meaning) depend on our commitment and assent to the vision which the New Testament documents present to us.

We are persuaded, then, in part to take Jesus' claims seriously because of how imaginatively they are presented, and the New Testament does not oversimplify the perplexities of faith. Yet we must not forget how specific and radical is the New Testament's basic challenge. This resides, as I have said, in the amazing claim that the chief character in the story is in fact God. Such a claim is startling enough, but it becomes almost overwhelming when we assess it in light of the crucifixion, the best-attested and most fundamental part of the gospel narrative and the close preoccupation of Paul's epistles, the earliest New Testament documents. It is all very well to affirm the world, with Jesus the restorer of health and normality, preacher of the Father's beneficence. But Jesus is also an innocent man made to suffer intolerably, and we are told that this, too, is God's way. In short, Jesus' death and the requirement that we imitate it face us with the fact that no religious observance or leap of faith will save us from pain and death. The world is a place where the innocent suffer, and insofar as God endures agony in Jesus, he directs us to see that such suffering is our lot, and faith must exist in spite of it. The degree to which the crucifixion criticises religion itself is easy to ignore but it cannot be evaded. Faced with the cross, how can we take joy in the world? By believing that God suffers here, we might find strength to endure, but the great conundrum remains: we are subjected to conditions where we must die, where there is untold, abominable suffering, and where guarantees of absolute meaning are denied to us.

In the face of these facts, the claim that Jesus is God is either a piece of wishful thinking (the merest fiction), or the most compelling of truths about the human condition, which we accept on faith. Such faith is, then, like a powerful, two-pronged pincer. It demands on the one hand that we take an affirmative attitude to the world, and, on the other that we accept that God's way in the world is to crucify the innocent.[20] This vision of faith provokes a high degree of existential anguish, which, as a literary document, the New Testament expresses vividly. It does so in part by making us acutely conscious of how suffering innocence challenges any belief at all in a good God. The startling conclusion that the transcendent, unapproachable deity comes among us to die and to be raised up (as we too will be), is therefore either a mere story expressing imaginatively our desire for absolute meaning, or a historical revelation compelling our assent because it alone permits us to reconcile God and the world. The following chapters concentrate on various aspects of such a rendition of faith, and I will turn first to the gospel according to Mark, whose concern for signs directly engages some of the main questions I have raised.

2
Mark: the Anointing at Bethany

Mark is preoccupied with signs and with the problem of their indeterminacy. Jesus is repeatedly called upon to provide signs to legitimate his claim, and refuses to do so. When the Pharisees question him, 'seeking of him a sign from heaven' (8:11), he replies even with a degree of vehemence: 'Why does this generation seek a sign? Truly, I say to you, no sign shall be given to this generation' (8:12). Later, when the disciples ask what signs will precede the last days, Jesus delivers an apocalyptic discourse (13:5–37). I will deal more fully with apocalyptic writing in the chapter on Revelation: suffice it now to say that the genre flourished at the time of Christ, and basically offered visionary interpretations of the world's end and of judgement whereby the elect would be separated from the damned, and would reign in paradise. The apocalyptic mood is especially intense in Mark's gospel, whether in his distinctive depiction of human turmoil and confusion, or in the sense that in such strange times as he records we are urgently under the burden of portentous promises, and judgement is soon to come on our disoriented and amazed humanity. The so-called 'little apocalypse' of chapter 13 expresses this mood directly, as Jesus responds to the request for a sign. But we should notice how much of the discourse is taken up with warnings against false messiahs, rumours, and prophets who will 'show signs and wonders, to lead astray, if possible the elect' (13:22). Jesus' attitude to signs here is largely negative (watch out because they will mislead you),[1] and even these warnings are further relativised. Earthquakes, famines, wars and troubles, we are told, are 'the beginning of the sufferings' (13:8): they are not the sufferings themselves, but only a prologue,[2] for 'the end is not yet' (13:7). The disciples thus learn that they will suffer in a good cause, but they ought not to be over-hasty in interpreting what exactly their suffering means.

At one point in this 'little apocalypse' (which as we see is turning out to be a critique of naive apocalypticism)[3] we do indeed seem to be given a clear indication of the real beginning of the end: 'But when you see the desolating sacrilege set up where it ought not to be (let the reader understand), then let those who are in Judea flee to the mountains' (13:14). In the opinion of one distinguished commentator, however, 'This passage presents the exegete with difficulties as great as any in the gospel',[4] which is no slight statement. I need not go into the arguments attempting to reconcile Jesus' apparent historical prediction in this verse with an annoying evasion of specificity on the matter. Briefly, as Nineham points out, such passages as Daniel 11:31, 12:11, and 9:27 are recalled here to remind us that Antiochus Epiphanes had profaned the Temple in 168 BC and placed in it an altar to Zeus. Yet Jesus does not mention the Temple, and the Greek participle 'standing', or 'set up' (*hestekota*) is masculine, as if to indicate a person rather than an object. Profanation, it seems, is less a particular, concrete event (a statue in the Temple) than the malign activity of a lawless personal agency. The odd parenthesis '(let the reader understand)' also seems designed to ensure that the events in Daniel are not applied too literally. It can not have been part of Jesus' oral discourse, and has been added either by Mark or by someone who worked with the literary materials before him. The point is that the reader (whether the person addressing the early churches to explain the gospel to them, or you and I, seems to make little difference) is distinguished from the disciples and is invited to take into account different layers of response to Jesus' words and deeds. The parenthesis puts the reader on guard at the very moment when Jesus seems to be offering the disciples a clear sign.

Towards the end of the apocalyptic discourse we encounter a further disconcerting statement by Jesus about the second coming: 'But of that day or that hour no one knows, not even the angels in heaven, nor the Son, but only the Father' (13:32). Understandably, exegetes have balked at this from the beginning. St. Ambrose argued that it was an Arian interpolation supporting the heretical claim that the Son is subordinate to the Father. Cyril of Alexandria thought that Jesus was testing his hearers by pretending not to know – an example of how powerless texts can become in the hands of determined interpreters.[5] And so the debate continues to present-day Form-critical arguments suggesting that Jesus did not use the title 'Son' of himself in a theological sense.[6] Still, the plain meaning of the statement seems to be that Jesus does not know what the Father knows.[7] Given the amount of debate on the subject, it is a modest enough conclusion that verse 32 offers us a statement which, at face value, a believer in Jesus' divinity is likely to find theologically uncomfortable.

The message the disciples receive as a result of their request for signs is, then, highly equivocal. The apocalyptic genre – with its stages of development towards catastrophe and judgement – becomes the opportunity for a careful warning by Jesus against seeking after apocalyptic signs. Nevertheless the reality which the discourse promises is clearly affirmed: 'And then they will see the Son of man coming in clouds with great power and glory' (13:26). Just so, in his refusal of a sign to the Pharisees (8:12) Jesus does not deny that he is indeed from God: his point is that the Pharisees are wrongheaded in asking for naive proof. Moreover, the absolute nature of the statement 'no sign shall be given to this generation' (8:12) suggests that Jesus *is* in touch with the divine intent, despite the fact that he does not know 'that hour'.[8] The problem is not that signs are meaningless; rather that they are ambivalent. Signs, that is, are basic to human discourse (and as such convey Jesus' message), but they are shifting and uncertain. There is no question, it seems, of somehow standing back and assessing some kind of proof sign as a preface to belief. As is well known, Mark portrays the disciples more harshly than do the other gospels, and stresses their groping incomprehension of the faith to which they are summoned. It is not clear whether Mark's account is the closest to historical fact, or whether he wanted to make a special point about the difficulty of reading signs. Certainly, he is everywhere concerned to impress upon us that faith is not subject to unambiguous demonstration. Indeed, he grasps this point with a degree of complexity and insight which forces his own rhetoric to turn repeatedly on itself, setting up a series of closely-woven oppositions and contrasts through which the dynamism of faith – the partial knowledge that we have of God in this life – is expressed.

In this context we can consider Mark's so-called 'messianic secret'.[9] This term arises from Jesus' peculiar insistence on secrecy in circumstances where it could scarcely be maintained: for instance, because a miracle was performed in public. Debate on this subject has remained active since William Wrede first drew detailed attention to it in his famous book on the subject. Put simply, Wrede's point is that lack of faith in Jesus as messiah during his lifetime needed to be explained by the church. Wrede holds that Jesus in fact did not make messianic claims, and Mark therefore invents a number of mysterious injunctions to secrecy initiated by Jesus. Mark is thereby able to read back the messianic claims into Jesus' life.

Although Wrede's thesis has stayed very much alive in modern scholarly debate, it has been refined and modified. For instance, critics argue that Mark possibly intended us to see that the secret could not be kept. Thus, the cured leper at 1:44 is told to say nothing, but immediately disobeys, as does the deaf-mute at 7:36: 'But the more he charged them, the more zealously they proclaimed it.' Or again, no one is to know about the cure of Jairus' daughter (5:43), and of the blind man (8:22), but it is unlikely that these events could be kept secret, being matters of public fact in such a plain way. Perhaps in all this Mark intends his readers to see how irrepressible is Jesus' power, which cannot help but declare itself, and which we cannot ignore.[10]

Oer perhaps there are two kinds of secret, as Ulrich Luz suggests.[11] The first, or 'miracle secret' is either transgressed or impossible to keep (1:44, 5:43; 7:36; 8:22; 9:30); the second, or 'messianic secret' is enjoined upon Peter when he confesses 'You are the Christ' (8:29) and is told to keep this knowledge to himself. Likewise, after the transfiguration the apostles are charged 'to tell no one what they had seen, until the Son of man should have risen from the dead' (9:9). The implication is that Jesus' identity cannot be properly grasped until after the passion and resurrection.[12] Yet, again this scheme is not quite consistent because the demons recognise Jesus as messiah (1:34), and so does blind Bartimaeus (10:46), and so, perhaps, might the woman who anoints him at Bethany (14:3). Nonetheless, Mark does stress how easily Jesus' messianic status is misunderstood if interpreted separately from the passion. Thus, as we see, at the transfiguration Peter confesses Jesus as Christ and is charged to secrecy (8:30). Jesus immediately talks of how he must suffer, and Peter objects (8:32), but is smartly rebuked ('Get behind me, Satan' [8:33]). Peter, it seems, is happy to acknowledge Jesus as Christ, but does not really understand the transfiguration, or his own confession, because he does not understand the cross. The acid test of his faith is yet to come: we who know about the cross, presumably, should have fewer illusions about what it takes for Jesus to be the messiah. By contrast, the privileged disciples looking at the transfiguration, the clearest of signs, can not accept what Jesus tells them it means. They still cling to the kind of easy comfort and secure interpretation which the cross denies.

The cross, we should therefore notice, is the opposite kind of sign to the miracles, because on the cross the powerful acts of a divine wonder-worker or wise man (the Hellenistic *theios aner*)[13] are so conspicuously not used to legitimate Jesus' claim. In his trenchantly brief account of the crucifixion, Mark goes out of his way to repeat that Jesus was mocked and tempted to come down from the cross to prove that he is Christ (15:29–32). Jesus once again does not provide a proof-sign, and his death rebukes those who would desire a *theios aner* Christology. The cross is, paradoxically, Jesus' chief sign, but is also a warning against seeking security from signs: the sceptic remains free to say that Jesus did not come down because he was so securely nailed up.

At various points throughout the gospel, the passion is intimated so that the reader is kept alert to how deeply the entire story is charged with its significance (or rebuke of significance). The miracles – those world-affirming restorations of damaged human beings to normality – are thus held in tension with the terrible event which undermines the very confidence they induce. For instance, when Jesus cures the withered hand, the Pharisees immediately take counsel 'how to destroy him' (3:6). Later, we learn that Jesus 'could do no mighty work' (6:5) because of unbelief among his own countrymen, and already we feel an ominous warning that those close to him will reject him. The cure of blind Bartimaeus is preceded by the statement that the Son of Man is 'to give his life as a ransom for many' (10:45). Likewise, the story of the widow's offering is held up to the disciples as an example because she 'put in everything she had, her whole living' (12:44). Jesus is also to give all he has by laying down his life, but it is unclear whether or not the disciples understand this. In each of these cases (and there are many others), we are reminded that whatever kind of interpretation of Jesus' mission we propose, it will be inadequate unless it takes into account the fact that Jesus' divinity participates, however paradoxically, in our suffering humanity.

The anointing at Bethany is of special interest in this context, because it also relates the process of signification to the passion in a way that exemplifies Mark's characteristic attitude to sign-making. The anointing (14:3ff.) occurs immediately after Jesus' apocalyptic discourse which, as we have seen, is enigmatic and ends with the doubtfully reassuring imperative, 'Watch'. Jesus is now well set upon his road to the cross, and is full of intimations of violence and suffering. The last supper is then described but, immediately before it, an unnamed woman approaches and pours precious ointment on Jesus' head. She is rebuked by those present (Mark does not identify them; Matthew says they are the disciples), and accused of wasting money which could have been spent on the poor. Jesus in turn rebukes the objectors, telling them that she is anointing his body for burial. Immediately, Judas departs and betrays Jesus to the chief priests, who promise Judas money.

J. Jeremias[14] approaches this episode by distinguishing between a Rabbinic teaching on gifts of love and works of love: the woman offers a gift of love, a spontaneous token of her appreciation, as distinct from a work of love, which is a duty. When she is rebuked, however, Jesus defends her by shifting the interpretation: 'she has anointed my body beforehand for burying' (14:8). Jeremias suggests that we are meant to see how the woman has inadvertently done a work of love, a duty for which there might not be time after the turmoil of the execution, or even because the resurrection will prevent the anointing, as is the case at 16:5.[15]

Clearly, the woman herself could not anticipate such a meaning. Still, her action is more darkly suggestive than the theory of spontaneous appreciation alone permits, for in anointing Jesus' head she might be recalling the ritual anointing of a King of Israel. In 2 Kings 9:1–13 (cf. 1 Sam. 10:1), Elisha gives instructions about anointing Jehu: 'Then take the flask of oil, and pour it on his head, and say, Thus says the Lord, I have anointed you king over Israel' (2 Kings 9:3) and at verse 6 this instruction is carried out. Could it be that the woman glimpses something of Jesus' messianic stature, or is she an enthusiast who hopes that he will rule as a political king?[16] There is also the detail of her breaking the container, presumably by snapping off its neck. This could simply indicate her lavish intent: all of the ointment is to be poured on Jesus. But it was contemporary practice to leave broken ointment-containers beside corpses at burial, and so there could be a hint here that she does indeed anticipate Jesus' death.[17]

If in the first instance there is a contrast between what the woman intends and Jesus' interpretation, on closer scrutiny this distinction begins to blur, and at last becomes multivalent. Perhaps the woman recognises Jesus as messiah; perhaps, even, she sees that Jesus will die. But we cannot be sure; perhaps our own 'watchfulness' is excessive, or perhaps deficient like that of the objectors. They see only the value of the ointment: it is worth 'more than three hundred denarii' (14:3), they remark, prudently. Again, however, their deficiency might be another kind of excess. The objectors would be well aware of Jesus' concern for the poor, and here they interpret the woman's gesture in what they feel is the master's spirit. The objectors have leapt enthusiastically to a conclusion, and it happens to be wrong. The reader could just as well do the same thing. 'Watch' is easier to say than to do. Watching too much might cause us to attend too little to the larger significance, but too much attention to higher meanings can blind us to the obvious.

There are further intriguing details in this episode. The objectors for instance make a fairly exact assessment of the value of the ointment – more than three hundred denarii. Then, immediately following upon Jesus' reply, Judas goes to the chief priests, who 'promised to give him money' (14:11) in an unspecified amount. This exact sequence occurs only in Mark. Matthew's version (which is very close to Mark's) says that the ointment 'might have been sold for a large sum' (26:9) – that is, an unspecified amount – and Matthew has Judas agreeing with the chief priests to betray Jesus for an exact sum: 'they paid him thirty pieces of silver' (26:15). John says that the ointment was 'costly' (12:3), and postpones the betrayal by Judas to a later chapter. Luke, whose story is quite different and might not belong to the same tradition, mentions 'an alabaster flask full of ointment' (7:37) without referring to its value, and the story is disconnected from Judas' betrayal.

The sequence, then, of precise evaluation, betrayal, and a non-specific promise is peculiar to Mark. It is, I suggest, one variation of a structural principle throughout his gospel whereby signs are misinterpreted (their saving potential betrayed, as it were) and then followed by a provocative message about the future. Certainly, there are signs galore in the various stories, exorcisms and miracles. These in themselves are usually quite specific, and yet, as I have noticed, Mark notoriously presents the disciples as obtuse when it comes to making the right interpretation.[18] Jesus, however, offsets this confusion by his eschatological promises,[19] even though they in turn are richly indeterminate.

Interestingly, Mark alone among the evangelists has no resurrection appearances, and instead ends his gospel with a promise (it is generally agreed that Mark's original ending is at 16:8, and that the 'long ending' material [16:9–20] is by another hand). Thus the women find the tomb empty. Again, this is a definite fact, a clear enough sign of some sort, but evaluating it is difficult, for no New Testament writer claims that the empty tomb itself is evidence that Jesus is risen. We learn from the event only that Jesus is not there, and to seek him at the tomb, where the women quite reasonably expect to find him, is to seek in the wrong place.[20] Mark's gospel then concludes abruptly with a note of consternation and amazement (16:8), and instead of a resurrection appearance, Mark substitutes the promise of the young man (presumably an angel): 'there you will see him, as he told you' (16:7). As Louis Marin says,[21] the women go to the tomb expecting a material reality and they are given a message.

My main point is the analogy between such a pattern and Mark's account of the anointing. There, too, a specific sign is misevaluated and this failure leads, in Judas' case, to a denial of Jesus and a promise about future reward. This promise, however, issues into suffering, loss, and death, and so reverses Jesus' redeeming eschatological messages. But within the series of oppositions thus proposed – life and death, fulfilment and betrayal, knowledge and ignorance – lies the turmoil of human beings seeking commitment to action, their search evoked all the more poignantly and richly through the play and counterplay of images. What exactly does the woman who anoints him see? What do the disciples see? And what the reader?

Mark's gospel consistently shows us how uneasily we are played upon by our own uncertainly affirmative and negative attitudes to signs. Let us again consider the anointing, which some scholars have read as a legitimation of art itself in the service of Christianity. This kind of interpretation was current in the Middle Ages, and has its modern advocates. St. John Chrysostom, for instance, comments as follows on Jesus' defence of the woman's action:

> Do thou likewise, if thou shouldest see any one provide sacred vessels and offer them, and loving to labour upon any other ornament of the Church, about its walls or floor; do not command what has been made to be sold, or overthrown, lest thou spoil his zeal.[22]

The church, that is, should receive art and ornament as a glorification of God. In his commentary on Matthew, St. Thomas Aquinas refers to Chrysostom and goes on to make a distinction between anointing the head (as in Mark and Matthew) and the feet (as in Luke). A good work (*opus bonum*) which is useful and natural is associated with anointing the feet; one offered to God's glory is associated with the head.[23] St. Augustine follows the same general line, but works a variation upon Chrysostom's argument by making the woman herself a type of the church.[24] And in his key work on signs, *Of Christian Doctrine*, Augustine refers again to the anointing at Bethany.[25] The ointment, he says, is indeed a sign, but we should notice its secondary position in the story, which consists primarily of verbal signs. The anointing is thus a sign within a further sign-system.

In Augustine's *Of Christian Doctrine* we see how exegesis is already at grips with semiology. Nor is Augustine's approach merely antiquarian, for it has its modern exponents. For instance, in his Neo-Thomist study of aesthetics, *Art and Scholasticism*,[26] Jacques Maritain holds that signs participate in the reality to which they point. Through his material medium the artist discovers an objective, intelligible order of being which his sign-making reveals, to our edification and delight. Maritain's emphasis can be broadly described as 'realistic' in the old-fashioned sense, as distinct from 'nominalist'. Like Aquinas and Augustine, that is, Maritain advocates a certain broad trust in the real relationship between sign-making and the god-created nature of phenomena. As Augustine says, we read signs to discover through the world a transcendent reality which gives the world meaning, and which links us to it through language and art. According to this manner of thinking, the realities which our signs indicate themselves become higher-order signs, until we are led to contemplate the Originating Mystery, the divine source of all signs and all signification. Augustine therefore acknowledges the opacity of signs, but he also affirms the real meanings they discover to us:

> Thus in this mortal life, wandering from God, if we wish to return to our native country where we can be blessed we should use this world and not enjoy it, so that the "invisible things" of God "being understood by the things that are made" may be seen, that is, so that by means of corporal and temporal things we may comprehend the eternal and spiritual. (I, III, 4)

This kind of interpretation, however, is directly in the teeth of that most energetic community of modern critics whose chief preoccupation is, precisely, the discontinuity between signs and meaning, literature and the world. As I have mentioned in the previous chapter, Ferdinand de Saussure's *Cours de linguistique générale* has deeply influenced such a body of opinion. Saussure insists that words do not bear real resemblances to their objects, but signify because of their differences from other signifiers. The word 'pin', we might say, differs from 'bin', 'sin' and 'din', and in the network of differences we come to grasp its meaning. But the word in itself does not signify a stable object: 'pin' can mean a metal fastener, a hold in wrestling, a wooden peg, or a foolish, inconsequential person.

Such insistence on the contextual, and on how meaning shifts amidst a network of differences has given impetus to literary critics intent on showing how literary language undermines stable meanings which it seems to express.[27] As Paul de Man says, 'the statement about language, that sign and meaning can never coincide, is what is precisely taken for granted in the kind of language we call literary'. He goes on to claim that literature 'asserts, by its very existence, its separation from empirical reality, its divergence, as a sign, from a meaning that depends for its existence on the constitutive activity of the sign'.[28] This could scarcely be further removed from the 'realist' camp, and for de Man, as for his mentor Jacques Derrida, the hankering after unified meaning such as we find in Maritain and the others (and, indeed, in the mainstream of Western philosophy, according to Derrida) is a kind of childish nostalgia for origins and for comfort which is never satisfied in human experience.

Just at the point where the contrast between these two camps seems strongest, however, we can also notice the beginning of another kind of complexity. The words 'which is never satisfied in human experience' could just as well come from Augustine. The story told in the *Confessions*, for instance, expresses existential anguish, confusion, and inability to read the signs. And Maritain warns us about the struggle for meaning in language consequent upon the opacity of words.[29] Likewise, Derrida depends on the persistence of those very meanings he would deride as 'metaphysical' in order to make his attacks cogent. As de Man tells us: 'To understand something is to realise that one had always known it, but, at the same time, to face the mystery of this hidden knowledge.'[30] The experience and allure of such 'mystery' gives impetus to our questing thought, and Aquinas here would not have raised an eyelid.

There is, clearly, a large contrast between the evaluation of human sign-making represented by Maritain and de Man, and yet, to make that contrast humanly recognisable, both sides, as we see, share a middle ground of uncertainty and doubt, condemned nonetheless to the pursuit of meaning. Mark's gospel evokes for us especially this sense of a turbulent middle ground whereby on the one hand we are summoned by the signs and promises to affirm a transcendent, beneficent reality even as, on the other hand, we are warned against naive interpretations of signs. Thus we are invited to read the narrative in a realist sense as a true revelation of God, providing us with reassurance of an objective, transcendent design for our salvation. But we are invited also to expect our hopes to be confounded and our securities dashed. Christ himself, after all, was left in abandonment, and his story in Mark's version especially presents us with warnings about the unreliability of interpretation.

To explain this further, I would like to turn briefly to another structural pattern of which Mark is fond. It involves dedication, ensuing dissolution and reconstitution on a higher plane. It is a version of the ancient *katabasis* and *anabasis*, descent and renewal, and is analogous, Mark holds, to Jesus' self-dedication, death and resurrection. However, Mark's deployment of this theme is of special interest because he also carefully inverts it, causing it to stand across itself, as it were, in a manner confounding easy conclusions about how we are to read it.

Sometimes the main stress falls on the high price of dedication. Thus, after the theophany at the baptism, Jesus enters the desert (1:12); after the transfiguration, he takes the road to the cross (9:12ff.); the promptness with which the disciples follow him (1:18; 2:14) leaves them vulnerable to all kinds of misunderstanding of his mission; their willingness to enter into a boat (4:35) leads them into a storm; giving all that you have to the poor (10:21) will only set you on the way of the cross; the woman at Bethany gives the precious ointment and is castigated. It seems, in short, that devotion and self-dedication do not guarantee happiness but tend to lead to pain and rather prompt humiliation.

Yet others who are humiliated and cast themselves down are raised up: the leper kneels and is cured (1:40); the sick man's bed is let down (2:4) so that he can be told to arise; Jairus' daughter seems to be dead and is told to get up (5:41), as is the Syrophonecian woman who falls at Jesus' feet (7:25), and blind Bartimaeus (10:49). The afflicted, whose faith is exigent and might well seem compromised to us because of their desperation, are nonetheless cured. The free self-givers, by contrast, are driven to shame and ignominy.

Once again, we hesitate to read the pattern too confidently. We cannot simply moralise and conclude that faith yields either security or loss of security. Yet there is a certain hard, punishing consistency even to this seemingly self-stultifying message. The kind of self-giving called for by faith is uncompromisingly radical. Its conditions are not met unless the strategems of security and self-congratulation even in the act of self-denial are quite burnt away. Paradoxically, for those with no hope hope might spring alive, just as the executed criminal who promises to come alive as the Son of Man, judge of the universe, might indeed do so, and just as the story, full of fantastic claims as it is, might be true.

Mark's narrative reminds us, then, that faith is not formal or aesthetic, and the special test of faith's reference to the world is the cross, the problem of suffering innocence in history. It is worth noticing that the gospels provide a strikingly consistent account of the cross, which occupies a commanding role in all four narratives. The event clearly threw the disciples into disarray in an embarrassing fashion which is unlikely to be invented. The Roman procurator who ordered the execution is named, and the events are described to emphasise their historical concreteness, even though the narratives are also theological and were written in light of the resurrection kerygma. It seems that if we doubt the historicity of the crucifixion narratives, we must doubt even more radically the historicity of everything else that the gospels tell us.

Here, then, the gospel as literature, concerned with signs and the interpretation of signs, pushes us, as it were, to the very edge of its own universe of discourse. In Mark especially, the cross is the sign which stands for the failure of signs to provide solace or certainty, and it is not just another play of the text. It is an event, the place of abandonment where even the Son of God cries out, 'My God, my God, why hast thou forsaken me' (15:34). It is a place where the rhetorical pattern of *katabasis* and *anabasis* is most vigorously turned inside out, as Jesus' mockers call on him to provide a sign to come *down* from the cross, on which, in his vulnerability, he has been raised *up*. The usual pattern of raising up to significance what has fallen down into suffering and emptiness is pointedly inverted: the story of the cross confounds (as far as a story can) the paradigm of the narrative which presents it, and in showing us this, the narrative once more lurches at the brink between sign and event. And we are asked to assess what this means. We might, for instance, read Jesus' cry of abandonment as a quotation from Psalm 22, and thus through further exegesis see him calling on God even in forsakenness. Yet such a reading might be sentimental, a desire, still, to read significance into a situation where there is none. The cry could just as well mean – as it has no doubt for many subjected to extreme suffering – that 'God' at last is an empty word. How are we to know? How are we to read such an event, such a narrative describing the significance of such an event, and derive knowledge from it that faith will sustain us *in extremis*? The striking achievement of Mark's treatment of this, and of the other signs in his gospel, lies in the way he presents the arduous human experience of such questions.[31]

I have tried to point out how Mark's narrative is both imaginative and self-reflexive, and how his writing has a distinctive set of emphases. His is the gospel especially aware that for Christ's followers there is no easy consolation, no finally secure interpretation of faith. His is the gospel of peculiar secrets, strange indeterminacies, and the one that most shows the disciples' obtuseness and the difficulties of following Christ. His is the most apocalyptic gospel, the one most pervaded by the mood of imminent, terrible judgement, and which depicts us blundering in fear and amazement at God's ways, his frightening invitations to suffering and his startling claims. The other synoptic gospels deal more circumspectly with Mark's apocalyptic urgency, especially by developing Jesus' story through the birth narratives and resurrection appearances. Jesus is thus seen more fully to take a place in history, whereas in Mark history itself, as it were, is threatened with imminent dissolution. In this context of apocalyptic anxiety filled with dark signs and amazing revelations, Jesus the Christ makes his claim upon us. His miracles restore the sick and outcast to health and community, and Mark's 'good news' is that God has sent us our salvation. Yet without the cross there is no true understanding, and the cross is precisely the event which removes us from our worldly comfort and security. The event of Calvary would therefore confound the narrative itself which describes it, even as the sign of the cross invites us to a faith which the story compellingly describes.

3

Matthew: the Centurion's Earthquake

Matthew is everywhere concerned with the identity and mission of the church: indeed, his is the only gospel to use the word *ekklesia* (16:18; 18:17).[1] As Edward Massaux[2] has shown, Matthew's was the most-often quoted gospel among the Fathers before St. Irenaeus, who seem to have recognised its special relevance to a newly-fledged institutional Christianity. It is still referred to as the 'first gospel' and is printed that way in most bibles, even though there is now a wide consensus that the honour of precedence should go to Mark.[3]

I cite Matthew's concern for ecclesiology because it has an immediate effect on his writing. He wants especially to provide an ordered discourse on which the church at large could draw to identify its duties and teaching on a number of subjects. At the same time, he is constrained by the traditional narratives about Jesus, which he undertakes to recount faithfully. He therefore tells the broad story as we have come to know it, but arranges the elements in large, clearly-identifiable blocks. He collects the miracles into one section, the parables into another, the missionary discourse into another, and the spiritual sayings into what has become known as the Sermon on the Mount.[4] It has long been recognised that his narrative falls into five main parts, each marked off by a transitional formula, and that these perhaps are meant to recall the five books of Moses.[5] The five sections deal with the sermon on the mount (5:1–7:27), the missionary discourse (10:5–42), the parables (13:1–52), the rules for the community (18:1–35), and the 'little apocalypse' (24:3–25:46). Each concludes with a formulaic phrase, such as 'when Jesus finished these sayings' (7:28), as we find at 11:1, 13:53, 19:1, and 26:1. Implicit in such an arrangement is Matthew's favourite idea that Jesus as messiah 'fulfils' the Mosaic law (to cite Matthew's favourite word),[6] bringing out its essence, as it were, and extending it to the gentiles. In all this, the author as literary craftsman balances the narrative facts against his design to instruct.

Matthew's intent is observable in numerous details, and one way to confirm it is to observe how he alters Mark's miracles. St. Augustine, who thought Matthew wrote first, argued that Mark's much shorter gospel was a botched abridgement of Matthew's prototype.[7] But had Augustine looked more closely, he would have seen that in most passages where they overlap – and this is especially true of the miracle stories – Mark gives us all the interesting detail and local colour. Matthew cuts it out.[8] The modern opinion of Johannes Weiss, that it is among 'the greatest riddles of gospel criticism how Matthew could deny himself the use of these living details'[9] is perhaps overstated, but it shows how far some modern assumptions are from Augustine's, and it raises a real critical point.

For our present purpose it is not crucial to have Matthew derive from Mark (though I assume that this is the case), because the contrasts between the stories as they stand are themselves instructive. An example is the healing of Jairus' daughter (Matt. 9:18–26; Mark 5:21–43). Even a brief glimpse shows how much longer and more detailed is Mark's account. Matthew's is sufficiently compact to quote in full:

> [18] While he was thus speaking to them, behold, a ruler came in and knelt before him, saying, "My daughter has just died; but come and lay your hand on her, and she will live." [19] And Jesus rose, and followed him, with his disciples. [20] And behold, a woman who had suffered from a hemorrhage for twelve years came up behind him and touched the fringe of his garment;[21] for she said to herself, "If I only touch his garment, I shall be made well." [22] Jesus turned, and seeing her he said, "Take heart, daughter; your faith has made you well." And instantly the woman was made well. [23] And when Jesus came to the ruler's house, and saw the flute players, and the crowd making a tumult, [24] he said, "Depart; for the girl is not dead but sleeping." And they laughed at him. [25] But when the crowd had been put outside, he went in and took her by the hand, and the girl arose. [26] And the report of this went through all that district.

Clearly, this is the same story as Mark's. It is unusual in being the only miracle within a miracle in the gospels, and many duplications in language make the interdependency plain. And yet Mark gives us about three times as much as Matthew, and the differences are largely in detail. For instance, Matthew's account of the ruler is quite straightforward: the daughter is dead, and if Jesus touches her she will live. By contrast, Mark connects the ruler with the synagogue, gives him the name Jairus, and has him say that his daughter is 'at the point of death'. If Jesus comes, 'she may be made well, and she shall live' (5:23). Mark's Jairus is pleading; there is not much time left and he appeals for sympathy with the diminutive 'little' (5:23). Also Jesus 'may' do something: Mark's verb is subjunctive. The outcome is less certain than with Matthew's nameless petitioner whose faith shows no such signs of nervousness or exigency. The daughter in Matthew is already dead, and if Jesus chooses, she will be cured.

The fact that the child is not yet dead in Mark's version has the further effect of making the episode with the haemorrhaging woman an interruption. Instead of hurrying to the sick girl, Jesus stops for a bit of perplexing interrogation of the crowd, one of whom has touched him. Mark has prepared for this by emphasising the crowd from the beginning, a thing Matthew (who otherwise is fond of crowds) does not do. Mark tells us that 'a great crowd gathered' (5:21) around Jesus, and when Jairus makes his request 'a great crowd followed him and thronged about him' (5:24). The haemorrhaging woman then 'came up behind him in the crowd' (5:27), and Jesus 'turned about in the crowd' (5:30) to ask who touched him. The disciples, obliging but slow as usual, point out that there is a 'crowd pressing around you' (5:31); surely lots of people are touching you, they imply, so there is no sense in being upset about a particular instance. Mark does not mention the crowd again in this story, and clearly he has emphasised it to show Jesus' sensitivity to the one woman among so many who touched the hem of his garment in faith. Nonetheless, Jesus does not seem to know who touched him until the woman comes forward and falls down and admits it. Of course he might be testing her, or testing the disciples, but we cannot be sure. Mark, as ever, highlights the difficulty of reading the signs.

Matthew omits most of these fine points. He spares the disciples embarrassment by dropping their advice about the crowd, and indeed he drops the crowd too. Jesus simply turns when he is touched, and tells the woman that her faith has made her well. This has the directness of the ruler's statement of faith that his dead daughter can be raised, and both verses combine to create a sense of Jesus' solemn power, responsive to faith. Jesus then proceeds to the dead girl, and performs the miracle.

Unlike Matthew, Mark also creates a degree of suspense by having Jesus dally on the way to the sick girl's house. Mark even has a messenger interrupt Jesus 'while he was still speaking' (5:35), with news that the girl has died. Jesus responds by telling Jairus not to be afraid, and then addresses the professional mourners: 'Why do you make a tumult and weep? The child is not dead, but sleeping' (5:39). They laugh at him, but he puts them outside and raises the girl, uttering the phrase 'Talitha cumi' (5:41). Everyone is amazed. Jesus tells them to say nothing about it, and to get her something to eat.

Matthew pointedly omits the unsettling suggestion that dallying on the way caused the girl to die, and there is no interruption by a messenger, and no fear and amazement. Instead of provoking the onlookers with a question, Jesus makes a magisterial and commanding statement: 'Depart; for the girl is not dead but sleeping.' Matthew also omits the magic words, the order to secrecy, and the detail about eating. All of which no doubt evokes in us something akin to Weiss's exasperated puzzlement about how he could have missed out on so much.

One answer is simply that Mark's purpose is different. He wants to show us the wonder-working Jesus and also warn us against the wrong kind of wonder-working. Mark's Jesus seems not to know, he provokes, he utters a healing formula like a magician, and he is disconcertingly concrete (this girl now needs something to eat). Mark alone gives us the girl's age ('for she was twelve years old' [5:42]), and we notice how this corresponds to the twelve-year haemorrhage of the woman whose healing interrupts Jesus' journey to the house. Frank Kermode speculates on the kind of antithetical contrasts established here between the girl's uncleanness (being dead) and the woman's (her menstrual disorder); between the two-fold, symmetrical approach to 'a healthy sexual maturity' (the young girl is pre-pubescent, the woman is ritually unclean; both are restored to society), and between the unwilled and willed exercise of Jesus' power.[10] By contrast, Matthew's Jesus is serenely efficient, and takes on something of the clear, powerful line of the story that describes him. Matthew's intent is to show how plainly messianic glory is present, and how it vindicates faith. His lesson is less murky than Mark's, but so also, we might conclude, his story is less interesting. This, we remind ourselves, is the author who changed Mark's statement that Jesus '*could* do no mighty work there' (6:5, my emphasis) because of unbelief, to 'did not do many mighty works there' (13:58). If Mark has an eye for details that will make a plain fact puzzling, Matthew equally has an eye for details (or the lack of them) that will make something teachable out of something dark.

Though Matthew's version of the story we have been examining is indeed shorter, the fact remains that his gospel as a whole is much longer than Mark's. Matthew therefore does not just abbreviate Mark; he also adds material from other traditions, including a number of elements peculiar to himself. Among these are the parables of the wheat and tares (13:24–30), the treasure in the field (13:44), the pearl of great price (13:45), the labourers in the vineyard (20:1–16), the two sons (21:28–31), and the wise and foolish maidens (25:1–13). In each case, his selection serves his own special emphasis on Christ's power and the church's discipleship. And in each case, he is concerned about order, arrangement, and the kind of balance that facilitates catechetical instruction.

For instance, the parables of the wise and foolish maidens and of the talents in chapter 25 are carefully measured opposites, deliberately placed after the eschatological discourse by way of illustration. The five maidens who prepare their lamps and consequently meet the bridegroom are matched by the servant who is given the five talents and invests well. Both stories deal with a delayed return of the Lord who is to judge, and both deal with the resourcefulness of those who are prepared for his coming. The application of all this to the church is obvious and Matthew seems aware that the second coming (the technical word *parousia* is used by him alone among the gospel writers) is likely to be delayed. But the stories are also antithetical. The maidens are women, and the servants who receive the talents are men. The maidens initially are active, going out to seek the bridegroom, and the oil carried by the wise ones prepares them to wait – that is, to be passive. The servants by contrast are initially passive, and are given the talents so that they can go off and invest actively. Also, we are warned against opposite faults: the foolish maidens are too reckless and do not count on a long delay; the foolish servant who hides his talent is too timid, and his expectation of a long delay ('a long time') makes him negligent. Proper watchfulness requires a balance between these extremes, in the midst of the complementary oppositions which the stories depict. Admittedly, there are some unsettling details in both stories which I am passing over for the moment. Suffice it to say that this kind of carefully-orchestrated statement is characteristic of Matthew, and there is evident artistry here, different from Mark's indeed, but considerable in its own right.

I would like to dwell on this aspect of Matthew's gospel a little longer, because much of his special contribution comes from the sense of pleasing and suggestive symmetry, of balance established among contending elements. Matthew signals his fondness for such patterns straight away in Chapter 1 by noticing how Jesus' genealogy breaks down into three sets of fourteen generations (1:17). As the first verse tells us, the key to this arrangement is the fact that Christ is 'the son of

David, the son of Abraham' (1:1). That is, he bears in himself the promises made to Israel through King David as well as to the gentiles through Abraham.[11] Throughout his gospel, Matthew wants to show how the church belongs at once to Israel and to the gentiles, and how Christ mediates between them. Christ, as it were, is in the balance, a point which Matthew confirms by an insistent fondness for rhetorical structures suggesting complementary opposition, such as we have seen with the stories of the maidens and the talents.

For instance, the wise kings who visit the infant Jesus stop first at Jerusalem to consult the scriptures: gentile recognition of the messiah, the narrative implies, must give Israel its due. Also, Matthew refers to Jesus' kingship only in the infancy and passion narratives, again to suggest balance between opposites.[12] Just as the birth stories show the mighty one in David's line become vulnerable, so the passion narratives show the vulnerable servant rise up again as king. And just as the birth narratives contain a story about death connected with kingship (the massacre of the innocents), so the passion narratives find their significance in the resurrection inaugurating the Reign of God.

A dense tissue of such antitheses runs throughout the gospel. The Sermon on the Mount is developed within the antithetical framework 'You have heard that it was said ... But I say to you' (5:27ff.). Two senses of fire are counterpointed in John the Baptist's promise that the Holy Spirit will baptize with fire, but also that 'unquenchable fire' will burn up the chaff (the unrepentant) when the wheat is separated out (3:11–12). A man cannot serve two masters (6:24), and houses built on rock and sand are compared (7:24–7), as are the fruits of good and corrupt trees (12:33). Whoever saves his life will lose it, and whoever loses it will save it (16:25); so also, the first shall be last, and the last first (19:30). There is talk of binding and loosing on earth and in heaven (18:18), and of you falling on a stone and a stone falling on you (21:44).

A further clue to Matthew's fascination with this kind of pattern is his interest in doubles, underlined by the peculiar habit of giving us two where Mark has one.[13] Thus, in the country of the Gadarenes Jesus meets two men possessed with devils (8:28); after he cures Jairus' daughter, two blind men follow him (9:27), and again, later, he cures two blind men (20:30). He sends two disciples for an ass and a colt and is strangely said to ride into Jerusalem on both animals (21:1). Other examples readily come to mind: if a man takes your coat, give him your cloak also (5:40); if you are forced to walk a mile, go two (5:41); there are parables about two brothers (20:24) and about two sons (21:28); two shall be in a field, and one will be taken (24:40); two women shall be grinding (24:41); two false witnesses give testimony (26:60), and two thieves are crucified (27:38).

Techniques of parallelism in Hebrew poetry have no doubt influenced these passages, and antitheses and dualities are evident also in the other gospels. But no other gospel shows such a concentrated interest in binary structures,[14] and, as I have said, part of the reason is pedagogical: symmetry facilitates teaching. Yet Matthew's emphasis is also connected to the fact that he alone of the evangelists gives an account of the last judgement in which the Lord's pronouncement divides the opposites: on the one hand, 'Come, O blessed of my Father, inherit the kingdom prepared for you from the foundation of the world' (25:34); on the other, 'Depart from me, you cursed, into the eternal fire prepared for the devil and his angels' (25:41). As Günther Bornkamm and Gerhard Barth point out, Matthew's strong feelings about judgement reflect everywhere in his ecclesiology.[15] His church is the discipleship which his powerful, serene Christ will judge at the *parousia*, and in the various examples of binary structures and dualities we are to see Christ's judgement-in-the-making.

There is a disturbing side, however, to Matthew's preoccupation with judgement, for it seems that the balance we associate with Christ is preserved only by the rejection and destruction of those who upset it. Matthew is severe on such matters. The Son of Man will gather those who do iniquity 'and throw them into the furnace of fire' (13:42, 50), and everywhere we are threatened with weeping and gnashing of teeth (13:42, 50; 8:12; 24:51). The Pharisees and Sadducees are cursed repeatedly as a 'brood of vipers' (3:7; 12:34); they are 'sons of those who murdered the prophets' (23:31), and they shall continue to persecute and crucify 'that upon you may come all the righteous blood shed on earth' (23:35). The unprofitable servant who is too timid to invest his money will be cast into outer darkness (25:30), and the wedding guest who turns up improperly dressed will be bound and cast out (22:13). We are to account for every idle word (12:36), and if our eyes (5:29), hands or feet (18:8) give offence we are to cut them off. Even the idealistic Sermon on the Mount becomes appalingly rigorous when seen in the light of judgement and everlasting fire.[16] A lustful look is adultery in the heart (5:28), 'whoever says, "You fool!" shall be liable to the hell of fire' (5:22), and we are to be perfect as our Father is in heaven (5:48). Over these injunctions to superhuman purity hangs the threat of the meek Jesus' iron promise: 'And then will I declare to them, "I never knew you; depart from me"' (7:23).

Matthew's eschatological rhetoric, then, is unsettling and frequently terrible, and I would like to consider it further in connection with his fondness for the word *seismos*, which means a commotion or shaking, and is translated as 'tempest' or 'earthquake', and in the verb form (*seio*) as 'to shake' or 'to move'. There are only two instances of these words in the other three gospels (Mk. 12:8; Lk. 21:21), but Matthew uses them seven times.[17] This frequency is matched in the New Testament only by Revelation, but even there the verb is used as a doublet in two cases, so that there are five main instances.[18] The fact that Revelation is Matthew's only contender is not surprising, for *seismos* is readily associated with eschatology and the disturbances which accompany the Son of Man coming in judgement.

Of Matthew's seven uses of the word, however, only one is directly associated with the second coming. In the apocalyptic discourse we learn that 'there will be famines and earthquakes (*seismoi*) in various places' (24:7). Elsewhere, the word is used to describe the tempest battering the boat in which the disciples are alarmed while Jesus sleeps (8:24), the commotion in Jerusalem when Jesus enters (21:10), the earthquake which occurs as he dies (27:51), frightening the centurion (27:54), as well as that which accompanies the angel's rolling back the stone from the sepulchre (28:2), and, finally, the terrified shaking of the guards at the tomb (28:4). In each of these instances, Matthew attaches eschatological significance to the word *seismos*, and in each case there is a violent breaking in of Christ's power upon the world, a radical upheaval, as it were, which upsets normal order and expectation. It is as if we are to expect crucial experiences wherein the established order of our lives is so disturbed that we must choose to commit ourselves to the powers of goodness and transcendent truth, or those of separation and the rejection of meaning. I use the word 'crucial' deliberately, for, as always in the gospel narratives, the cross gathers to itself the main issues. In Matthew, as we see, it is accompanied by earthquakes and a concentric series of seismic shocks that split stones and open graves and break the hardness of a Roman soldier. The cross indeed represents rejection, vulnerability and pain, but also judgement, power and revelation. It is an upheaval challenging us to balance its own powerfully negative and positive poles by understanding how Christ is discovered there.

Matthew's carefully patterned rhetorical designs, I am suggesting, become a kind of measure of the special, creative energy which disturbs them. Symmetry and organisation, that is, are of our own making, but by themselves they are inert. The creative force of redemptive love does not dispense with such foundations, but is brilliantly unsettling and makes of them the expression of something new and strange. Christ perennially disrupts our over-reliance on order and prescribed form, the designs for security with which we would save ourselves from anxiety and the finitude which is our lot. This is not to deny that he also brings form and order to those whose lives are threatened by the chaos of disease and mental derangement.[19] He remains the mediator, but preserves a perilous equipose, and his activity is forever surprising: 'For as the lightning comes from the east . . . so will be the coming of the Son of Man' (24:27).

In some such context, we should consider the controversy with the Scribes and Pharisees, which is strenuous in Matthew and is directly related to the mission to the gentiles. It seems clear that Jesus is upset by an over-reliance on formal order among certain Jews, and continually points to hypocrisy as a dangerous triumph of precept over practice, of external convention over inner disposition. He therefore advises us to give alms without show, and not for public approval (6:2); we are to pray in our closet and not make a public display (6:6); when we fast we should seem to prepare ourselves for dinner and not draw attention to the fact that we are fasting (6:16–18). The hypocritical Pharisees by contrast are like whited sepulchres, 'which outwardly appear beautiful, but within they are full of dead men's bones, and all uncleanness' (23:27). They are denounced as serpents and vipers mainly because they lay burdens on others, but 'themselves will not move them with their finger' (23:4).

Matthew makes clear that Jesus does not attack the Law, and indeed declares roundly that 'not an iota, not a dot, will pass from the law, until all is accomplished' (5:18). On the contrary, Jesus attacks antinomianism (*anomia*, 7:23) in the form of false prophets who call him Lord but are wolves in sheep's clothing (7:15). Rather, the Law is fulfilled by the creative lightning flash, the upheaval of the Christ-event energising it from within so that it can be extended to the nations, as promised to Abraham's seed. Analogously, such strategies of upheaval repeatedly enliven and irradiate Matthew's carefully-ordered text, thereby enacting rhetorically the creative and redemptive event they describe.

In the infancy narrative, for example, we have already seen that Matthew arranges Jesus' genealogy in three sets of fourteen. Yet they do not add up: the numbers are slightly off, and Raymond E. Brown has a section in his magisterial study of the infancy narratives entitled 'Could Matthew Count?'[20] In the first genealogical set, from Abraham to David, there are fourteen names but only thirteen generations. Still, as Brown says, 'Abraham, whose name is listed first, had to be begotten' (82), and this could make up the fourteen. The second set, from David to the Babylonian exile, does list fourteen generations, 'but at the price of omitting four historical generations and six kings who actually ruled' (82). The third section, from the Babylonian exile to Jesus, again has thirteen generations, and this time we cannot count the first names because the first person in section 3 is also the last in section 2. As Brown shows, a good deal of ingenuity has been spent on seeking the fourteenth in section 3, but he concludes, with some ruefulness, that only 'with ingenuity' can one 'salvage Matthew's reputation as a mathematician' (83–4).

Whether or not Matthew intended his pattern to appear almost symmetrical, that is the effect he achieves. But lest we too quickly discard the possibility that he knew what he was doing, we should consider his inclusion of the four women.[21] These are Tamar, Rahab, Ruth and Bathsheba, and the relationship of each to her consort is irregular. Tamar deceived her father-in-law Judah into an incestuous union (Gen. 38); Rahab was a prostitute who sheltered Israelite spies in Jericho and was subsequently received into Israel (Joshua 2); Ruth's marriage to Boaz was irregular because she was a foreigner from a nation said to have had its origins in incest (Gen. 19); and Bathsheba ('the wife of Uriah' [Matt. 1:6]) committed adultery with David. The scandalous nature of these relationships prepares us for the irregularity of Mary's conception of Jesus, a fact which, as Matthew alone points out, gives Joseph pause: 'he resolved to divorce her [Mary] quietly' (1:19). Clearly, God's ways can be surprising, but the measure of such surprise is the very fact that there is a foundation of expectation, a pattern to fulfil. Matthew seems quite aware of presenting us simultaneously with order and with its disturbance.

This effect is repeated throughout the gospel and is apparent, for instance, in the parable of the labourers in the vineyard (20:1–16). Those who are hired early in the morning quite reasonably expect to earn more than those hired at the eleventh hour (20:9), but the householder overthrows this expectation by paying them all the same. The lesson is that the gentiles have come late into Israel's history, but are no less worthy. Yet the story on the face of it is unsettling: the labourers who have worked all day have a right to object, and the householder's action is a surprise. Perhaps he is concerned that everybody gets a subsistence wage, which one day's pay provides. Nevertheless, the parable is effective because we detect so clearly how the calculated order of expectation breaks down before certain over-arching moral and spiritual concerns. Human worth cannot be added up like money, and our expectation of what ought to happen is remade at the very moment when it is overthrown. Interestingly, Matthew shows more concern with money than does any other gospel author,[22] and this preoccupation is partly explained by his fascination with how things really add up, as distinct from how they seem to add up from the point of view of predictable order and utilitarian design.

These remarks on the parable of the labourers can bring us back to the parables of the maidens and the talents, in which, as I noticed earlier, there is a certain strain. The parable of the talents deals with money, but seems initially to reverse the emphasis of the story about the labourers in the vineyard. Here, the man who invests his five talents and makes five more is highly praised. The man with one talent, who is afraid to lose it and returns it safe and sound, is reproved for not at least having put it in the bank to make interest. The talent is taken away from him and given to the man with ten talents, and the unprofitable servant is then cast into darkness. As we have seen, this story warns us against timidity, and initially it seems a reasonable expectation that the successful investor should be praised. But it is upsetting that the man with one talent should be so harshly treated. To rescue the story, we rush to its spiritual significance, but not without some uneasiness: while we wait for the lord to return, we tell ourselves, we should work to promote Christian truth to the best of our ability, and it is wrong not to do so. Whereas in the parable of the labourers we encounter a disconcerting generosity, here we encounter a disconcerting severity. In both instances, our worldly expectation is broken in a way that forces us to try to see what the story is getting at spiritually.

The same kind of observation can be made about the wise and foolish maidens. The wise ones seem to meet the bridegroom because they refuse to share their oil. This action, we might reflect, sits ill with Jesus' earlier instruction to 'Give to him that begs from you, and do not refuse him who would borrow from you' (5:42). Indeed, by the standard of the Sermon on the Mount, the wise maidens ought to have given all their oil away, on the principle that if you are sued for your cloak, you should give your coat too (5:40). Had they done so, that might have been praiseworthy. Instead, the door is barred against the foolish maidens who are late because they had to go to buy oil.

According to Eduard Schweizer, this sort of reading misses the point. 'The only point that matters for the story', he argues, 'is that the foolish girls are not there when the time comes.'[23] Schweizer also assures us that the refusal of the wise girls to share their oil should not be interpreted allegorically, but then he seems to take his own injunction as justification for not interpreting it at all. Yet it is a rankling detail, and again it involves money (the other five go off to buy what they lack). Once more we are forced umcomfortably upon the counterpoint between worldly calculus and spiritual economy.

A main characteristic of the gospel parables in general (and not only Matthew's) is that they are at once homely, illustrative examples, but also force us to re-examine our conventional assessments of the world and other people.[24] As such, they are disruptive, and so in Matthew's gospel they quite naturally belong with those other provocative upheavals and deliberate asymmetries that fire our curiosity and imagination. As Hans Georg Gadamer says, imagination is the bearer of life into 'a cultic or social context',[25] and its special distinction is to seize our whole being, and open us to ever-new integrations and possibilities, especially by showing us the limits of our cultural horizons and unconscious prejudices. We all inherit the biases implicit in our language and social mores which enable us to take hold of the world and engage it in a human manner. Gadamer argues that tradition enables understanding, but a work of art surprises us, to a degree, out of the received forms which shape our horizons. We are thereby able to come into more open relationship with others who likewise allow their prejudices to be tested and unsettled. Indeed, the sign of a work of art is that it perennially provokes the surprise and illumination that inflame our desire to understand it, and Gadamer points to a potentially endless search for meaning through interpretation.

Matthew's thinking has little in common with modern hermeneutic theory, but it is a token of his artistry that his work provides such a pertinent example of Gadamer's claims. Matthew, as we have seen, is everywhere concerned with tradition, especially the sort which has hardened in some minds into prejudice, and which he would have irradiated by the creative upheaval which he calls Christ. The Scribes and Pharisees are denounced mainly for closing their horizons. Matthew here does not attack all Jews,[26] though his gospel does reflect what Harold Bloom describes as anxiety of influence[27] – that combined dependence on and resentment of one's strong predecessor by a poet who is forced to incorporate yet transcend (or otherwise evade) such indebtedness.

For instance, in the notorious statement of 27:25, the multitude describing Jesus' crucifixion are said to cry out, 'His blood be on us, and on our children.' Matthew might well have included this in light of the disastrous events of AD 70 when Jerusalem was destroyed by the

Romans, as an indication of how these events might be explained. But the statement is a dangerous example of the negative kind of anxiety: how much anti-Jewish sentiment it has stimulated in the history of the church is impossible to assess, but clearly it could all too readily do so.[28] The mob, of course, is not identifiable with all Jews any more than are the hypocritical Pharisees, and insofar as any Jew, or anybody else, was responsible for having an innocent man crucified (or any man at all) we must abhor such action, along with that of the Romans who either would permit or carry out such an execution. The most that can be said for Matthew's inclusion of 27:25 is that it is the utterance of some individuals whose prejudices have so hardened them that they destroy their own credibility. To identify this group with all Jews would itself be a prejudice of a sort that the meaning of Christ contradicts.

We should, instead, recall that the Law itself is never denounced by Jesus in Matthew's gospel, but is the necessary condition for understanding God, and so its influence is positive. The Law, or any religion and mythology truly open to God, can manifest Christ, as some, at least, of the early Church Fathers were willing to state.[29] Christ the mediator between legalism and antinomianism can bring to any tradition the imaginative and surprising challenge which would extend its horizons, opening it up to the richest possibility of understanding. And yet Matthew remains distinct from Jews who do not accept the historical claim that Jesus of Nazareth is the messiah, as he does from a critic like Gadamer, whose hermeneutic theory invites us to pursue meaning through the inexhaustible glide of language. For Matthew, the promise is fulfilled and is present, and his faith rests there.

The gospel then is not just a story, but a story that claims to be true, and in which the strategies and achievements of imagination are offered as examples of God's process in history. 'When the centurion and those who were with him, keeping watch over Jesus, saw the earthquake (*seismos*), and what took place, they were filled with awe, and said, "Truly this was the Son of God" ' (27:54). Faced with the stultifying event of the cross, the centurion is shaken into a knowledge of what good in fact means. Matthew alone adds the phrase 'and those who were with him'. The nameless others taken by the event or, even, by the story of the event insofar as it captures the strangeness and extravagance of the fact it claims to describe, or those taken by the imagination of the fact and then by the fact which so assaults the imagination that imagination yields assent: these are, for Matthew, the church, the assembly of all who have encountered the earthquake, and are 'with' the centurion through the ages.

4

Luke-Acts: the Ironic Travellers

Journeys have always been a favourite subject of literature. In a way, what occurs in a journey matches what happens to the reader of a narrative. There is an end, though *in medias res* it is not evident how it will turn out. Adventure and novelty arise from displacements and interruptions of the predictable path, and yet a certain secure purpose keeps things on track. As in journeys, so in narratives we proceed anticipating a satisfactory conclusion: there is a point of arrival, a coming home.[1] Otherwise, instead of a journey we have a mere series of incidents, and instead of a narrative, a random collection of anecdotes.

Our oldest recorded literature takes easily to journeys. Odysseus wanders the Aegean on his way back to Ithaca after the Trojan war, and his travels make up Homer's epic. The Israelites start on their exodus from Egypt, and wander in search of a promised homeland from which they had been taken into captivity. By the time of Plato, for whom Homer's treatment of the gods was embarrassingly over-literal, the journey home had become a philosophical quest which could not be fully realised on earth because of the preponderance of human and natural evil. The immortal soul would be judged after death and would either come to rest or continue to be tested. Correspondingly, by the time of second Isaiah (who preceded Plato by slightly more than a century)[2] the hope of Israel restored had been tempered by reflection on the cruel facts of history and experience. Israel is now a suffering servant, and the righteous remnant living by faith extends God's offer of salvation to the world. His word is to encompass the earth, and our successful homecoming will be declared by our righteousness.

As Thorleif Boman[3] points out, the Greek imagination of this high quest for a homeland tends towards spatial metaphors, whereas the Hebrew imagination tends towards temporal. And as Erich Auerbach[4] says, Homer carefully describes foreground details, giving us a brightly-lit, evenly-externalised account of phenomena. By contrast, the Hebrew Bible is impressionistic, and full of a sense of the mysterious depths out of which historical decisions are made. Plato, we might reflect, was a teacher of geometry, who represented the relationship between God and the human mind in terms of a visual metaphor of the sun and a cave, and who saw the universe as a geometrical arrangement of concentric spheres, describable mathematically from the smallest particle of matter to the grandest sweep of the stars.[5] The Hebrew Bible shows no interest in geometry and mathematics, and the universe is pictured as a historical manifestation of God's creative power.[6] We are not asked to speculate about judgement: we are assaulted by it, confronted by the weight of history already upon us, and by the promise of history's fulfilment through the terrible uncertainties of its unravelling.

This space–time contrast of course is not hard and fast, and Boman correctly emphasises the profound similarities between Hebrew and Greek culture. Their shared monotheism – philosophical among the Greek thinkers (especially the Platonists), theological in Israel – and similarly affirmative engagement with the world remain the foundations of a synthesis upon which Western civilization continues to draw. Part of my claim in this chapter is that the author of Luke-Acts offers a highly suggestive treatment of the journey motif, blending a characteristic Greek emphasis on geography with an over-arching Hebrew eschatology which treats the human journey as a historical opportunity for personal decision-making about God.

It has long been recognised that Luke's gospel is the first section of a two-part work, of which *The Acts of the Apostles* is the second part.[7] This is indicated by the promise in Luke's prologue 'to write an orderly account for you, most excellent Theophilus' (Lk. 1:3), to which Acts refers back: 'In the first book, O Theophilus, I have dealt with all that Jesus began to do and teach' (Acts 1:1). There has been wide recognition also of a close similarity between Luke's concluding chapter 24 and the first chapter of Acts, and critics have found a variety of other stylistic and structural parallels.[8] For instance, there are special emphases on salvation history,[9] on universalism, and on the idea of Christian witness. Both books show a carefully accommodating treatment of Rome, and both stress Jesus' name and word. Both are fascinated by Jerusalem, and share a sophisticated literary irony. To these we can add a common interest in journeys.

Luke departs from the other gospels in his development of a long journey-section (9:51–19:28) in which Jesus makes his way to Jerusalem, and in Acts Paul's missionary journeys and the geographical spread of Christianity are central concerns. In the gospel, Jesus conspicuously does not preach to gentiles, and as Vernon K. Robbins points out, Luke carefully avoids any mention of Jesus travelling by sea.[10] To do this consistently, Robbins goes on to say, Luke alters Mark's references to the Sea of Galilee and instead talks of the Lake of Gennesaret (5:1; 8:22, 23, 33). When Jesus travels by water, he is pointedly said to go on the lake (*he limne*). Mention of sea-travel appears for the first time in Acts 13, and further sea voyages are then described, climaxing in Paul's shipwreck adventure on the way to Rome. These descriptions include the much debated 'we sections', where narration shifts suddenly into the first person plural.

It seems clear that the author of Luke-Acts reserves journeys by sea to describe the word spreading to the gentiles, and when he does so, his narrative draws on gentile literature. As Robbins shows in detail, the 'we sections' deploy conventions of Greek and Roman writers for describing sea voyages: transition to a first person plural narrative suggests immediacy and indicates the corporate personality required of a sea-going crew. In drawing upon this precedent, the author of Acts not only suggests that discipleship is a corporate effort, but also evokes the atmosphere and climate of the Graeco-Roman literary world. Consequently, the journeys in Acts remind us of an epic voyage. Jesus' spirit (16:7) fills the disciples, and their mission carries them to Judea and Samaria (ch. 8, 9), Syria (ch. 9), Cyprus and Galatia (ch. 13, 14), Greece (ch. 16, 17, 20), Asia (ch. 19), and finally to Rome (ch. 23, 27). We thus watch the gospel spread from the heart of Israel (Jerusalem) to the intellectual centre of the ancient gentile world (Athens) and then to the political hub of the Empire (Rome).

By contrast, the journey section in Luke is towards Jerusalem rather than away from it. After preaching in Galilee, Jesus suddenly decides to make for the holy city: 'When the days drew near for him to be received up, he set his face to go to Jerusalem' (9:51). It is almost as if he were responding to a demand, and the expression 'set his face' is a semitism suggesting that he is to encounter hostility.[11] As Jesus sets out, the indications are already ominous. Jerusalem is a place of destiny to which he must travel, but it is also a place of rejection. In a consequent dynamic interplay throughout Luke-Acts of journeying to and from Jerusalem, of centrality and outreach, exile and home, acceptance and rejection, we are to grasp the meaning of Christian pilgrimage in the world.

I LUKE

Commentators often notice that Jesus' initial decision in the journey section of Luke's gospel stands in odd relationship to the dilatory account of the travels which follow. Despite his firm intent, Jesus does not go straight to Jerusalem, and there is no urgency about his getting there by any direct route. Instead, the section has a variety of teachings in a number of circumstances: the sending out of the seventy (10:1), the parable of the good Samaritan (10:30–7), casting out a devil (11:14), a sermon against hypocrisy (11:39), the cure of a crippled woman (13:11–13) and of a man with dropsy (14:2–4), the parable of a prodigal son (15:11–32), and the blessing of little children (18:15–17) are some examples. Throughout, an assortment of geographical references is provided: Jesus visits a Samaritan village (9:52) and the house of Martha and Mary (10:38), which according to John's gospel is situated in Bethany (11:1). We learn, rather vaguely, that he travels through 'towns and villages' (13:22), and 'along between Samaria and Galilee' (17:11). He meets a blind man near Jericho (18:35), which he enters and passes through (19:1). At such points we are reminded that he is all the time aiming at Jerusalem. The Samaritans, for instance, reject him 'because his face was set towards Jerusalem' (9:53); as he goes through the cities and villages he is 'journeying toward Jerusalem' (13:22); he passed through Samaria and Galilee 'on the way to Jerusalem' (17:11), and as he approaches Jericho he assures the disciples, 'Behold, we are going up to Jerusalem' (18:31).

As K. L. Schmidt remarks, 'although Jesus is travelling to Jerusalem all the time, he never really makes any progress'.[12] Indeed, his route is strikingly roundabout. Bethany (if that is where Luke thought Martha and Mary lived) is a few miles from the holy city, and yet soon after we learn that Jesus is in the midst of Samaria, much further to the north. This leaves him no closer to his goal than he was at the beginning, when he also visited a Samaritan village (9:52). Clearly, the journey section is of central importance to Luke,[13] but the geographical itinerary by which Jesus reaches Jerusalem is scarcely important at all. The suggestion that Luke was confused about the geography does not withstand close scrutiny,[14] and the notion that he re-organized John's account of several visits to Jerusalem into a single account might be plausible,[15] except that Luke seems to have effected this re-organisation rather badly. Such carelessness certainly stands in sharp contrast to equally strong indications of precise organisation of other sorts.

For instance, there is the so-called 'great omission' at 9:17, immediately before the journey section. Since 8:4, Luke had followed Mark's gospel quite closely, but suddenly skips over Mark 6:45–8:26, in what is surely an editorial decision. Within the journey section itself is a series of threefold patterns: three stories about vocation (9:57–62), three passages on prayer (11:1–13), three parables about mercy (15:1–32), three statements about law (16:16–18), and three about scandal (17:1–6).[16] Also, Kenneth Bailey has detected a detailed chiastic structure, with Jerusalem at the extremities (9:51–6 and 19:10, 28–48) and at the centre (13:22–35).[17] Ten points on the way to the centre stress rejection, and are paralleled exactly by ten points in the second half stressing the offer of the gospel to outcasts.

Among these examples, the patterns of three are easy to detect, and should alert us to the author's literary intent. The less obvious issues of the 'great omission' and the chiastic structure gain relevance from the fact that they mutually re-enforce a single intent. As I have indicated, Luke avoids having Jesus preach to the gentiles, and avoids having him travel by sea. Understandably, therefore, Luke drops the material in Mark 6:45–8:26 – the so-called 'great omission' – because it deals with Jesus' calming of a storm at sea, and preaching to gentiles.[18] Likewise, the chiastic structure of the journey section stresses Jerusalem, but in so doing suggests how rejection there prefaces an extension of the word to the gentiles, described more fully in the journeys of Acts. In both cases, Luke seems bent on treating the journey as a linking device in a two-volume work wherein Jesus' journey to Jerusalem and his death there become the means by which salvation will eventually extend to the edges of the world.

The geography of Luke's journey section is less important than his understanding of the spiritual course of salvation history. This is not to deny that there is an itinerary, and that human feet trod the earth to Jerusalem, by however circuitous a route. Still, it seems clear that this section is also theological, and a further clue is provided by the opening verse in which Jesus expresses his determination: 'he set his face to go to Jerusalem' (9:51). The main emphasis here is on making a decision at a crucial point of time, and Luke's entire journey narrative will appear less full of digressions when we notice how its various episodes revert to this central theme. Jesus' teaching, his cures, and his rebuke of hypocrisy *en route* to the holy city challenge his hearers to make direction-changing decisions in their own lives, analogous to his. Appropriately, the stories of the lost sheep, the lost coin, and the prodigal son are unique to Luke and occur within the journey narrative, thereby drawing our attention to how the way can be lost, whether by accident, or unwitting foolishness, or by irresponsible decision. Nonetheless, God searches, calls and forgives (as for a coin, a sheep and a person). Everything depends on whether or not our wandering and our decision, insofar as we have one, lead us to him.

The story of the good Samaritan (10:30ff.) is again unique to Luke and also occurs within the journey section. It is a story about a journey, indeed about a series of journeys: the traveller's, the priest's, the Levite's and the Samaritan's. We are reminded of the larger narrative frame because the man who falls among thieves has just been to Jerusalem. The priest comes upon him 'by chance', finding him by the roadside, rather as one might find a lost coin. Although the story does not tell us explicitly that the priest also has been at Jerusalem, the same verb 'was going down' (*katebainen*) is used, and the word 'likewise' (*homoios*) is then deployed to describe the Levite's coming upon the place. They are, so to speak, 'insiders', both by religion (the priest and Levite are co-religionists), and by association with Jerusalem. The Samaritan, by contrast, is an outsider by religion and seems to arrive from another geographical direction: 'But a Samaritan, as he journeyed, came to where he was' (10:33). The encounter is by chance, but the moment of decision which all three travellers face, ironically reverses the insider–outsider contrast. This is indicated by the fact that the priest and the Levite 'passed by on the other side', whereas the Samaritan 'went to him'. The outsider who has no association with Jerusalem crosses over, both literally and metaphorically, becoming by his merciful action the true insider. The priest and Levite also cross over, but in so doing make themselves outsiders to the true spirit of Israel. Once again, topographical details are barely sketched in, and are significant insofar as they relate to the spiritual consequences of a crucial change of direction.

Within the journey section, as I have begun to suggest, a variety of subordinate stories helps to develop the significance of Jesus' main journey to Jerusalem, and to suggest how it should be imitated. On the one hand, we are exhorted to make a decision and take a direction: we are to let the dead bury the dead (9:60), and when our hand is on the plough we are not to turn back (9:62); like the good Samaritan we are to cross over and pick up the wounded (10:34); we are to seek so that we may find (11:9); are to gather, not scatter (11:23), and we are to forsake all that we have, or else we cannot be disciples (14:33). On the other hand, we are told not to worry about exact geographical directions, for although we should seek in order to find, one consequence of our seeking might be that we are found. In this spirit the seventy are sent out with 'no purse, no bag, no sandals' (10:4), in the expectation that circumstances will reveal their work to them. Even the Son of Man has nowhere to lay his head (9:58).

There are obvious difficulties, however, in seeking and also allowing oneself to be found. These are indicated by the coolly crushing paradox which familiarity should not be allowed to blunt, that 'Whoever seeks to gain his life will lose it, but whoever loses his life will preserve it' (17:33). As with the rich man and Lazarus (16:19–31), positions can be reversed in a trice, and the solid ground of our confident proceeding turn to quicksand. Indeed, Luke's narrative consistently shows how by indirections we find directions out, and how perplexingly initiative and response can combine. This is so with the parable of the prodigal son (15:11–32), who turns around and makes his way back home, dependent on his father's mercy and forgiveness which, as it turns out, are extravagant.[19] Within the parable, however, the further story of the elder son is disconcerting to our easy correlation of reward to merit. The elder son, who has been dutiful to his father and has worked hard, wonders why the prodigal deserves such attention and expense. His indignation even causes him to become the outsider, for we are told he was so angry he 'refused to go in' (15:28). His father entreats him (15:28), but in the end reverts to the scarcely-convincing reassurance that the younger son 'was lost, and is found' (15:32). Part of the initiative indeed lay with the prodigal who changed his direction and came home, but the response of mercy and acceptance is incalculable.

These stories all tell us something about Jesus' journey to Jerusalem. The sketchy geography and indirect route are less important than the decision to act in response to a call – the divine *dei* of which Luke is so fond.[20] Jesus travels as a homeless one performing works of healing and love, preaching and exemplifying his dedication to God as circumstances require or permit. And yet the question remains: Why did he decide at that point?

In a sense, the meaning of Jesus' decision lies in the events that occurred at Jerusalem, and in their consequences. Chief among these are the crucifixion and resurrection (unlike the other synoptists, Luke has the resurrection appearances occur in and around Jerusalem, rather than in Galilee). Of course Luke also lives in a wake of historical consequences which are in turn part of his interpretation of the original events. Relationships between actual history and its theological interpretation remain obscure,[21] and once more we are left with that sense of mysterious depth out of which God calls his chosen ones in Biblical narrative. The variety of the subordinate journey stories and the indirect conduct of the main journey contribute to this effect. We are left with no unambiguously clear itinerary, but rather a set of exempla and a series of provocative gaps which our own questing imaginations strive to shape into a coherent pattern. Such, we might conclude, is the quest of faith itself.

Jerusalem, then, is the focus of Jesus' journey, but he also expects Jerusalem to reject him.[22] In contrast to Mark, Luke's parable of the vineyard (20:9–16) says that the young man was cast outside and killed, and the vineyard will be given to others. This suggests how Jesus' redemptive death is significant for outsiders and not just for those within Israel (traditionally a vineyard) who reject him.[23] Consequently, Jesus laments for the holy city: 'O Jerusalem, Jerusalem, killing the prophets, and stoning those who are sent to you! How often would I have gathered your children together as a hen gathers her brood under her wings, and you would not!' (13:34). The preceding verse contains an even more sombre observation: 'for it cannot be that a prophet should perish away from Jerusalem' (13:33). Luke clearly implies that continuity with Israel and departure from Israel are both necessary, and neither should be stressed to the point of denying the other. Thus the universalist implications of the birth narrative, in which, unlike Matthew, Luke traces Jesus' genealogy back to Adam (3:38), are offset by stories of such pious Jews as Zechariah and Simeon, who affirm continuity with tradition even as the new thing is breaking into history.[24]

Luke's interlayered structure of journeys therefore points consistently to the single challenge of our choosing a way to God, whether as insiders or outsiders, sinners or Pharisees, women or men, healthy or diseased, and whether our direction is forward or backward, up or down, to home or away. The spirit of this choice and an extravagant self-dedication based on service to others is the real meaning of Jesus' way. It is an extension of God's declaration of himself to the prophets of Israel, but it is not contained by Israel as a geographical entity. W. D. Davies correctly observes that 'Luke fully recognises Jerusalem as the geographic centre of Christian beginnings. . . . But he deliberately and clinically transcends this spatial dimension. Christianity is a way which began at Jerusalem, but passes through it.'[25] Thus Jesus clears the Temple to make way for his teaching the same message we have seen delivered in a number of localities and to a variety of people. We might even see here a tendency in later Judaism to spiritualise the Temple, developed to the point where Jesus does not identify it with a geographic location at all, but with his own word.[26] This is consistent with the fact that no other gospel places such emphasis on Jesus' name and word.[27] He returns to the Temple in order that it should be identified with his teaching rather than with any more specific, nationalistic hopes about the kingdom.

Indeed, both Luke and Acts contain clear warnings against such expectation. In Luke, Jesus tells the parable of the pounds 'because he was near to Jerusalem, and because they supposed that the kingdom of God was to appear immediately' (19:11). Even after the resurrection, the disciples are still confused about this issue, and ask, 'Lord, will you at this time restore the kingdom to Israel?' (Acts 1:6). The fact that Luke consistently tones down Mark's harsh depiction of the disciples' obtuseness makes this point even more telling: continuity between Israel and Jesus is to be dissociated carefully from literal expectations of a new kingdom. Rather, the Reign of God is 'within',[28] and ironically the survival of Jesus' name and spirit occurs because of the destruction of their material vehicle, the temple of his body. The rude reversal of a traditional homecoming clarifies the true meaning of Jesus' journey to Jerusalem.

The kingdom of God is not therefore of this world, and a journey to find it cannot be charted on any map. Still, we are creatures of this world, confined to a certain geography and a certain bodily space through which we must travel despite the fact that we are all, in the end, equally cast out from our home in the world because we all must die a material death. As we see, the constant play of continuity and discontinuity, of direction and indirection, of finding and being found, reminds us of how particular are the circumstances of our entering upon the Way. Not surprisingly, Luke's refined sense of irony is especially effective in his treatment of this subject.

Irony occurs when the real import of a speech or action is understood by the reader but remains hidden from or misunderstood by others in the story. For instance, Mary and Joseph find the boy Jesus in the Temple 'after three days' (2:46). They had been looking for him 'among their kinsfolk and acquaintances' (2:44), and do not understand when their son tells them he has been attending to his Father's business. The reader sees that the parents were on the right track, seeking among their kinsfolk, but they would have done better to attend to Jesus' family in a spiritual sense. Their journey – like so many other journeys in Luke – is fruitless until they turn to the Temple, that is, the spiritual centre. They do not see themselves as examples of excessive literalism, and of course they do not see the allusion to resurrection in the number of days they have searched for their absent son. In a similar fashion, he will be taken from the world at his death, to come again in the Spirit.

The gospel is full of examples of words and actions described by Luke or interpreted by Jesus differently from the speaker's intent. At one point, in an episode unique to Luke, 'a woman in the crowd' cries out in well-meant enthusiasm, 'Blessed is the womb that bore you, and the breasts that you sucked' (11:27). Jesus' reply is on the edge of dismissiveness: 'Blessed rather are those who hear the word of God and keep it!' (11:28). He does not exactly rebuke her for praising him, but makes clear that she has got it wrong, or not sufficiently right. Her words contain the seeds of a truth more profound than she manages to express. In a similar vein, Jesus has Simon cast his net one more time after a fruitless night's fishing (5:4). Simon grumbles (5:5) but complies, and is amazed to catch so many fish that two boats almost sink with the weight. His surprise then turns to fear and he falls down, asking Jesus to leave him, but Jesus turns the tables in his usual disconcerting fashion. Fishing is not the point, but rather bringing in souls. Simon is so smitten that he follows Jesus forthwith.

A brief glance at the parallel stories in Matthew 4:18–22 and Mark 1:16–20 shows how much more carefully Luke develops Simon's misunderstanding. In other versions, Jesus passes by and simply calls out: 'Follow me, and I will make you become fishers of men.' The details of Jesus' preliminary teaching from the boats, Simon's reluctance to cast the net, the fact of the catch itself and the large number of fish (more than Simon can handle alone), the astonishment and reversal from anxiety to allegiance, all belong to Luke alone. His treatment of the incident cultivates both a sense of Jesus' extraordinary power and also of the ironic indirection by which it is communicated to others.

A further, provocative example of irony is Luke's version of Jesus' journey to the Mount of Olives. One possible reading of this episode is especially testing for Christian readers because the irony encompasses Jesus, and very likely Luke as well. The key passage is again unique to Luke, and describes how the disciples are advised after the last supper to bring a sword: 'and let him who has no sword sell his mantle, and buy one' (22:36). Jesus goes on: 'For I tell you, that this scripture must be fulfilled in me, "And he was reckoned with transgressors"; for what is written about me has its fulfilment' (22:37). The disciples reply, quite soberly, that they have two swords already, and Jesus says 'It is enough' (22:38). They then proceed to the Mount of Olives and Jesus' suffering in the garden, which in Luke is more terrible than in the other gospels. Jesus is in 'an agony' and his sweat falls like blood. These details again are peculiar to Luke, for whom the crucified Jesus is, by comparison, a model of compassionate control. Luke omits Mark's cry of desolation from the cross, and Jesus dies instead uttering the calm pronouncement, 'Father into thy hands I commit my spirit!' (23:46).

In the midst of his agony in the garden Jesus is further galled to find his disciples 'sleeping for sorrow' (22:45), and once more this odd detail is Luke's alone. Matthew and Mark provide the more plausible, if redundant, explanation: 'for their eyes were very heavy' (Mk. 14:40; Matt. 26:43). Jesus is then betrayed, and the disciples waken up sufficiently to ask him if it is time now to use their swords: 'Lord, shall we strike with the sword?' (22:49). Not waiting for an answer, one of them cuts the ear off the high priest's servant, but Jesus immediately heals it, indicating that indeed, no, that is not what the swords are for. He is then taken into captivity.

There is some evident irony in all this, consistent with the pattern we have been noticing whereby Jesus intends a statement spiritually and his hearers take it literally. Thus the disciples who are told to take their purse, bag and swords (22:36) are being advised to prepare themselves spiritually for the long and testing period ahead. The disciples, however, do not see themselves as early conscripts into the spiritual warfare of the church militant, and show off their real swords instead. Jesus resignedly says 'It is enough', as if shrugging off their literal-mindedness, and proceeds to the Mount of Olives. Luke stresses the agony there because he is especially concerned with Jesus' spiritual suffering, which the disciples do not fully understand.

An alternative, rather more challenging interpretation of this episode is offered by Robert Graves in his novel, *King Jesus*.[29] According to Graves, when Jesus refers to 'what is written' and sees himself numbered among the transgressors, and then asks about swords, he is referring to Zechariah 13. There the prophet is rejected by his own people, and even by his own family: 'and his father and mother that begat him shall thrust him through when he prophesieth' (13:3). A prophet will be humiliated and even killed by the sword by those close to him: 'Awake, O sword, against my shepherd, against the man who stands next to me, says the Lord of hosts. Strike the shepherd, that the sheep may be scattered' (13:7). When the prophet is run through by his followers – this rejection being a sign of his authenticity – his disciples will be dispersed.

Jesus' allusion to Zechariah suggests that he expects his disciples to kill him in the garden. That is why he asks them to bring swords. He thinks that they understand, and his words 'It is enough' are then coldly literal: he is looking at the instruments of his own execution. His agony is intense because he is waiting for them to strike, but they do not. The odd expression 'sleeping for sorrow' would indicate how Jesus thought they were unable to kill him because to do so would have caused them too much grief, and they had fallen instead into a torpor of inactivity. Jesus, of course, over-estimates his disciples, for they seem to miss the allusion to Zechariah, and think that the swords are to defend him against those who come to seize him. Graves adds the captivating detail that the only one at the supper who did understand was Judas, who had Jesus taken into custody to save him from death. By a fateful but dreadful twist, Jesus is thereby launched upon the road of the cross.

Most readers, believers or not, are likely to react against the idea that the time-honoured stories of the supper and the Mount of Olives record a bungled suicide attempt, and indeed Luke does not make such a point explicit. He does, however, build a story on how misunderstanding leads people to act at cross purposes, and his method is ironic. This is true of both our interpretations. The first places the passage among a series of episodes where literal and spiritual are ironically confused, and whereby Luke develops his key emphases on the mission of the church and the spirit of Jesus' teaching. By this account, Jesus knows what he is doing, but the disciples do not: Luke and the reader appreciate the *contretemps*. The second interpretation emphasises the fact that Jesus chooses the road to Jerusalem in fear and trembling, as a suffering servant indeed. He knows himself to be a rejected prophet after the debacle in Galilee, and comes to understand the chilling truth that total rejection is his only chance of vindication. But Jesus also misunderstands how his death is to come about, a fact which enhances his human suffering and vulnerability, making the story more touching and resonant.

This second interpretation differs from the first mainly because the irony includes Jesus. Certainly, both Jesus and the disciples (with the possible but only partial exception of Judas) are confused, and there is a strong sense that Luke does not see the full implications of the sword episode, from whatever special source he derives it. Perhaps he thought of the episode in the manner of our first interpretation, and tried to fit it to his narrative accordingly. But in the odd details we still feel the presence of a story with another import.

Having said all this I must now admit that I prefer the first interpretation on the ground that it is more probable, given the story of Jesus recorded not just by Luke but elsewhere in the New Testament. If indeed there was a story of the Zechariah sort, there is no reason to feel that it was suppressed because it was right, but because it was wrong. I do not pretend, here, to dispel the mystery of Jesus' journey to the Garden of Gethsemane, or to discount the provocative strangeness of Luke's special materials. Whatever way we view it, we are faced with ironies of misunderstanding, and our imaginations are called into play in the service of judgement. That this judgement should be accompanied by some perplexity and a sense of the imponderable is quite in keeping with the journey motif throughout Luke's gospel. After all, despite warnings about not turning back (17:32), the one leper who does so is correct (17:15). When Zechariah asks the angel how it is that his wife will conceive (1:18), he is struck dumb for his importunity; when Mary asks the same question about her own conceiving (1:34), she gets a gracious and friendly answer. We cannot be too confident that we are doing the right thing. For all his resolution in setting his face for Jerusalem, we cannot be sure that Jesus did not suffer crises of conscience based on fear and doubt rather like our own.

As a last example of Luke's irony, I would like to consider the Emmaus story, which duplicates the main emphases of the journey narrative. We are not told why the two disciples are travelling to Emmaus. Indeed, today we do not even know where Emmaus is, and Luke's text does not provide much help, except to situate it 'about seven miles' from Jerusalem (24:13). As the disciples walk, the risen Jesus joins them, but they do not recognise him. At his prompting, however, they tell him about the crucifixion and the hope they once had that Jesus 'was the one to redeem Israel' (24:21). They explain how the women found the empty tomb and claim to have had a vision assuring them that Jesus is alive. To check the story, certain disciples visited the sepulchre which they indeed found empty, 'but him they did not see' (24:24). Jesus then expounds the truth about himself by citing scripture, until they arrive at the village. He then makes as if to continue ('He appeared to be going further' [24:28]), but they ask him to stay. Later, when he blesses and breaks bread, they recognise him and he vanishes. They reflect on how indeed their hearts had burned while he discoursed with them.

Clearly, the two disciples are dispirited because of the fiasco of the crucifixion, and consequently are sceptical about the empty tomb story. The women's words 'seemed to them an idle tale, and they did not believe them' (24:11), and partly because of their state of mind they do not recognise the risen Lord. The crucial moment in the story, however, can easily be passed over. It occurs when Jesus is about to walk on, and they invite him in. His journey, wherever he was headed, is unexpectedly interrupted and their own journey takes an unexpected twist, based on a moment's generosity and fellow feeling. That is the true ground of their understanding the resurrection as an extension of Jesus' spirit into our everyday behaviour and meeting with others. The fact that they know him at the moment of breaking bread warns us against any purely spiritual or abstract interpretation. The risen Jesus is concrete, but we cannot recognise him until we act in the spirit of his teachings.

Otherwise we too will look in the wrong places and in the wrong manner.

As with all the journey stories in Luke, this one does not stress geography so much as the moment of decision by which our spiritual direction is changed. The time (that mysterious moment) is more important than the place, and yet our commitment to a place, and to the concrete realities which constitute our being in the world, is a condition of our decision. This is true of Jesus' journey to Jerusalem, and of the various other journeys and stories which develop its central theme. It is true of the search by Mary and Joseph for their son, and the various tales about lost objects and people; the seventy disciples going their various ways and Peter's reluctant venture in casting the net; the journeys of Lot's wife (17:32) and the healed leper; and, finally, the adventure of the distracted apostles on the road to Emmaus. The geographical conditions of our finding the way are manifold, and our going forth is likely to be fraught with the kinds of ironies and blundering indirection which Luke so imaginatively describes. The moment of decision might well change our course surprisingly, but also we might never know that we have passed it by.

Luke's ironies are thus different from the misunderstandings of the messianic secret in Mark. As we have seen, Jesus' interlocutors in Mark especially misunderstand the cross, but Luke does not stress the cross so much as the imitation of Jesus' journey. Likewise, Luke tends to play down Mark's eschatological urgency, and does so partly by developing the birth narrative through a series of vignettes and by dealing with the resurrection appearances as a means of offering instruction to the church about how to develop its teaching through the long historical journey ahead. The journey, however, both for the church and for each of the faithful, is likely to be full of perplexities and painful turns: we are called upon to imitate Jesus and to take a course, engaging the world. Yet the token of our acceptance might well be the pain itself of the world's rejection.

II ACTS

Acts, Dibelius says, is the diary of a journey.[30] It records the consolidation of the early church in Jerusalem, and its subsequent spread to Samaria, Greece, Asia and Rome. Just as in Luke the journey narrative is a kind of central massif, so in Acts are Paul's missionary travels (19:21–8:31). Also, the chiastic structure which critics find in

Luke's journey narrative can be read as parallel to a similar chiastic organisation of Paul's travels, so that the rejection and promise of outreach in the gospel are duplicated by Paul's rejection in Israel and adventures to the gentile world.

Donald R. Miesner's[31] precise analysis of chiasmus in the missionary journeys, however, is inconsistent with another, briefer version of the same thing offered by Vernon K. Robbins.[32] Disagreements of this sort might cause us to wonder about how much the discovery of such structures is due to critical ingenuity rather than to the author. One rejoinder might be that critics discover what the text yields, and a sign of great literature is that incompatible interpretations can be made about it. Yet in the present case, the question of Luke's organisational intent cannot be so easily shaken off. A high degree of complex parallelism and architectural detail suggests deliberate planning, and if this is so, the narrative is more likely to be concerned with theological interpretation than with the bare, factual record of events. Indeed, an appreciation of Acts as literary – that is, as showing complex internal organisation – was the cornerstone of the attack by Dibelius and others on the documents as historically reliable.[33] An author might well be unconscious of patterns of plot and imagery detected by readers in the 'deep structure' of a narrative, but a device such as chiasmus requires a high degree of conscious deliberation, and so cannot well be divorced from the author's intent. The most thoroughgoing analysis of structure in Luke-Acts is by Charles H. Talbert,[34] and it is a mixture of fine-grained distinctions which might indeed stretch our credibility, and other correspondences which seem undeniable. In short, the boundary between conscious design and unconscious organisation is unclear, but there is sufficient evidence throughout Acts of considerable literary craft.

Debate along these lines usually leads to the speeches Luke gives to Paul, and to whether or not they are consistent with the Paul we know from his epistles.[35] Once more, the question is whether Luke is inventing for literary effect, or making an accurate record. Although it would be too much to claim there is a consensus on this issue, it is fair to say that the grey area is very much the same as for the debate about structure. The portrait Luke gives of Paul is consistent with what we know from other sources, though Luke the interpreter is also in evidence, forming and adapting his materials to the main theological emphases of his own two-volume work. In this context, critics tend to compare the speeches of Acts to other ancient historical writings. Josephus, Tacitus, Livy and Plutarch all invent speeches for their principal characters, rather than record the *ipsissima verba*. The kind of thing the famous person is getting at was held to be more important than the exact record of his words. For instance, in *How to Write History*, Lucian of Samosata advises the recording of what is important, essential and useful, as well as what actually happened. Invention of speeches in this fairly free spirit goes back at least to Thucydides, and is a well-established literary tradition in Luke's time.[36] Indeed, it is what Luke very likely thought historical writing to be.

Paul's speeches, then, deliberately evoke a kind of discourse appropriate for different audiences in the geographical locations in which they are uttered during his travels. As Miesner points out,[37] Paul's three main sermons are given in different locations: Antioch, Athens, and Miletus. The first is to Jews, and is delivered in a synagogue; the second is to gentiles, delivered in a city which is the symbolic heart of ancient culture; the third is to Jews and gentiles together, offered to the church elders. Moreover, the speech at Athens (17:16ff.) is unique in New Testament literature because it deals explicitly with natural philosophy, even citing the names of philosophical schools and quoting the Greek poet Aratus.[38] It has been suggested also that there is an implied parallel between Paul and Socrates, on the ground that both put their case dialectically to all-comers, and both are accused of introducing new gods.[39]

The uncertainly balanced claims of historical accuracy and literary interpretation which we find in Paul's speeches are again at the heart of discussion of the so-called 'we sections' in the travel narrative. At four places (16:10–17; 20:5–15; 21:1–18; 27:1–28:16), the narrative voice suddenly switches from third person to first person plural. Some critics have taken this to indicate Luke's personal participation in these sections of the journey: the 'we sections' are therefore especially reliable history. As we have seen, however, other critics suggest that Luke draws upon conventions of ancient sea-voyage literature, a sub-genre developed from epic tradition and especially marked by first-person plural narration into which an account can shift at critical moments when group effort is stressed. According to this interpretation, the 'we sections' are self-consciously literary. A third interpretation suggests that in the 'we sections' Luke is using an itinerary now lost to us.[40]

The intimation of special reliability in the first of these explanations is quite reversed by the special evidence of artifice in the second. The choice required of a critical reader confronted with such exclusive possibilities is unsettling, and the theory of a missing document does not really solve the problem, but re-introduces it on another level: Is the missing account literary or literal? Still, we might ask if the opposition really is so straightforward. Even if Luke were present, he would want to cast his account in the truest form, which means highlighting its universal elements as other historians of his day prescribe. The sea-voyage genre could be the most effective way for expressing what the spread of Christianity really meant.

In an excellent article on the subject, Vernon K. Robbins[41] demonstrates that the 'we sections' are indeed conventional. He points out the basic coincidence between a shift to first-person plural narration in Acts and the beginning of a sea journey. He also notices that sea travel begins at Acts 13, with the main geographical outreach of the Christian mission. The 'we sections' therefore begin as Paul starts to travel confidently abroad, and they grow longer as his travels extend outwards. Thus, the sea-voyage motif helps to join the gospel to Acts by developing the land—sea contrast. Moreover, a set of motifs found consistently in the sea voyage genre is duplicated especially in the 'we section' account of Paul's shipwreck. Typically, says Robbins, sea voyagers land in an unfamiliar place and establish friendly relations with the natives. Trouble then tends to occur, and the natives are divided about their visitors. The sea-voyage leader either performs some extraordinary deed or makes a convincing speech, and the voyagers are either driven out or continue on their way with the people's good will. Robbins goes on to show how these motifs occur also throughout the 'we sections', but are plainest in the last, most elaborately-described voyage, where Paul travels to Rome as a captive (27–8). During a storm, Paul saves those on board because he correctly indicates what is going to happen, and they are forced to follow his advice, or drown. They are cast up on the island of Malta, where they make friends with the natives. In a weird incident, a snake comes out of a fire and fastens on Paul's hand. The natives first think that the event shows Paul is a murderer, but then that he is a god because he is unharmed. Paul then cures the chief's sick father, and the good opinion of him is confirmed. After three months, the group departs on another ship.

The miraculous cure and praeternatural incident of the snake especially suggest a literary model, and other elements of the story conform closely to the criteria Robbins finds common to the genre. This of course does not mean that the voyage to Rome did not occur; only that Luke is also concerned to show us what it meant. It is indeed an adventure of heroic proportions, as powerful and significant as epic. Paul's adventure thus informs gentile audiences in their own terms that a Hebrew religion can now be theirs, and yet Luke's message also radically challenges the gentiles who hear it. Paul, after all, is captive on board the ship, so that his emergence as a conventional literary hero reverses the status which the gentile world accords him by bringing him bound to Rome. The sea-voyage motif is thus used subversively, because it seems at first to affirm how well Christianity accords with gentile culture, and then points out how it offers to transform that culture. Ironically, the captive held in bondage is the hero.

Because of its use of Graeco-Roman journey literature, Acts shows more interest in geography than does the gospel, but still this geography is sketchy. Much is obscure, as Marshall says,[42] and there is an exasperating incompleteness. Even the early account of the church in Jerusalem compresses into summary form such interesting matters as having all things in common and breaking bread from house to house (2:44–6). Again, the journey of Paul and Barnabas to Asia Minor (from Paphos to Perga and then to Pisidian Antioch) is compressed into two verses (13:13–14), leaving us to wonder how the travellers got to the mainland, why they left Perga, and even what they did at Perga. Similarly, the journey from Iconium to Troas (16:6ff.) is cryptically brief. We learn that the missionaries were 'forbidden by the Holy Spirit to speak the word in Asia' (16:6), and so, after having gone 'through the region of Phrygia and Galatia' (16:6), they 'went down to Troas' (16:8). The identification of Galatia in this account is itself a problem (giving rise to the 'South Galatian theory'),[43] and details of the extensive itinerary are simply missing. And when Paul later goes to Greece (after another vaguely sketched itinerary: 'When he had gone through these parts' [20:2]), we are told that he stayed three months, but there is no further information about what he did or where he went, except that certain Jews are lying in wait for him as he departs for Syria, so that he is forced to go back through Macedonia (20:3). Soon after, he takes an unexplained walk across the cape from Troas to Assos instead of going with the others by ship (20:13). Finally, when the voyage to Rome itself is complete, we learn that news of Christianity has already arrived there (28:22), but we are not told how. The sense we have had all along of Paul's pioneering outreach to Rome is disconcertingly qualified by this casual notice that he has been pre-empted – however ineffectively – by other, unnamed, travellers.

The degree to which geography in Acts is full of annoying gaps is roughly in proportion to the critical enquiry expended on attempts to make it come clear. Some of these attempts even highlight the problem rather than solve it. Thus we learn that the difficult details of 13:13ff.

are explained by Paul's having caught malaria, which caused him to seek high ground.[44] Lack of information about the journey from Iconium to Troas is because Luke himself joined the party there.[45] And perhaps Luke gives two accounts of a single journey to Jerusalem, thereby mixing the itineraries. Speculation of this sort has its own interest, but the text provides no evidence of malaria, and the theory that Luke himself joined the party is based on an interpretation of the ensuing 'we section' which, as we see, cannot be read so literally. The theory of conflated itineraries soon causes even more problems, for there is no end to possible applications of this sort of argument, which could reduce any number of discrete events to ideal uniformity.

Faced with such interest in geography, yet apparently casual concern for detail, we can choose between two main possibilities. The first is that Luke's account reflects the state of his knowledge, and in his desire to be true to what he knows, he allows the imperfections to stand. The second is that his account is incomplete to show us, rather in the manner of the gospel, that the spirit is unpredictable and does not follow direct geographical itineraries. Because of the obvious claims to historical truth made by Acts, the first of these interpretations is immediately plausible. Acts does indeed present us with a jagged account, full of rough edges and disconcerting tensions. Insofar as this leaves us with unsatisfactory and not especially evocative gaps, it does not make much claim on us as literature. It seems straightforward to suggest that such structure reflects the author's incomplete knowledge.

The second interpretation, however, cannot be dispelled completely. For a start, the word 'literature' indicates an uncertain quality. The very roughness of certain parts provides a sense of truth-to-life – as the term 'diary-like effect' suggests – a kind of rugged authenticity such as Helen Gardner finds also in the gospel according to Mark.[46] Besides, whether Luke contrived the effect or not, the geographical gaps and various scattered journeys and abrupt departures do serve Luke's central, driving insistence that our geographical destinations and our finding the spirit do not always coincide. In short, there is a distinctive tension throughout Acts between a pleasing sweep of the geographical compass and particular invasions and compulsions of the spirit, expressing the same interplay as in Luke's gospel between continuity and discontinuity, offering and response, prescription and surprise.

I am aware that I have now used the first interpretation to dispel irony, and the second to re-admit it, and there is, at last, no easy way to reconcile the contending claims of these two points of view. The moment at which historical data, geographical place-names and itineraries disclose to a reader the spirit of Luke's theological message is likely to be as unpredictable for individual readers as it was for Paul on the road to Damascus and for his audiences in the other journeys. The author of Acts is well aware of pulling us two ways simultaneously, as becomes evident especially in his development of the Jerusalem motif.

We recall how, in Luke's gospel, Jerusalem is at once the goal of Jesus' journey and the place where he will be rejected. Concentration on Jerusalem is a prior condition, as it were, of the church's development beyond Judea, recorded in Acts. And yet Acts calls our attention to Jerusalem even more strenuously than does the gospel. The word itself (in Greek and Hebrew spellings) occurs thirty times in the gospel, but sixty-four times in Acts.[47] Far from turning his back on the holy city, therefore, the author of Acts reminds us at every opportunity that it is the church's doctrinal centre, and Paul makes six separate journeys there. Paul (9:26), Peter (11:2), Barnabas (11:22), and various other missionaries (11:27) carry their message from Jerusalem. The peculiar little record of choosing a successor for Judas (1:22–26) – one Matthias, who is not heard from again – is mainly to consolidate the authority of the original twelve in the holy city. Although Paul receives the Spirit on the way to Damascus, the missionary enterprise itself takes its authority from the Jerusalem base. Clearly, Luke is guarding here against spurious innovations in Christian teaching, and works to establish an authoritative tradition. Jerusalem's rejection of Jesus indeed precipitated a geographical outreach, and the Spirit does not belong to any local habitation. Still, we must take our place in the world, preserving such continuity with the past as enables us to take our bearings towards the future. And, as in the gospel, irony throughout Acts is a principal device for expressing the perplexities and indirections of such an understanding of the way of faith.

Significantly, Acts begins with a reminder to the disciples that their hopes for a restored Israel should not be too literal, and that they do not know when they will be taken by surprise by the kingdom. Luke has the disciples ask the resurrected Jesus, 'will you at this time restore the kingdom to Israel?' (1:6). They are told, bluntly, 'It is not for you to know times or seasons' (1:7). They are then instructed that their journey in power of the Spirit will take them from Judea and Samaria 'to the end of the earth' (1:8). They are to travel with a purpose, but their clear intent can become the vehicle of an unsuspected, higher design. In some such fashion, the lame man being carried to the Temple to beg for alms happens to meet Peter and John. He turns, 'expecting to receive something from them' (3:5), but instead of money he is given a cure.

Structurally, the episode suggests how journey, intent, and outcome are at once interconnected and ironically discontinuous.

Likewise, we appreciate the irony of Saul's holding the coats of those who stone Stephen (7:58). If we missed the point initially, Luke forces it on us when Paul himself comes with some bitterness to see it: 'And when the blood of Stephen thy witness was shed, I also was standing by and approving, and keeping the garments of those who killed him' (22:20). The re-direction of Paul's allegiance from prime persecutor of Christians to prime missionary involves the interruption of journeys he undertakes willingly (to persecute Christians), and the completion of a journey (to Rome) where he travels in bonds. At one point, the Lord reassures the understandably suspicious Ananias that despite appearances to the contrary, Paul is 'a chosen instrument of mine' (9:15). It is a chastening statement: we cannot be sure that even a cruel persecutor does not work God's will despite himself, and yet it would be dangerous to excuse our own evil-doing on such grounds. Indeed, when Sapphira tells the same lie as her husband (also called Ananias), not knowing that he has fallen down dead, there is a chilling predictability in the account which leads her to the same fate. There is irony indeed in her not knowing what the reader knows, as she repeats her husband's answer to the question about whether or not they had made a full financial offering. In the first instance, irony shows us how unpredictable can be God's ways to man; in the second, how they can be all too predictable. In both cases, the principals themselves are unaware of their true circumstances, which the reader perceives.

The two examples I have just discussed are admittedly limit cases, and most of the irony in Acts occupies a place between the suggestion that wrong-doing is part of God's plan, and the suggestion that even minor wrong-doing will be punished inflexibly. As with the cure of the lame man, expectation and discovery, direction and re-direction are caught up in a tissue of cross-motivations where responsibility and circumstance, initiative and response, meet in complex ways. Thus the Ethiopian eunuch reads scripture, but without understanding; only on meeting Philip does he learn to apply his reading to Jesus, and subsequently he interrupts his journey to be baptised (8:27ff.). By contrast, Simon Magus thinks he understands and is baptised, but then offers Peter and John money in exchange, he hopes, for the power of imparting the Holy Spirit (8:18). The juxtaposition of these two stories multiplies the ironies in each attendant upon the shifting relationships of intention to truth.

Again, after Paul and Barnabas are forced to flee from Iconium to

Lystra and Derbe (14:6), they cure a crippled man and the people think they are gods. The apostles tear their clothes and insist on their ordinary humanity: even a good deed like curing a cripple can suddenly take on an unexpected and threatening aspect. The people do not see the sign as the apostles intend it, and public enthusiasm turns easily to idolatry. For his trouble, Paul is then stoned and left for dead (14:19). A parallel to this ironic story occurs two chapters earlier, when Herod gives an oration and also is praised as a god by the people (12:22). Immediately he is smitten, and is eaten by worms because he did not give God the glory. In this case, the main ironic juxtaposition is between Herod's throne and 'royal robes' (12:21) and the nasty, humiliating manner of his death. The high is made low at the very moment it thought itself most high.

There is a similar ironic play in the story of the vagabond exorcists who call upon Jesus' name (19:13). One evil spirit, rather in the manner of an illegal resident to a bailiff without a warrant, says 'Jesus I know, and Paul I know; but who are you?' and the exorcists are then set upon by the man they would have cured. Likewise, the story of the plotters who swear neither to eat nor drink until they have killed Paul (23:12, 14, 21) is left incomplete in a manner which I have found intriguing since childhood. Paul, of course, avoids their trap by rearranging his journey, but we are not told what became of the 'more than forty' men (23:21). Did they keep their rash oath and dwindle by dehydration and starvation, or did they, as it were, eat their words? We are not told, but are left with yet another instance of thwarted intent in the context of a redirected journey.

And so we come to Paul's voyage to Rome itself, the central city of the gentile world. As we have seen, the voyage by sea draws upon gentile literary models which it duplicates but reverses in the ironic account of Paul's captivity. Epic heroism and Christian heroism are analogous but also opposed, for the real meaning of Paul's journey is to transform the spirit of classical literature from within, much as the captive Paul takes over the beleaguered ship. There is further irony in the fact that Paul might have been set at liberty by Agrippa (26:32) had he not appealed for liberty to Caesar. Again, however, the very condition of Paul's bondage enables him to preach at Rome 'quite openly and unhindered' (28:31). Finally, it is worth noticing that despite the assumptions of some critics, the 'end of the earth' (1:8) to which the gospel is to travel is not simply identifiable with Rome.[48] As we have seen, the Christian message has arrived there before Paul, and Rome does not offer an epic homecoming for the Christian mission, for Paul remains in bonds.

Unlike Odysseus (who comes back to the home he left), and unlike Aeneas (who finds a new home), Paul does not come home to the kingdoms or places of this world.

Acts, we might conclude, places more emphasis on geography than does the gospel, but the two books are interdependent. In both, journey narratives are used to place before us the challenge of taking a spiritual decision which is not determined by the physical world, but which cannot be divorced from it. We are bound to take a direction, but the spirit in which we do so might transform the meaning of our travel, or make of our journey the means of having us arrive at another goal altogether. The way of life Jesus demands is, as he himself says, a way of the cross. This means, partly, that the experiences of continuity and discontinuity, of rejection enabling development and development causing rejection, are perennial in the life of faith. The central challenge is simple enough, but our experience is frequently difficult. We are all travellers of one sort or another, bent on homecoming, but the ways of our choosing are fraught with complex ironies and indirections.

5

John: Seeing and Believing

John's gospel presents the challenge of belief in an especially insistent way. As Edward Schillebeeckx says, the entire action is governed by a dialectic of belief and unbelief.[1] Jesus testifies repeatedly to what he has seen and heard with the Father (3:32), and those who accept his testimony will not perish (3:15), but those who do not are condemned already (3:18). A pervasive use of court-room images keeps before us the sense of critical decision,[2] and John never uses the noun (*pistis*), but only the verb (*pisteuo*):[3] belief, he implies, is not only a judgement made from within ourselves, but also an active relationship.

The main message of the fourth gospel is repeated even to the point of monotony. Jesus keeps telling us that whoever believes in him believes also in the Father who has sent him, and that the world is divided between those who believe and those who do not. This is the source of John's so-called dualism, which is not based on world-rejecting gnosticism as has sometimes been claimed, but on a conviction about radical differences of attitude and experience between believers and unbelievers.[4] Jesus is the light, and those who do not accept him are in the dark; he is the truth, and those who reject him dwell in falsehood; he is of the Father, and those who do not acknowledge him are of the 'world'. No man, that is, has seen the Father save Jesus, 'who is from God' (6:46). We others are assured: 'His voice you have never heard, his form you have never seen' (5:37). Jesus goes on: 'He who has seen me has seen the Father', and 'The words that I say to you I do not speak on my own authority; but the Father who dwells in me does his works' (14:10). The superb corollary is delivered unflinchingly: 'I and the Father are one' (10:30).

Such statements are likely either to draw our affirmation because Jesus' authenticity compels us, or provoke our rejection because they are preposterous. Those who prefer to live without faith will always suspect that it casts an enchanted, reassuring glow on a landscape that is really more grim and ought to be accepted as such. But to those whose knowledge is by faith, the others appear merely to crouch in their own darkness. 'I am the light of the world,' says Jesus, and 'he who follows me will not walk in darkness' (8:12).

This insistence on Jesus' unique relationship with the Father, and the firmness with which it is presented through the dialectic of belief and unbelief, light and dark, truth and falsehood, give John's gospel its particular character. As is often noticed also, Jesus in the fourth gospel is especially the omniscient Christ whose crucifixion is a kind of exaltation and enthronement where the victim stays very much in control. Just so, instead of providing a birth narrative, John takes an extraordinary step outside history altogether, claiming that Jesus pre-existed as the divine principle, the logos through whom God made the world (1:1ff.). One effect of this high Christology is to play down Jesus' human abandonment on the cross. This is not to say that the cross is unimportant: Jesus dies a terrible death in the fourth gospel as he does in the synoptics, but John presents the problem of faith with a distinctive emphasis because we are confronted so directly and unremittingly with the alarming claim that Jesus, the pre-existent logos, is one with the Father. Throughout the gospel, Jesus has a way of knowing what will happen in advance, and he is, emphatically, a divine figure come down among us. Consequently, there is an unsettling sense that our belief or unbelief, our choice of light or dark is as much a matter of him choosing us as of us choosing him. In short, those who regard Jesus' claims as preposterous and imaginary are not chosen, whereas those are chosen who take them as the living truth and not just a story. Indeed, in our very reading of the gospel the problem of choosing and being chosen is already upon us. Why, we might ask, did we pick up the book in the first place? Was the initiative our own, or were we somehow providentially directed to it? It is of course fruitless to pursue such enquiries too vigorously, because there is always more in events than reason can grasp. But a special achievement of John's gospel is to make us feel how complex our actual experience of faith is, because our particular responsibilities are often unclear. This helps to explain why we are addressed so consistently – albeit paradoxically – both as responsible free agents and also as creatures incapable of helping ourselves.

On the one hand, the message is clear and imperative: 'He who does not obey the Son shall not see life, but the wrath of God rests upon him' (3:36). This is echoed by Jesus: 'he who hears my word and believes him who sent me, has eternal life; he does not come into judgment' (5:24). Repeatedly, Jesus badgers his listeners: 'How can you believe, who ... do not seek the glory that comes from the only God?' (5:44); the Comforter, he assures us, will reprove the world 'because they do not believe in me' (16:8–9). We are condemned, threatened, admonished

and questioned because we are responsible. Otherwise, Jesus'
statements are merely cruel jibes assuring us of God's anger. Plainly we
bear some responsibility for what we believe or do not believe. We must
work at resisting evil and doing good according to our lights, in
however groping a fashion and in whatever semi-darkness we find
ourselves.

On the other hand, we cannot save ourselves, and we require
assistance. Jesus states that 'You did not choose me, but I chose you'
(15:16), and again, 'because ... I chose you out of the world, therefore
the world hates you' (15:19). At one point we learn that some 'could not
believe' (12:39) because their hearts were hardened so that a saying of
Isaiah might be fulfilled (12:38). Such statements imply that we have no
choice about being chosen, and it is clear from the general reception of
Jesus that the world felt itself confronted by something arbitrary for
which it ought not to be held accountable.

With a certain amount of ingenuity it is possible to reduce the first set
of these examples to the second, and vice versa. Calvin's *Institutes* is
perhaps the most thoroughgoing reduction in one direction, and
gnosticism in the other. Yet one of the main fascinations of John's gospel
is the skill with which he presents our uncertain experience of
combined responsibility and dependency, initiative and response. The
clear opposition between light and dark therefore paradoxically
becomes a way of showing us also how in actual experience evidence
and belief are in perpetually unstable relationship. John, that is, keeps
returning us to the half-lights where the faith of most of us resides.

As is frequently noticed, Jesus' statements are often misunderstood
so that he can show his audience what they have missed. In being set
right, his hearers come to grasp the point in a different way. Sometimes,
indeed, neither faith nor understanding emerges, but frequently both
do. For instance, the well-disposed Nicodemus learns what it means to
be born again (3:4ff.), and the Samaritan woman declares that Jesus is
Christ, but seems not to understand his offer of living water (4:11). The
main point about the cure of the man born blind (9:1ff.) is that he
gradually comes to understand what has happened to him. At first, the
only thing he knows certainly is that he has received his sight: 'one
thing I know, that though I was blind, now I see' (9:25). Pressed by the
authorities, he is moved to defend his benefactor ('If this man were not
from God, he could do nothing' [9:33]), and for his pains he is cast out of
the synagogue. On re-encountering Jesus, the blind man at least sees in
a spiritual sense, and declares his belief (9:38).

At this point, some reflection on how we come to know a work of literature might be pertinent, because I am now claiming that John's presentation of developing faith is imaginative as well as prescriptive. Let us take the example of John Donne's famous *Holy Sonnet XIV*, a poem about the desire for grace, and about being chosen. The sonnet begins with four lines describing the speaker's yearning for God to invade his soul:

> Batter my heart, three person'd God; for, you
> As yet but knocke, breathe, shine, and seeke to mend;
> That I may rise, and stand, o'erthrow mee, and bend
> Your force, to breake, blowe, burn and make me new.[5]

At first we feel the impact of the verbs, and the contrast between gentleness in 'knocke, breathe, shine, and seeke', and powerful action in 'Batter', 'breake, blowe, burn'. Aware of his own recalcitrance and the flaw in himself that needs mending, the speaker calls out for violent invasion. The vigorous imperatives, 'Batter', 'o'erthrow', 'bend', suggest the pent-up energy of a desire for grace which cannot compel grace.

We might also notice the symmetry between the three-fold activity described in line 2, and the similar pattern of line 4, each directing us back to the 'three person'd God' of the opening. For the Father knocks, the Spirit breathes, and the Son (developing a favourite seventeenth-century pun) shines and seeks. Just so, to 'make new' the speaker's flawed heart, the Father must break, the Spirit blow, the Son burn.[6] The single action of grace is therefore three-fold, in keeping with the single threefoldness of God as the Trinitarian formula describes him. Yet these lines express God's single threefoldness also in another way, for an implicit metaphor unites all six actions. God is depicted as an ironworker or blacksmith,[7] who at first knocks upon the metal, and then breathes on it to shine it, seeking the crack or flaw. To make the repair, God must exert force, breaking the crack open in order to fuse it ('blowe', 'burn').

We now begin to see that the poem draws upon a sophisticated theology but this does not much help the speaker, as the second quatrain shows us. There, he reflects on his alientation (despite his knowledge) from the good he desires: he is like a captive within a walled city, 'betroth'd unto your enemie', and must await invasion. The poem ends with a passionate desire for divine violence: 'For I / Except you enthrall me, never shall be free, / Nor ever chast, except you ravish mee.'

Throughout Donne's sonnet, transcendent mystery engages us by contact with ordinary human longings to be free of anxiety and uncertainty, as a rational mind seeks to come to rest in that kind of order which satisfies the heart's desire. By attending to contrasts between gentleness and force, imperative mood and submissive desire, impersonal martial imagery and personal urgency, acquired knowledge and given illumination, we come to understand something of the perennial condition of the human soul seeking God's grace.

Not all of this is likely to strike a reader straight away, and part of my point is that we must labour to open up the text. Still, insight when it comes strikes us somehow as *sui generis*, and surprising. An inexperienced reader could well ponder Donne's sonnet and still not truly 'see' it. Even practiced readers might overlook the implicit metaphor of the ironworker, and some might regard it as over-interpretation. The process remains open-ended, and this is one reason Donne's poem continues to engage us. Competency in reading a literary text is to some degree the reward of discipline, practice and desire, but the quality and depth of one's insight and understanding are unpredictable. Biographical circumstances and psychological makeup, the occasion in which the text is encountered, other people with whom it is being discussed, familiarity with other literature of the kind, and so on, have a complex relevance to interpretation.

John's presentation of belief also has this kind of literary fullness and open-endedness. Just as the poem shows theological knowledge coming to grips with entanglements of experience, so the word made flesh engages the world. Through the Son's actions and words, belief is mediated to a variety of people disposed in a variety of ways to receive it or not, or partly to receive it, or to learn gradually to understand it. Insight into 'the light of the world' is neither produced automatically by the labour of seeking to find it, nor divorced entirely from such labour. Illumination is a surprise, but we must learn to seek it, even while expecting it to surprise us. The real life of faith is precisely in the poise of such contrary energies, and to surrender its exacting tension is to falsify the peculiarly resonant achievement of John's gospel.

There is, however, an important difference between the gospel and the poem, because Donne expresses for us a psychological conflict that we might appreciate or leave aside: he does not say, 'If you reject this poem you are damned.' But the gospel says precisely that about Jesus' message by making an absolute, extra-literary claim upon us. This claim, as we see, is boldly presented, even though it is everywhere held in tension also with a literary sense (such as Donne's sonnet also gives us) that faith is a special way of seeing things, and the difference between having it and not having it is often perilously fine. We are all the man born blind, learning to read our experience to discover what is most real in it. That reality, always unexpectedly new, is the Father. As we have seen, Jesus alone knows what he has 'seen and heard' with God, and throughout the gospel conveys his message through further acts of seeing and hearing.[8] Yet in John's gospel the evidence of sight and hearing bears no straightforward relationship to the faith (or lack of it) that ensues, and is often highly personal and unpredictable. Sometimes, indeed, seeing and hearing do provide direct evidence for faith, but John also suggests how equivocal is the relationship between what is given to the senses and what we choose (or are permitted) to believe as a result.

For instance, the Galileans receive Jesus, 'having seen all that he had done at Jerusalem' (4:45), and many others who 'had seen what he did, believed in him' (11:45). People come 'also to see Lazarus' (12:9), and many believe. 'You have seen me and yet do not believe' (6:36), says Jesus, and the gospel itself claims to be based on first-hand eyewitness: 'He who saw it has borne witness — his testimony is true' (19:35). As C. K. Barrett points out, the miracles of the fourth gospel are offered as visible signs to promote belief, 'in marked contrast' to the synoptic tradition, where the word 'sign' tends to be used of something Jesus' adversaries seek and which he refuses.[9] In John, the first sign is the miracle at Cana, which causes the disciples to believe (2:11), and John says he has selected a number of such examples so that readers might believe too (20:30). Norman Perrin points out that Jesus is presented in the fourth gospel as a divine man or wonder worker in a less tentative way than in the synoptics.[10] People, in short, do believe because they see.

Likewise, people believe because they hear: 'As he spoke thus, many believed in him' (8:30). 'Every one who is of the truth hears my voice' (18:37), says Jesus, and 'he who hears my word and believes him who sent me, has eternal life' (5:24). The Samaritans believe because of the saying of the woman who testified (4:39), and the official at Capernaum believes in Jesus' word (4:50). At the tomb, Mary Magdalene does not recognise Jesus when she sees him, but does when he speaks (20:16). John also is concerned with early traditions about how belief was conveyed by word of mouth, and his gospel stresses that witnesses talked about Jesus to one another before actually meeting him. Thus, John alone tells us that Jesus' earliest disciples had previously been disciples of John the Baptist (1:35ff.), and in John alone Andrew calls Peter, and Philip calls Nathanael (1:40ff.). John's stress on the continuity of verbal witness partly reflects the fact that the gospel's final redactor (or redactors) had to deal with an especially complex textual tradition. Even as we have it, the gospel is full of seams and interpolations of a striking sort.[11] Paul S. Minear concludes that with one exception (which is explained on textual grounds), 'no person in the gospel became a disciple save through the mediation of some other person'.[12] Hearing, therefore, does promote belief.

As Walter Ong points out,[13] sight is the human sense which most permits the distancing of its object, and the more we define knowledge in terms of sight, the more we deal with surface appearances held over and against us. The need to give distinctness, edge and clarity to knowledge moves us to describe its contents visually and impersonally. Sound, by contrast, reveals interiors and tends to the personal. Sound, Ong says, places us in the midst of a situation and calls us to the expression of present power; sight fixes things over and against us. This difference corresponds roughly to the contrast between subjective and objective, interior and exterior, personal and impersonal.

Without drawing on Walter Ong, critics have applied something very like these broad distinctions to the fourth gospel. Bultmann, for instance, followed by Dodd, compares, a Greek conception of knowledge based on sight (external, distanced, static), to a Hebrew conception based on intercourse with God (interior, immediate, dynamic).[14] In John's gospel, says Dodd, Christ's knowledge of the Father has the Hellenic, spatial quality of direct vision, and is mediated in a Hebraic manner through the words of a living person.

We can easily extend this suggestion to John's entire treatment of belief. Insofar as he wants to avoid reducing belief to subjectivity (any reading of a text is as valid as any other), he insists on the fact that Jesus entered history and was visibly evident. Insofar as he wants to avoid limiting the significance of that fact to a single place and time (this text has one sense only) he creates the impression of Jesus' present relevance through his words and the verbal testimonies of those who believed in him. At this point, further reflection on Ong's theories as distinct from those of Bultmann and Dodd is pertinent, because Ong avoids the abrupt Hellenic-Hebraic contrast. He develops instead the interesting notion that the New Testament was written at a time when a predominantly oral culture was being shaped towards visualism by means of alphabetic writing.[15] The alphabet allows words to be fixed in space as never before, to be taken out of time and ordered objectively. The word can thus be seen in the text analogously to being seen by the historical eyewitness. Paul S. Minear[16] is entirely correct to say that the author of the fourth gospel presents his book as a substitute for the 'signs' which he describes, and that the reader can come to faith by 'seeing' the book. Of course, this kind of seeing is not the same as actually seeing Jesus in the flesh, just as 'hearing' his word in the written text is not the same as hearing it in his own voice. The concrete, actually observed, human Jesus has passed beyond our reach, as he said he would, but now he sends another comforter, or paraclete, by whose spiritual aid we may come to understand the real meaning of the text we are looking at instead. 'A little while, and you will see me no more,' says Jesus, and 'again, a little while, and you will see me' (16:16). Some of the disciples find this hard to fathom, for the word 'seeing' is used in two senses. You will not see me, Jesus assures them, because I will be dead and gone. But you will understand me better ('see' in a spiritual sense) because the paraclete will provide insight and help you to interpret the story, and even to write a book about it.

The plain distinctions between seeing and hearing on which I initially relied will now begin to seem too simple. Seeing the actual Jesus and seeing the text are analogous but different, and seeing the miracles can be different from seeing what they mean. Likewise, hearing Jesus' actual words and reading them in a book are analogous but different, just as hearing the words and hearing their spiritual sense are different. Hearing can be merely literal unless we 'see' what the words say, and the visible signs are superficial unless we 'hear' the word spoken through them. At this point we might consider again the famous declaration that Jesus is the logos, or 'word'. As is generally known, the Greek *logos* means 'reason', 'story', 'word' and translates the Hebrew *dabhar*, the 'word' or deed by which God creates. John's logos thus combines the sense of something heard with something made visible, and the pre-existent, divine Christ contains within himself the sum of what we correctly 'see' and 'hear' through faith. John works upon such differently-shaded senses of seeing and hearing with the loving ingenuity of a musician composing a fugue, as Dodd says.[17] The gospel's fundamental injunction to believe is thus developed in a complex manner captivating of our imaginations and challenging to our powers of interpretation, for despite our responsibility to choose the light and hear the word, we might not recognise what we see, nor correctly interpret what we hear. The very forcefulness of Jesus' declaration of the Father's will therefore confirms how problematic is our human response. If faith is a gift, can we be blamed for thinking that Jesus' claim to be with the Father is simply untrue?

For instance, Jesus sees Mathanael under the fig tree in more than one sense. His words, 'when thou wast under the fig tree, I saw thee' (1:48) evoke what might seem to be an exaggerated response, for Nathanael immediately declares Jesus the Son of God. We are not told what Jesus 'saw' under the fig tree,[18] but clearly he 'saw into' Nathanael, who is shocked and impressed. Certainly, Jesus did not just casually spot Nathanael under the tree as an object occupying space. Yet John also addresses the reader here, by having Jesus draw attention to Nathanael's response: 'Because I said unto thee, I saw you under the fig tree, do you believe? You shall see greater things than these' (1:50). The reader is provoked also to acknowledge Jesus' special insight, and to apply to himself the promise that there is even more to 'see'.

Likewise, in the declaration, 'he who does not obey the Son shall not see life' (3:36), the word 'see' stands for 'know' or 'experience' in a larger sense. And when Jesus says, 'Yet a little while, and the world will see me no more, but you will see me' (14:19), he contrasts the two meanings of 'see' in accordance with his own advice delivered earlier: 'Do not judge by appearances, but judge with right judgment' (7:24). Seeing, that is, has a superficial and an interior meaning, and the first of these is insufficient for faith: 'You have seen me, and yet do not believe' (6:36). This lesson applies also to the book. Jesus, we are told, did 'many other signs ... which are not written' (20:30), but 'these are written, that you may believe' (20:31). The visible words on the page are as open to superficial reading as the other signs, and likewise require the 'right judgment' of insightful interpretation.

At this point we might recall that when the 'other disciple', whom the gospel presents as a model true believer, visited the empty sepulchre, 'he saw and believed' (20:8). Clearly, he did not see in any straightforward sense, because there was nothing there, but Jesus' absence to literal sight opens the eyes of faith. It is not too much to suggest that written language likewise entombs meaning, which is in a way always partly absent. As St. Paul says, 'the written code kills, but the Spirit gives life' (II Cor. 3:6), and Walter Ong points out that spirit here is breath, 'vehicle of the living word in time'.[19] The text itself, we might say, is a kind of sepulchre which provides evidence of the living reality which written words do not present directly, but which is affirmed by faith. The things seen and heard in the text alone do not compel faith, or enable readers to declare that the gospel story is true.

Hearing also has different senses. 'Every one who is of the truth hears my voice' (18:37) says Jesus to Pilate, who has trouble really hearing what is meant. His ironic words of mockery – 'Here is the man' (19:15); 'Here is your King' (19:14) – are then doubly ironic because

inadvertently affirming the gospel truth: Pilate does not only fail to
'hear' what Jesus says; he also fails to 'hear' his own words. And others
beside Pilate have similar trouble: 'Many of his disciples, when they
heard it, said, "This is a hard saying; who can listen to it?" ' (6:60). They
hear the spoken words, but do not 'hear' with the ears of understanding.
Labouring amidst similar perplexities, the Jews ask one another, 'What
does he mean by saying . . . ?' (7:36). As we have seen, Jesus is not shy to
state the importance of his words: 'he who hears my word and believes
him who sent me, has eternal life; he does not come into judgment, but
has passed from death to life' (5:24). Yet any madman might say as
much and be rightly disregarded. However, Jesus himself acknowledges
that plain statement is not sufficient for what he wishes to convey: 'I
have said this to you in figures' (16:25). Proverbs or 'figures' need to be
'heard' in a spiritual sense, and only by speaking in a manner that
stimulates our emotions and desires, our senses and feelings as well as
our reason, can Jesus engage us in the kind of personal relationship that
faith requires. It seems we are to know the Father 'plainly' (16:25) as an
object, and also through a complex meeting of interiors. 'In that day'
Jesus says, 'you will know that I am in my Father, and you in me, and I in
you' (14:20). Sight and hearing, in short, interpenetrate as they reach
towards a higher kind of knowledge which preceded and which will
subsume them.

A similar complex deployment of sight and hearing could well be a
clue to the puzzling episode in the story of the woman taken in adultery,
where Jesus twice writes on the ground. (I am treating the story as part
of the gospel because it appears in most bibles and is well known,
despite strong evidence that it is not from 'John's' hand). Critics have
spent a good deal of effort trying to decide what Jesus might have
written,[20] but without considering the importance of the act itself:
omission of any information about the words suggests that content is
not the important thing, and we notice that Jesus wrote on the ground
as if he does not hear the accusers (the Authorised Version contains the
statement 'as though he *heard* them not' [8:6]). He then stands and
speaks to the woman's accusers, inviting anyone without sin to throw
the first stone, and 'when they *heard* it' (8:9) they were smitten
inwardly. Jesus meanwhile turns away and writes again.

Speaking and hearing in this account are in counterpoint to writing
and not hearing. Those who hear are affected inwardly, but when they
are not so affected, they want to stone the woman. Stoning, like
crucifying, requires the depersonalization of the victim, who is set apart
for the purpose and treated as an object. We are told, however, that the

woman is 'in the midst' (8:3): that is, she is among her accusers and is more part of them than they know while they treat her as one set over and against. When Jesus stoops to write, the action precludes hearing, and in itself therefore becomes part of his accusation of the accusers. The letter objectifies and kills just as surely as the stones in their hands. The word, by contrast, turns the accusers into themselves (into the midst, as it were). They then realise their affinity with the woman, and none of them casts a stone.

The whole episode can be interpreted as a comment on reading the gospel itself. Writing – like the empty tomb, another kind of stone – objectifies and fixes, and the living word enabling faith is not found in it. However, the empty tomb may occasion belief, just as writing on the ground points the accusers to better understanding. And even though the story as I have described it seems to favour hearing over seeing, Jesus' words directly after dismissing the woman help to fill out the picture: 'I am the light of the world; he who follows me will not walk in darkness, but will have the light of life' (8:12). Again, 'hearing' Jesus' word leads us to 'see' the truth, and the senses interpenetrate at a higher level, for there is a real vision to believe in, if we have ears to hear. But insight, it seems, is not just for the asking, and in some sense must be delivered up to us.

Still, the fourth gospel assures us that we can detect the father's 'glory' in and through Jesus' adventure among us. The word 'glory' is a favourite of John's, and indicates God's presence visibly manifested. As Bruce Vawter says, 'glory' is an old Testament term, used especially 'in connection with the Tent of Meeting (cf. Ex. 40:3ff.) and the Temple (I Kings 8:11)'.[21] Thus, the Johannine Jesus refers to 'the temple of his body' (2:21), and by coming in the flesh to take up an abode in the midst of us, he is himself the tabernacle, the tent of witness, the glorious manifestation of his Father.[22] When the word became flesh we 'beheld his glory' (1:14). Similarly, the miracle at Cana 'manifested his glory' (2:11), and Jesus later reminds Martha: 'Did I not tell you that if you would believe, you would see the glory of God?' (11:40).

G. Wilson Knight correctly points out that in John's gospel 'Physical sight symbolises another "sight",' but then regrets that 'there is no exact name' for this.[23] The word 'glory', however, provides exactly such a name, for it indicates the illumination or radiance bespeaking God's presence in Jesus' actions, visible to the eyes of faith. It is the recognition of what the signs reveal, and, by extension, what the book reveals. Indeed, readers of the book have an advantage over those present at the actual events, because when Jesus' earthly life is complete it is easier in retrospect to see the significance of the parts. We are even told that 'the Spirit had not yet been given, because Jesus was not yet glorified' (7:39). When Jesus is 'glorified' by his death and resurrection – and this is indicated by the repeated references to his 'hour' – the spirit will be sent to open the eyes of believers, among whom are discerners of the book's true meaning. The process of insightful reading – of 'hearing' the word through seeing the written text – also participates in God's glory, and the same challenge is offered to the reader as to Jesus' own interlocutors: Do you believe? As we have seen, the gospel stories depict the complex dynamism of belief seeking rest in certitude but often having to struggle through various degrees of seeing and hearing in search of its object. The same process applies to reading and interpreting the book in which the truth about Jesus is written down.

For instance, Nicodemus comes by night (3:2) to confess that he believes Jesus is from God, but he does not understand what Jesus tells him about being reborn. It seems likely that he approached Jesus under cover of darkness to avoid detection and there is no need to discount this interpretation, even if we also think that darkness is the condition of Nicodemus' understanding. This, we remind ourselves, is the case also with Judas who goes out (John alone tells us) into the night when he has betrayed Jesus (13:30). Further, because Nicodemus is a Pharisee, a member of the Sanhedrin (3:1) and a rabbi (3:10) there is a strong suggestion that he represents Judaism itself. His partial acknowledgement of Jesus and the darkness of his own understanding therefore indicate in an imaginative way John's view of the privileged position of Jews in relation to Jesus, and their difficulty in acknowledging him.[24]

Similarly, the encounter with the Samaritan woman is particular and detailed, but hovers on the boundaries of allegory. The woman is briskly aggressive: 'How is it that you, a Jew, ask a drink of me, a woman of Samaria' (4:9). She is also practical, though literal-minded: 'Sir, you have nothing to draw with, and the well is deep' (4:11). And she is perhaps a bit credulous: 'Sir, I perceive that you are a prophet' (4:19). Again, none of the impress of particularity needs to be surrendered when we see that the woman also represents certain general problems of Jesus' mission to the Samaritans. They are outsiders, and a Jew would not be expected to converse with one, and especially not with a woman. The disciples 'marvelled that he was talking with a woman' (4:27), and she herself is surprised by the encounter, reminding Jesus that 'Jews have no dealings with Samaritans' (4:9). Like her, Samaritans in general are less knowledgeable than Jews about God's plan, and Jesus is rather blunt about this: 'You worship what you do not know; we worship what we know, for salvation is from the Jews' (4:22). Nonetheless, opportunity is also offered to the Samaritans to acknowledge Jesus as Christ, and Jesus insists that 'the hour is coming, and now is' (4:23) for God to be worshipped 'in spirit and in truth' (4:23) unconfined to a particular group. Clearly, the woman does not grasp all that Jesus tells her, and misunderstands his saying about the living water (4:10ff.). Instead, she is impressed by the vulgar fact of his telling her about her many husbands. Her subsequent confession of Christ to the other Samaritans preserves something of her coarse understanding, combined with tentativeness: 'Come, see a man who told me all that I ever did. Can this be the Christ?' (4:29). Such is the nature, John suggests, of the entire mission to outsiders. Jesus breaks with tradition in order to deliver this message, and the soil in which he sows his word here is less well-prepared, though also worthy to receive him.[25] Not surprisingly, he is less than fully understood; yet he is accepted in faith.

Unlike the stories of Nicodemus and the Samaritan woman, the story of the official whose son is cured (4:46ff.) has a synoptic parallel in the cure of the centurion's son, and there are similarities also to the cure of the Syrophonecian woman's son.[26] John's version, however, is placed in close proximity to the stories about Nicodemus and the Samaritan woman so that they form a group.[27] It is even possible that the story of the official's son has been displaced from its position after the first Cana miracle (2:1–11), described as the first of Jesus' signs (2:11). The cure of the official's son, we are told, is 'the second sign that Jesus did when he had come from Judea to Galilee' (4:54), even though other signs have been mentioned at 2:23. This is a key argument for the claim that John worked from a special 'signs source', and it has a strong following. Yet, as Raymond E. Brown points out, John could also mean quite literally the second miracle *en route* from Judea to Galilee, and this is one way of solving the difficulty without resorting to a theory of displacement.[28]

The significant point for our purposes, however, is John's reproof of the official's request for a cure: 'Unless you see signs and wonders you will not believe' (4:48). We notice that the official had first 'heard' (4:47) of Jesus before asking for a cure, and Jesus' reproof suggests that the mere seeing of signs and wonders is insufficient for faith: Jesus is not just a wonder worker, and there are different kinds of seeing and hearing. When Jesus then says 'Go; your son will live' (4:50), the official believes, and subsequently learns of his son indeed being cured 'As he was going down' (4:51).[29] It is not so clear in John as in the synoptic stories that the official is a gentile. But the formula 'himself believed, and all his household' (4:53) is used in Acts only of the conversion of gentiles, and might here also indicate that the official is such.[30] If this is the case, then Jesus offers a firm warning against simple pagan expectations of seeing a wonder, and we should notice a carefully-graded progression through the three stories from Jerusalem to Samaria and the gentiles. John's point is to show us different kinds and qualities of belief among different groups, and in each story different kinds of seeing and hearing coalesce in acts of belief which are more or less adequate to the challenge at hand. For all of us, faith, like reading itself, is an adventure towards true interpretation conducted through the impedimenta of our prejudices and wordliness. Our response to the challenge of faith, however, is as unpredictable as the challenge is imperative.

As in these three stories, so throughout the gospel John has a special interest both in particular details and in structural patterns. For instance, he tells us the number and size of the pots at Cana (2:6) and the value and weight of the ointment Mary used (12:3–5). He tells us the time of day Jesus sat at the well in Samaria (4:6), gives us the name of the pool of Siloam (9:7) and the distance from Bethany to Jerusalem (11:18). He tells us that Jesus is tired (4:6) and troubled (12:27) and, uniquely, that he wept (11:35). His interest in structure is reflected in a fondness for sevens and threes: there are seven miracles, seven 'I Am' sayings and seven references to his 'hour'. Jesus goes three times to Galilee, three passovers are mentioned, and three other Jewish feasts. John the Baptist appears three times as witness, Jesus speaks three times from the cross and there are three resurrection appearances.[31] The repeated references to Moses and to Jesus as an eschatological prophet (the one greater than Moses) invite us to see a further pattern of typological parallels between the gospel and the pentateuch.[32] As Moses lifted up the serpent in the wilderness, so the Son of Man will be lifted up on the cross in the wilderness of the world (3:14), and as Moses provided manna from heaven, so Jesus provides bread for the multitude (6:32).

Incident and design thus equally lay claim to our attention, and John implies that belief is engendered in the embrace of particulars which in varying degrees lead us towards larger patterns of meaning. Experience is, as it were, many-layered, and the ways evidence brightens into faith are as various as the ways we discover in a text how patterns are imminent within particulars. Once again, the act of reading is analogous to the process by which we come to faith, but just as the text does not determine our individual response, neither does the claim it makes that Jesus is God determine our belief that such a claim is true. The general principle here is clear enough, and I would like to conclude by dealing with a set of incidents peculiar to John, exemplifying not only his compositional strategy but also how it relates to hearing and seeing.

My first example is the pair of resurrection appearances to Mary Magdalene and Thomas (20:11ff.; 20:26ff.). The chapter in which these appearances occur is carefully divided in two, so that the parallel is plain. Each half has two scenes, and each scene begins by drawing our attention to a specific time (20:1, 19).[33] In the first scene of each half, Jesus appears to his disciples, and in the second scene to an individual who is perplexed about whether or not this is really Jesus. In both scenes there is a careful counterpoint of hearing and seeing.

Magdalene sees the resurrected Lord but at first thinks he is a gardener. When he calls her name she recognises him, but Jesus then says 'Do not hold me, for I have not yet ascended to the Father' (20:17). It appears that she wants to hold, or more precisely, 'cling to' him in the old way, and she must learn that Jesus will not be present just as he was. By contrast, Thomas hears the disciples bear witness, but does not believe that Jesus has appeared to them. Jesus then invites him to probe his wounds, at which point Thomas says 'My Lord and my God!' (20:28), the highest Christological pronouncement of the gospel.

Contrary to what is sometimes thought, there is no indication that Thomas actually touches Jesus. Indeed it seems more likely that he does not, just as it seems that Magdalene is touching him when he tells her not to.[34] As Walter Ong points out, the sense of touch is more fundamental even than sight for our recognition of something as an object. By touching, we come to know a thing most basically as not ourselves, and yet touch is also an especially intimate sense. Confirmed by sight, touch would therefore establish the presence of the object not-ourselves; confirmed by hearing, it would establish the object's intimate relation to us. In short, touch mediates between hearing and sight, so that we can say without strain that we have been touched by something we have heard, or have seen a touching sight.[35] Thus Magdalene's hearing the Lord's voice moves her initially to capture the intimate moment of recognition through the medium of touch: she would objectify and hold what she has heard. However, she must temper her belief and learn that the visible sign will pass, but her inner love and faith must endure. By contrast, Thomas does not listen to what the disciples tell him, and says he will give his interior assent only when he has seen and touched. He is initially moved to interiorise the visual object through touch, but he seems in fact to believe by seeing alone, and, indeed, by hearing Jesus' invitation. He too learns that over-insistence on the concrete dulls the spiritual sense by which we recognise the Lord's presence. For Thomas, as for Magdalene, the evidence of sight and hearing bears no predictable relationship to the interior assent which is faith. We are to learn therefore that Christ the Word and bringer of light gives us faith despite our intentions to lay hold on him for ourselves. The gospel invites us to grasp this truth imaginatively, and once again hearing and seeing interpenetrate to bring us to a sense of how elusive faith can be.

In the stories of the man born blind (9:13ff.), and of Jesus' trial before Pilate, seeing and hearing are carefully deployed to depict the dynamics of belief. At first, the Jews do not believe that the blind man received his sight, and so they interrogate his parents, who attest that their son was born blind. The parents are nervous about the whole affair, and direct the authorities to hear the man's own account: 'Ask him; he is of age, he will speak for himself' (9:21). The authorities seek out the man, and state that they know Jesus is a sinner. The man replies, evasively though firmly, 'Whether he is a sinner, I do not know; one thing I know, that though I was blind, now I see' (9:25). When the authorities persist, the man scolds them for not listening: 'I have told you already, and you would not listen. Why do you want to hear it again?' (9:27). The authorities then claim that whereas they know the source of Moses' authority, 'we do not know where he [Jesus] comes from' (9:29). As the conversation continues, the man becomes increasingly secure in his conclusions: 'If this man were not from God, he could do nothing' (9:33). When at last he is ejected from the synagogue, he openly acknowledges Jesus, who says: 'For judgment I came into this world, that those who do not see may see, and that those who see may become blind' (9:39).

The interrogation of Jesus by Pilate also raises the question of Jesus' origins ('Where are you from?' [19:9]), and the process of enquiry again is ironically reversed so that the judge becomes the accused. Like the man born blind, Pilate at first tries to be neutral and inoffensive to the Jewish authorities. 'I find no crime in him' is repeated three times, but Pilate is compelled, partly by Jesus himself, to take a firmer position. The very moment after having allayed anxiety about the primary charge concerning the kingdom, Jesus tactlessly insists: 'Every one who is of the truth hears my voice' (18:37). Pilate is thus forced to attend to a more over-arching claim. His celebrated reply, 'What is truth?' is essentially an evasion, a refusal to listen. It is as if one should say, 'This is the happiest day of my life', only to hear in return 'What do you mean by happy?' Further to distract himself from having really to hear what Jesus is saying, Pilate decides to make a visual display, and Jesus is scourged and dressed up like a king. 'Here is the man' (19:5), Pilate tells the crowd, hoping that such a battered and pathetic sight will seem no threat to anyone. But the Jews insist still that Jesus claims to be the Son of God, and Jesus' refusal to speak ('You will not speak to me?' [19:10]) must appear to the pragmatic secular official to imply consent. When Jesus does reply, the words are disconcertingly close to insolent: 'You would have no power over me unless it had been given you from above' (9:11). Perhaps concluding that such reckless behaviour could come only from a crank, Pilate seeks to release his captive, but the Jews still press their point: 'every one who makes himself a king sets himself against Caesar' (19:12). This strikes the most sensitive nerve, and Pilate's verdict follows.

The story of the man born blind is mainly about coming to see properly (that is, in a spiritual sense, with the eyes of faith), and listening to accusations and answering questions are subordinate but significant parts of this process, unpredictably related to the end result. By contrast, the trial before Pilate is mainly about the difficulty of coming to hear properly, and is about spiritual obtuseness. In both stories, the interrogators are ironically judged by their own questions and accusations, and in both, belief in Jesus is the central point. The structural symmetries invite us to make these detailed comparisons, and in the tensions and ironic reversals, the complementary emphases and contrasts, the delicate mystery of faith being granted or withheld is expressed with a subtle and complex artistry.

My final examples of John's depiction of belief through seeing and hearing are Jesus' prediction of his death in the conversation with Nicodemus (3:1ff.), and the crucifixion itself. The words spoken to Nicodemus early in the gospel already foretell the cross: 'And as Moses lifted up the serpent in the wilderness, so must the Son of man be lifted up' (3:14). The reference is to Numbers 21:9ff., where the brazen serpent was raised up on a pole in the wilderness and cured those who looked upon it. John's emphasis is on the act of lifting up, and is repeated twice more (8:28; 12:32–4). The humiliation of the cross, John implies, is also an exaltation, despite appearances. The reference to Moses is a further reminder that Jesus is the one greater than Moses, but it also refers Nicodemus the Pharisee to the authority of scripture. Wisdom 16:7 says of the serpent story that 'They had a symbol of salvation to remind them of the precept of your law. For he who turned toward it was saved, not by what he saw, but by you, the saviour of all.' The visual sign is not as important as what one 'sees' through it, in a spiritual sense.

Just so, in the crucifixion Jesus is exalted as saviour of the world. It is often noticed how, unlike the other gospels, John describes the cross as an enthronement ritual revealing God's glory.[36] Again we are invited to compare an external spectacle which alienates with an internal revelation which sustains. As with the story of the woman taken in adultery, Pilate's inscription is a sign of the victim's alienation, and just as Jesus' writing and not hearing is part of his rebuke of the woman's accusers, so Pilate does not hear, and his written proclamation, though intended as a mere label for a despised object, is ironically (for us who have eyes to 'see' it) a self-accusation. Likewise, the stones held by the woman's accusers resemble the executioners' nails, and once more the accused is depersonalised by being hoisted aloft as an object to be viewed, a public spectacle. Also as in the story of the woman, the term 'in the midst' (*meson* [19:18]) is ironically used. Jesus is 'in the midst' between the two thieves, symbols of belief and unbelief. He is not just the executed alien set over against us, but a judgement among us.

Jesus' reference to the serpent in the wilderness reminds us that visual appearances have to be 'seen' with the eyes of faith to reveal God's glory. Later, on the cross, which is fore-shadowed by the serpent story, we learn how words have to be 'heard' in a spiritual sense and not just seen externally if we are to grasp their true meaning. John alone among the gospels refers to the serpent and, in parallel, he provides details about the written proclamation on the cross. Each of these incidents helps us to interpret the other, deepening our understanding of the interrelationships between objectively seen and subjectively heard elements of belief, and of how alternative readings and interpretations can just as easily cause us to avoid faith as to discover it.

Throughout the fourth gospel the challenge of belief remains fierce and clear, and is divisive of those confronted by it. We are to believe that the Son has special knowledge of the Father to which neither human seeing nor hearing can attain directly. In short, the Father is the origin of the light by which all things are seen, and of the word by which we communicate. The challenge of belief according to John is radical and existential, as Bultmann says, because it calls us either to acknowledge our creaturely dependence on a single beneficent source which would put us apart from separation and pain, or to deny that dependence. This is the difference between light and dark, as the gospel uses these terms. Although we cannot hear and see the originating source directly, we can see something of his glory in creation, and through the contactual immediacy of our everyday experience. We find what the Son has come to tell us in water and bread, in burials and gardens, in casual words and words of the prophets, among the accused and the blind, in the ironies of circumstance and the vacillations of politicians, the doubts of friends and the encounter with strangers, in eating and drinking, travelling and fishing, and all the ordinary impedimenta of life. The choice is before the reader no less urgently than it was before Jesus' interlocutors, as our labour with the text waits upon insight partly meeting our intent, yet always ready to surprise us. But, like the evidence of his divinity that Jesus presented during his life, the text alone does not compel assent. The pre-existent logos is also the crucified man, suffering in the midst of us: Christ comes down among us not only with his imperative demands, but also to enable our suffering desire for truth to discover him by faith. As in Donne's poem, the psychological experience of choosing to believe is deeply pervaded by a sense of one's own unworthiness in the matter, for we must also be chosen. The very insistence in the fourth gospel on Jesus' power shows us precisely how elusive a thing faith is in human experience: how perplexing is the evidence; how uncertainly related seeing and hearing are to the insight which compels assent; how easily we might miss by a hair's breadth what will deliver us to the light or consign us to perpetual darkness – or permit us to remain the interested readers of a fascinating story.

6

Paul to the Corinthians: 'As deceivers yet true'

T. S. Eliot's poem *The Journey of the Magi*[1] is spoken by one of the wise kings from the East who visited the infant Jesus. This king, or magus, recalls his journey many years afterwards, but he is not quite sure about the significance of what he has seen. And so he tells his story yet again, as if by rehearsing the details he will discover some larger, relieving insight that eludes him. He recalls the events carefully and deliberately:

> A cold coming we had of it,
> Just the worst time of the year
> For a journey, and such a long journey:
> The ways deep and the weather sharp,
> The very dead of winter.

He is taken up with how bothersome it all was, and complains of 'the camel men cursing and grumbling / And running away, and wanting their liquor and women, / And the night fires going out'. His list of annoyances gives to the account a ring of truth: only someone who had really made the journey we feel would remember such things. But as we read, we also begin to detect through the details a limited understanding. 'A hard time we had of it', the magus says; yet given the event he is called to witness, the inconveniences he describes seem trivial. Although the wise king was sufficiently moved to make the journey, it seems that he did not quite know why he was doing so. As the first half of the poem ends, he tells how his party proceeded, 'With the voices singing in our ears, saying / That this was all folly.'

We then learn of a change in landscape, as at dawn they 'came down to a temperate valley'. Again the magus dwells on particulars: below the snow line they saw a running stream and a water mill, three trees on the horizon, and an old white horse; at a tavern they encountered six men 'at an open door, dicing for pieces of silver'. Still, all this is treated as incidental, and the narrator concludes that 'there was no information'.

When at last he describes 'the place' he remarks only that 'it was (you may say) satisfactory'.

In this section, readers are likely to feel increasingly removed from the wise king, mainly because the details which seem neutral and innocent to him appear significant to us. The dawn, vegetation, and freed water suggest rebirth after the barren winter landscape, and foreshadow the event at Bethlehem. The three trees remind us of Christ's crucifixion between the two thieves (Lk. 23:32–33). The pieces of silver and the dicing recall the money used to bribe Judas (Matt. 26:14–16), and the soldiers who drew lots for Christ's garments (Matt. 27:35); the white horse recalls Revelation 6:2; 19:11. When the magus concludes 'there was no information' we might feel pleased to rebuke him with our superior knowledge: he simply does not understand what is going on around him. Indeed, as the poem ends, he is left facing his own perplexity. He admits that he would do it all again, though the birth which he witnessed has indeed changed many things ('This Birth was / Hard and bitter agony for us, like Death, our death'), and he is not now at ease among his 'alien people clutching their gods'. He has grown old and weary, unable to forget the new thing which he does not quite grasp, or relinquish the old culture to which he belongs. His closing words are, rather sadly, 'I should be glad of another death.' Literally, this means his own death would be a relief. Yet even here the reader might look beyond the literal sense to that rebirth of knowledge beyond death, which is a reward of faith and of a life lived struggling to understand, such as we see in the case of this old man.

Although the reader is invited to feel better-informed than the stumbling narrator, however, the magus clearly could not be expected to know about the book of Revelation and the details of Jesus' death. The gospel story after all is closed to him, and he speaks, as it were, typologically. We see the types fulfilled in the New Testament books which we know but he does not. But before concluding that history is simply against him, we might notice how the old king's perplexity is also to some degree consequent on his personality. For instance, his remark on the place of Christ's birth has a kind of condescension not surprising in a person who feels that his superior social standing is compromised by visiting a stable: 'it was (you may say) satisfactory'. The words are full of elegant restraint: clearly he thought the place unsatisfactory, and he cannot easily humble his imagination to search the implications of the event with which he is now confronted. Also, we notice the learned precision of words like 'refractory', 'regretted' (used in the precise sense, meaning 'missed'), and 'old dispensation', which

Eliot places at the ends of the line to emphasise his speaker's educated habit of exact expression. The elitism of this learned king, the poem quietly suggests, is an impediment to the knowledge he seeks.

The magus thus is engaged in a personal struggle in the midst of circumstances which simultaneously privilege and confine him, and Eliot's conspicuous use of participles and gerunds ('coming', 'lying', 'bringing', 'grumbling', 'running', 'wanting', 'going', 'charging', 'sleeping', 'saying', 'running', 'dicing') suggests involvement in a process. Insofar as we, like the magus, participate in an event, we do not see it objectively. Caught up in the midst of something which has become more objective for us as history, the magus experiences an obscure, exciting potency which promises meaning, but he does not, for that very reason, identify the event or see the meaning clearly.

In this context, the opening lines of the poem are especially provocative because they show that Eliot does not exclude himself from his own lesson. These lines are placed in quotation marks, which might at first suggest that they are spoken by a voice within the poem. But this is not so: Eliot draws here on a nativity sermon by the seventeenth-century divine, Lancelot Andrewes,[2] and the quotation marks indicate his indebtedness. Putting these words in the mouth of the magus is thus conspicuously anachronistic, and the author signals to us that he, too, is groping for a way to make sense out of an old story. We are all caught up in our particular histories, the poem implies, and we all make use of the languages available to us in our search for meaning, our desire to fix the significance, to understand the events that move and draw us by the lure of an implied coherency. In this process, text calls upon text, and perspectives change and modify one another, but (as mystics and deconstructionists alike assure us) no human being enjoys an entirely privileged perspective.

It is fashionable these days to explain how poems are really about themselves, and something of this fashion has flavoured these last remarks about *The Journey of the Magi*. But I do not want to obscure Eliot's main achievement in expressing an enduring truth about the life of faith: this poem tells us that because we all have a place in history, we are more like the magus than we might think. We are all in the process, called by promises which demand assent, and required to discover their meaning in the particulars of our own landscape, our own journey. Indeed, we know more about the gospel story than the magus, but the mysteries of birth and death and the difficult ways of the journey are not less challenging and perplexing. We must therefore be cautious lest our patronising of the magus' comparative ignorance does not merely mimic his own condescending attitude to the stable at Bethlehem. The absolute remains a mystery to which we are drawn because it is desirable, and because we seek meaning. We are invited by the world to explore and to find out its informing patterns, and yet death prevents our information from being complete. Even the Lord of creation comes among us as a child who will die on the cross: it is as if God himself guarantees that the perplexed paths of human enquiry must engage the world only to be defeated by it. Thus Eliot's magus is caught up in pursuit of something he understands imperfectly and which delivers him to a bitter confrontation with death. So are we all caught up and confronted, according to the story of birth and death which the New Testament records. This is Eliot's real subject, and the poetry expresses it by creating a sense of the personality and particular circumstance of one man's struggle for clarity in the midst of a powerful, moving series of events. Participation (and we are all participants) is a kind of immediate knowledge, of which suffering is one unavoidable example. It prevents the abstract fixing of faith in concepts which would make faith a matter of propositions rather than an individual's experience. But we must not, it seems, allow ourselves to fall either into the fire of non-cognitive irrationalism (mere participation) or the ice of unlived abstraction (mere objectivity).

I have used Eliot's poem to introduce my discussion of St. Paul because *The Journey of the Magi* is in many respects analogous to the epistles, and can assist us in appreciating the literary dimensions of Paul's writing. Indeed, failure to appreciate this side of Paul's achievement opens us to the perils of fire and ice which I have just described, as Paul himself discovered even among his interpreters in the Christian communities which his letters address.

Like the magus, Paul is caught up by an event – his witnessing the crucified and living Christ – which he does not fully understand, and his letters record the struggle to clarify his experience. The epistolary form itself provides a strong sense of a voice addressing an audience in a personal way. Paul's journeys and dealings with early Christian communities are full of hardship, as he keeps reminding us, and the voices laugh in his ear too, saying it is all folly. Of course Paul takes this folly by the horns, asserting that it is in fact Christ's wisdom,[3] which will always seem folly to the world, but his acknowledgement of the problem indicates that he knew full well how imitating Christ would seem offensive to ordinary prudence.

In his attempts to clarify the revelation of Christ offered to him, Paul draws on the Hebrew scriptures (especially in the Septuagint translation),[4] on early Christian hymns, fragments of oral tradition, on doxologies and prayers, and the conventions of *diatribe* and epistolary form current in the ancient world.[5] His letters are thus deeply intertextual – indeed it is not clear how many of those ascribed to him are by his own hand – as he musters a variety of literary resources to awaken his readers to an imponderable redemptive significance in the death and resurrection of Jesus,[6] which Paul attempts to clarify through whatever language and in whatever terms he can.

Again like the magus, Paul is very much a participant, engaging his readers, exhorting them to love and mutual support and to their work in the world. Yet, as with Eliot's narrator, his personality does not always seem pleasing or well-enough informed. He can be sarcastic and severe, overweening and bitter; he seems almost certainly to have thought the last days would be upon the world during his lifetime, and was constrained to modify his views on that subject.[7] He oversimplifies the Jewish Law by often reducing it to a body of prescriptions,[8] and his attitudes to women (though complex and sometimes enlightened) are not always reassuring.[9] Like all of us, Paul suffers, struggling with his own limitations, and we should be prepared to acknowledge these without too much self-righteousness or too much indulgence. Indeed, a just appraisal of the balance between these alternatives is at the heart of Paul's own message to the Corinthians, so that we are invited to apply Paul's injunctions to Paul himself.

Also, just as Christ's birth causes Eliot's magus to ponder the interdependency of birth and death, so Christ's death causes Paul to ponder the relationship of the crucifixion and resurrection. He well knows how the blessings of life, light and unity are often in human experience inextricably entangled with experiences of death, darkness and separation, so that characteristically we come to know 'through a glass darkly' (1 Cor. 13:12[AV]). In this context, Paul's special vocabulary of semi-technical terms marks his attempt to clarity a truth in which, as his letters dramatically show us, he is quite caught up, but which he would nevertheless know – and have us know – objectively.

Admittedly, there are differences between Eliot's bewildered old man and the energetic, missionary Paul, but Eliot's poem nonetheless can help us to see how literary are the Pauline letters. They too express character in action, in the process of shaping memory to define a commitment and discover the meaning of human experience. Thus, Paul presents us with a broad set of oppositions between death, suffering, separation and ego on the one hand, and life, peace, union, and self-giving love on the other. The difference between these separate spheres is presented as objective, and Christ is the energy joining us to the second, whereas Satan and the powers of darkness are all that would move our allegiance to the first. Yet, however objective in theory, the complex of peace, union, and love which is for Paul the body of Christ, is not fully evident to us, and we must discover it tentatively in and through the textures and circumstances of our particular histories where we are all participants, and also prey to the powers of darkness. Thus, although Paul is full of passionate exhortation, he also preaches toleration based on a sense of our compromised position, belonging in historical events which we cannot see clearly enough.[10] But although he holds firmly to the idea that faith is imperfect knowledge, Paul does not allow us to conclude that faith is irrational. The lively vitality of our particular experience should yield some understanding about God, just as the abstract clarity of our theological concepts should enhance life. The balance between them, whereby thought and experience fructify one another, we could define as the act of imagination itself, and through such a dynamic relationship we can be said to dwell in the body of Christ.

I would like now to apply some of these observations to the Corinthian correspondence, and this very use of the word 'correspondence' can afford a place to begin. Ever since Adolf Deissmann claimed that an epistle is public and literary, whereas a letter is private and casual, critics have debated which of these two terms better suits Paul's writing. Deissmann concluded that Paul wrote 'real letters, not epistles', and was not a literary man in any formal way.[11] He is followed by scholars such as Willi Marxsen and Norman Perrin, but others, such as Bo Reicke and Ralph P. Martin, think that Paul used his writings to preach to congregations that he could not address in person, and that he wrote epistles.

This debate raises in an acute form the question of what Paul thought he was doing, and how much we ought to allow for the private circumstances of his particular addressees. William G. Doty's recommendation that 'the absolute distinction between epistle and letter should be dropped'[12] might seem to short-circuit the debate and afford an easy evasion, but it is a sensible compromise, because it draws attention to the fact that there are interesting intermediate positions between private and public utterance. Erasmus once complained that his letters were being published before they were delivered, and partly in consequence he also wrote for a general audience peeping over the shoulder, as it were, of the designated recipient – just as Robinson Duckworth tells us Lewis Carroll did in composing *Alice*: 'the story was

actually composed and spoken *over my shoulder* for the benefit of Alice
Liddell...'.[13]

The circumstances of letter writing in the ancient world (rather more
like Erasmus' Europe in this respect than our modern world) offered
little assurance of privacy, and less of punctuality. Although Paul wrote
to particular communities and even addressed particular individuals,
his letters – let me now call them that, without suggesting that I share
Deissmann's view – everywhere 'look over the shoulder' of their
designated recipients to the general issues of salvation in Christ and the
public declaration of the mysteries of his death and resurrection and
the development of his church. It is useful to insist on this point because
it prevents us from relinquishing that key tension between the
participant (the private letter-writer) and the *objectivist* (the epistolary
preacher bent on clarification), which a sharp opposition between letter
and epistle requires. Thus, for instance, 1 Cor. has private details about
Chloe (1:11) and Timothy (4:17) and an incestuous person (5:1), but the
famous chapter praising charity (13) is strikingly universal and public.
The letter creates the impress of immediate and wholehearted
engagement with others whose difficulties and shortcomings are
specifically addressed, but through whom a general truth is sought out
and declared. Since each person's circumstances are different, the
number and kind of impediments to true illumination are unspecifiable,
and no general prescription is sufficient to cover all the cases
adequately. Paul's particular letters therefore stand as examples of how
to proceed: that is, alive to the uniqueness of personal problems,
including his own, yet concerned with the truth which is Christ.

I am now close to saying that the spirit of Paul's letters and the
manner of his approach to problems are of singular importance for
understanding the faith to which he calls his readers. This 'manner',
insofar as it is a style of discourse, is pre-eminently a literary
achievement, and can lead us to consider the vexed question of Paul's
texts.[14]

In 1 Cor., Paul says he had written previously to the community: 'I
wrote unto you in my letter not to associate with immoral men' (1 Cor.
5:9). He seems to have received a reply ('Now concerning the matters
about which you wrote' [1 Cor. 7:1]), to which he addresses himself in
the passages beginning 'Now concerning...' (7:1; 7:25; 8:1; 12:1).
Paul's original letter is lost: some scholars think they have found a
fragment of it in 2 Cor. 6:14–7:1, but this claim is not widely accepted.
The letter we now call 1 Cor. is therefore Paul's second letter, and it
addresses issues his first letter did not resolve. 1 Cor. itself, however,

could well be made up of two separate letters. Paul's tone at certain points does not suggest that his differences with the community were profound (1 Cor. 11:18ff.), and yet the information from 'Chloe's people' dealt with in 1 Cor. 1–4 suggests that there is a more serious rift which needs to be checked. The several 'now concerning...' sections address this rift and belong with 1 Cor. 1–4. It is then possible to see in the remaining sections of 1 Cor. the outline of an earlier, less controversial address to the Corinthian community.

The tone of 2 Cor. is more distinctly adversarial, and Paul's differences with the community are now evidently serious. However, certain breaks in tone and subject-matter strongly suggest that 2 Cor. might be made up of several documents. One clue to identifying these is the number of visits Paul made to Corinth. It seems clear that there were at least three. He says he was determined not 'to make you another painful visit' (2 Cor. 2:1), and it is unlikely that this refers to his visit to found the community, for there is no suggestion of an initial painful experience in 1 Cor. Paul then says, 'This is the third time I am coming to you' (2 Cor. 13:1). It seems therefore that there was a visit involving difficulty which could well be the content of the so-called 'tearful letter' to which Paul refers: 'For I wrote you out of much affliction and anguish of heart and with many tears' (2 Cor. 2:4). Some scholars think that the 'tearful letter' is contained in 2 Cor. 10–13, and there is a good deal of support for this suggestion because of the vehemence and sudden switch in tone.

It is also arguable that 2 Cor. 2:14–7:4 is a separate letter. Paul's authority has not yet been as seriously challenged as in the 'tearful letter', but his tone differs markedly from the conciliatory language of the opening chapters. Again, 2 Cor. 8 has a doublet in Ch. 9 which could itself be a separate document. It is customary to designate this entire collection by letters of the alphabet, and I summarise here the hypothesis advanced by J. Weiss, modified by W. Schmithals and recently affirmed by Robert Jewett, though it is subject to many variations among scholars.[15] Letter A is made up of 1 Cor. 9:24–10:22; 6:12–20; 11:2–34; 15; 16:13–24. Letter B is 1 Cor. 1:1–6:11; 7:1–9:23; 10:23–11:1; 12:1–14:40; 16:1–12. Letter C is 2 Cor. 2:14–6:13; 7:2–4. Letter D is 2 Cor. 10:1–13:13. Letter E is 2 Cor. 9:1–15. And Letter F is 2 Cor. 1:1–2:13; 7:5–8:24. However uncertain the details, there are strong grounds for concluding that the Corinthian correspondence is a collection of letters. These address a variety of problems[16] associated with a number of missionary journeys and with other pieces of correspondence now lost.

I do not wish to suggest that fragmentation is in itself a literary virtue, and it is useful to turn again at this point to T. S. Eliot, whose famous words about the modernist movement at the beginning of the twentieth century advise how 'the poet must become ... more allusive, more indirect, in order to force, to dislocate if necessary, language into his meaning'.[17] Eliot talks here about artists making unity out of fragments, thereby reflecting the acute discontinuities and eclecticism of knowledge in our century. His own practice in *The Waste Land*, and elsewhere, is to create a sense of the effort itself entailed in making a sustaining synthesis out of so much disorder. A mere juxtaposition of fragments will not suffice, for these must be fused and illuminated by imaginative vision. Consequently, readers who approve of Eliot's *Waste Land* find in it combination of hauntingly evoked but lost order, of poignant sympathy for the disoriented and estranged, of denunciation of a dehumanising culture, and a profound diagnosis of our present civilizational phase in relation to its antecedents. Those who dislike the poem find it a pretentious jumble.

None of this is far removed from what I am claiming for Paul's Corinthian letters. The sense of fragmented discourse broken off by exigency or accident, or shading towards a horizon of confusing controversy and a turmoil of unstated counter-argument, punctuated by angry grief and pleased reconciliation, fitfully ordered and swiftly changing in tone and mood, constitutes one pole of the experience. The other pole consists of a visionary energy fusing the fragments into a synthesis of peace, unity and love whose name is Christ, whose way is the cross and whose promise is resurrection. Such a vision offers to interpret the course of human history itself, the absurdity of human suffering, the recalcitrance of human selfishness, the volatility of human love, the human fear of death and the deepest human desires for consolation.

Fragmentation and discontinuity, in short, draw our attention to the creative struggle, indicating for us the difficulty and intensity of the task. Again, as for *The Waste Land*, those who disapprove of St. Paul (and there have been many) find him pretentious and arrogant, a wanton obfuscator of Jesus' clear simplicity.[18] Yet, it might be objected that I have ignored the obvious fact that Eliot *causes* his poem to seem fragmented. The interlayered structure of the Corinthian letters is, by contrast, naively or unselfconsciously discontinuous: translators, for instance, often rather smooth out the seams than draw our attention to them. Nonetheless, the end result is comparable, and Paul, who had no hand in the collected edition – or any edition – of his writings, must have been well aware of the manifold, often paradoxical adaptations of his message to a variety of circumstances, and of how indirect and imperfectly finished his discourse often is. In terms of our reading experience there is a good deal of similarity between these two kinds of fragmentation, the origins of which are quite different. Perhaps, then, modernism alerts us to a fresh way of reading Paul's discourse.

Indeed, Paul is willing, as he says, to become 'all things to all men' (1 Cor. 9:22): 'to the Jews I became as a Jew. . . . To those outside the law, I became as one outside the law. . . . To the weak I became weak' (1 Cor. 9:20–2). Like Proteus, he assumes many forms, yet the single truth at the centre remains unshaken. 'Is Christ divided?' (1 Cor. 1:13) he asks the Corinthians, and the answer is, of course, no. Even the semblance of Christ's division from us by death is paradoxically the means of his eternal being with us. 'We preach Christ crucified' (1 Cor. 1:23), says Paul with a challenging plainness from which he does not swerve. And 'if Christ has not been raised', he later says, 'then our preaching is in vain, and your faith is in vain' (1 Cor. 15:14). This combination of single vision and manifold engagement gives to Paul's writing a distinctive, tense energy in which the scandalous fact of Christ's death becomes the reason why we are to engage the world, loving one another in the full knowledge that God himself dies among us so that we may know him in the fulness of time.

On the one hand, then, Paul is clear and objective, and this is especially so when he claims a direct experience of the risen Lord. Talking of Jesus' appearances to the apostles, Paul says that 'last of all, as to one untimely born, he appeared also to me' (1 Cor. 15:8). The appearance that Paul witnessed was of the same kind as those offered to the apostles, except that Paul was not present among them, and is a kind of malformed, imperfect example (*ektroma*, abortion).[19] Nonetheless, 'by the grace of God I am what I am' (1 Cor. 15:10), he says, and he received a vision even though he does not describe it. In 2 Cor., Paul again tells of a vision of ineffable splendour wherein he was 'caught up into Paradise . . . and . . . heard things that cannot be told' (2 Cor. 12:4). The truth communicated at these key moments remains fundamental not only to Paul's own life, but, he thinks, to all human lives, and he never tires of saying so. Christ is God's power and wisdom (1 Cor. 1:24), and there is but one God and we are in him (1 Cor. 8:6) through Christ, God's image (2 Cor. 4:4). The Father who raised Jesus will raise us too (2 Cor. 4:14), and if Jesus is not risen, preaching and faith are in vain (1 Cor. 15:14). Paul has been called to be an apostle 'by the will of God' (1 Cor. 1:1; 2 Cor. 1:1), 'For necessity is laid upon me.

Woe to me if I do not preach the gospel' (1 Cor. 9:16). He claims even to preach a hidden wisdom 'decreed before the ages' (1 Cor. 2:7) and now mysteriously made known. He holds that his experience of the risen Lord contains a revelation about the second coming when Christ will incorporate the faithful in himself: 'For just as the body is one and has many members, and all the members of the body, though many, are one body, so it is with Christ' (1 Cor. 12:12). Meanwhile, we must remember that we will 'all appear before the judgment seat' (2 Cor. 5:10): yet if we 'walk by faith' (2 Cor. 5:7) we are already 'in Christ' (2 Cor. 5:17), bearing in ourselves his earthly sufferings, and also building his ministry of reconciliation.

On the other hand, as we see, Paul also knows he cannot communicate his vision fully because it is beyond the reach of language. Thus, for instance, he deploys the key metaphor of the believer as a member of Christ's body. This comparison is based on our experience of physical bodies, and so we can easily enough grasp its intent, but it refers also to Christ's risen body in which we belong, somehow, in an ineffable, spiritual way:[20] 'we look not to the things that are seen but to the things that are unseen; for the things that are seen are transient, but the things that are unseen are eternal' (2 Cor. 4:18). The metaphor directs us, therefore, *imaginatively* to a prospect of intimate unity and harmony, even though our minds are confounded by attempts to picture exactly what kind of stuff Christ's spiritual body is made of, and how we might fit into it. We tremble here at the edge of the mystery, though many who do not go in for mysteries might well judge such language trembling on the edge of nonsense.

Paul, indeed, seems well-enough aware that to do full justice to faith he needs metaphors which are elusive and less plain than he would like. It is as if his cool reasons melt in the heat of experience to produce a warmly resonant, affective language. This process is evident also in the binary oppositions consistently used throughout the letters to contrast our negative experience of the everyday world with our desires for other, contrary kinds of gratification. On the negative side are suffering, death, separation and that kind of self-regard which engenders anxiety and aggression.[21] On the positive side are peace, unity, love and abundant life, for Christ is the living form of the good, the energy of all that would make for human happiness.

These opposites are often stated clearly. The brethren, for instance, should attempt to overcome divisions because Christ is not divided (1 Cor. 1:10–13). The world's confusion is opposed to God's peace (1 Cor 14:33), and the suffering of the cross is associated with the wisdom of this world (1 Cor. 1:20) which engenders only pain, confusion and selfishness. The 'carnal' who are attached to creature comforts and worldly power engender only 'jealousy and strife' (1 Cor. 3:3), but in Christ we are 'united in the same mind' (1 Cor. 1:10). Love of this world's material solace is like the love of a harlot (1 Cor. 6:15) – specious, transient, mercenary, and without a future. Such love is a parody of the way in which our bodies are members of Christ in 'one spirit' (1 Cor. 6:7), true and eternal. Trust in ourselves binds us to this world, subject to the fear of death, whereas we should trust in God 'who raises the dead' (2 Cor. 1:9). This body, where we 'sigh with anxiety' (2 Cor. 5:4) is associated with Christ's absence (2 Cor. 5:6), whereas in Christ's presence our mortality itself is 'swallowed up by life' (2 Cor. 5:4). In brief, Christ is unity, belonging, life and freedom, and once seen in such terms, it is impossible for us, short of perversity, not really to want him, the truly humanising content of our lives opposed to whatever we shrink from in horror or fear or pain.

These opposites, however, are not in fact so conveniently separate, as Paul acknowledges by often using his key concepts in a subtly figurative way, so that clear opposition yields to engaging suggestiveness. Words such as 'world', 'body', 'spirit', and 'flesh', among others become richly associative and convey various shades of meaning. 'Body' (*soma*) can be the observable human being (1 Cor. 9:27), but also human nature in general (2 Cor. 5:6), a sacramental relationship to Christ (1 Cor. 11:24), and the Church (1 Cor. 12:12). 'Flesh' (*sarx*) can indicate not only a material body, but the whole realm of the old law (1 Cor. 10:18): as Jewett says, Paul holds 'there is both confluence and opposition between the old fleshly aeon and the new spiritual aeon. Without these associations he could not admit living "in the flesh" and at the same time deny living "according to the flesh".'[22] Spirit, the main antithesis to flesh, is for Paul God's creative power (1 Cor. 12:7ff.), but Christ also is the Lord who 'is the spirit' (2 Cor. 3:17) and 'a life-giving spirit' (1 Cor. 15:45), and there is no clear distinction in Paul between the Spirit and the Son. Finally, the cross is both the event itself of Jesus' execution, and the mystery of salvation and all human suffering (1 Cor. 1:18).

Throughout his several controversies and despite his obvious doctrinal intent, Paul does not so much appeal to his opponents by reasoning as by calling upon their desire for happiness and meaning. As we see, his binary oppositions accommodate what Christ 'really means' to our love of life itself, so that we hesitate to dismiss either Paul's theological ideas, or his figurative language. His obscurity is not just the sign of a muddled head, for we feel the author working with traditional concepts to forge an understanding of his own deeply-felt experience of suffering and desire in a manner touching the wellsprings of moral consciousness. To be human, he tells us, happiness must involve the body; to be happy, the body must transcend death. In the resurrection, Paul insists, Jesus objectively transcended death, and his body is preserved in a spiritual form. Sent by the Father, the Son assures us that this way is God's, and so we ought not to fear death as we approach it in faith. Yet Paul also knew how complex and easily misunderstood is our participation in the Son's mission. Indeed, Paul's main teachings were often misinterpreted almost as soon as they were delivered, as was the case not least with the Corinthian community. Consequently, his rhetoric is often self-conscious, alert to the possibilities of dogmatic oversimplification or narcissistic wish-fulfilment which can so easily upset the exact understanding he requires.

At the beginning of 1 Cor. (Letter B), Paul complains that the community has divided into parties. It appears that the party of Christ consisted of Hellenistic 'divine man' missionaries, though it is difficult for us today to be certain.[23] This faction stressed that illumination came from the resurrected Christ, but tended to ignore the significance of the crucifixion. Paul therefore stresses that God's wisdom is Christ's cross, and says that he preaches 'not with eloquent wisdom, lest the cross of Christ be emptied of its power' (1 Cor. 1:17): 'I did not come proclaiming to you ... in lofty words or wisdom. For I decided to know nothing among you, except Jesus Christ and him crucified' (1 Cor. 2:1–2). Like every real suffering, the cross humiliates abstraction and confounds 'lofty words'. Christ is truly revealed in those intense particulars which beggar description, and where we, the participants, are most painfully in the midst. Suffering is the paradigm of such experience, and the fact that Paul addresses himself here to a definite audience in a certain historical situation helps to preserve the keen edge of his message.

Later, in a famous phrase, Paul says that 'now we see in a mirror dimly, but then face to face' (1 Cor. 13:12). This is part of his paean to charity, which follows an exhortation to the Corinthians to be unified as members in Christ's body (1 Cor. 12:12). The root of such mutual caring is self-giving love which 'does not insist on its own way' (1 Cor. 13:5), and which is called upon in unspecifiable ways according to the demands of a situation. 'For our knowledge is imperfect and our prophecy is imperfect' (1 Cor. 13:9), says Paul, just as we see 'in a mirror dimly'. Here once again in addressing the Corinthian factionalism, Paul draws attention to the limitations of concepts. Words give us partial knowledge, which is like an indistinct reflection from a mirror.[24] Hence words cannot prescribe the particular content of charity, just as we have seen they cannot adequately deal with suffering. Love and suffering are both participatory experiences, we might say, and although Paul firmly states an objective opposition between Christ's love and our human suffering, he is careful to maintain a sense of the personal ground of such experiences. There is consequently a certain tentativeness in his preaching the mystery, and in the balance between careful discernment and firm commitment, Paul's literary achievement is especially evident.

The same pattern can be found throughout 2 Corinthians. In chapter 3, for instance, Paul answers a charge that he spends too much time recommending himself. Rather disarmingly, he says that he does not need written letters at all, for 'You yourselves are our letter of recommendation, written in your hearts, to be known and read by all men' (2 Cor. 3:2). The Corinthians' good behaviour, he says, is a rhetoric better than words; once more, charity outreaches the power of language to describe it, and the particular instances of Christian love among the Corinthians do more to preach Paul's message than any amount of ink. Nonetheless, this message is itself written in words which express Paul's meaning most exactly by finding a position between conceptual remoteness and particular opacity.

Paul's exhortation takes a further interesting turn when he goes on to compare the letter of the Mosaic law, which is a kind of veil (equivalent to the ink), to Christ in whom the veil is removed (equivalent to the Spirit). Because this is the case, Paul says, 'we are very bold' (2 Cor. 3:12), and the community of believers, 'with unveiled face, beholding the glory of the Lord, are being changed into his likeness from one degree of glory to another; for this comes from the Lord who is the Spirit' (2 Cor. 3:18). Here Paul deploys the same kind of imagery as we have seen in I Corinthians, and he now associates the deficiency of words explicitly with the written law. In the 'Spirit' of the Lord, by contrast, our knowledge is clarified, but such knowledge is more direct, personal, and immediate than words can say. Precisely because words are such imperfect vehicles, Paul recommends boldness, or 'great plainness of speech', as the Authorised Version has it (2 Cor. 3:12). This connects back to his professed indifference to letters of recommendation: words are less important than behaviour, and so we need not try to make our words especially impressive, nor rely on them too much.

As with other gifted authors who commend plain speech, however, Paul's rhetorical practice contradicts his advice. His defence against his accusers is in fact a complex mixture of flattery, metaphor, typology, and dexterous redirection of the argument. There is a strong, though latent, implication that the attack on him by the Corinthians is really an attack on Christ, and Paul proceeds with vigorous mastery, maintaining a sense of solidarity with his auditors, yet giving them a firm lesson. Once more, he responds to a particular life situation, and deploys words to draw attention to the limited effectiveness of words, but also aims thereby to persuade his audience. He also advises us to proceed in like manner 'in honour and dishonour, in ill repute and good repute. We are treated as imposters, and yet are true' (2 Cor. 6:8). By this he means that even when they speak truth, Christians will be misunderstood because the special perspective of an individual auditor will cause the message to be misinterpreted. Bad reports of what they are saying and doing will mingle with good reports, and they will be represented as deceivers, even when they are not. Yet, in the words of another master of language, it is maddeningly the case also that the truest poetry is the most feigning, and despite his praise of plain speech, Paul finds the indirections of literary language often the fittest vehicle for what he has to say.

In both 1 and 2 Corinthians, then, Paul draws attention to the fact that his writing cannot adequately convey the full 'participatory' reality of love and suffering, and yet a sense of such participation is necessary for conveying what is meant by belief in Christ, the supreme reality. Paul's sensitivity to the uses and limits of language is especially evident in his accounts of glossalalia (1 Cor. 14:2ff.), and of his visionary experiences (2 Cor. 12:1ff.).

The treatment of glossalalia or speaking in tongues in I Corinthians is carefully ambiguous. Insofar as a person's inspired talking in an unidentifiable language is a sign of the private workings of Spirit, Paul respects it, 'For one who speaks in a tongue speaks not to men, but to God' (1 Cor. 14:2). Yet he is uneasy, because an entirely private language is not really a language at all.[25] There are 'many different languages in the world', Paul reminds us, 'and none is without meaning; but if I do not know the meaning of the language, I shall be a foreigner to the speaker and the speaker a foreigner to me' (1 Cor. 14:10–11). Paul does not exactly say here that speaking in tongues is mere babble signifying nothing. It might indeed indicate a private revelation of the Spirit to the inspired talker, but not far below the surface Paul is worried that there is no clear way to distinguish genuine private inspiration from mere barbarian chatter. He therefore discourages speaking in tongues at church meetings, and calls for interpretation when possible. Personally, he says, 'in church I would rather speak five words with my mind, in order to instruct others, than ten thousand words in a tongue' (1 Cor. 14:19). Besides, if everyone spoke in tongues, unbelievers might think the whole church mad (1 Cor. 14:23).

The opposite extreme is encountered in Paul's brief allusion to his visionary experience. 'I know a man in Christ who fourteen years ago', he says, 'was caught up to the third heaven – whether in the body or out of the body I do not know, God knows.' In this condition he 'heard things that cannot be told, which man may not utter' (2 Cor. 12:2–4).[26] At first glance, the immediacy of the 'things that cannot be told' brings to mind speaking in tongues. But Paul's account here is not in an unknown tongue, and is in fact quite the opposite of speaking in tongues. He even casts the account in the third person ('I know a man'), in order to distance it: the vision itself was beyond words, but this description is in deliberately clear words. Indeed, Paul's language is so clear that it carries hardly any sense of the actual content of the experience, and the author suggests that he will thereby be prevented from glorying too much in himself.

Both of the above examples deal with the limits of language, as Paul probes the point at which communication crumbles away under the world's weight. On the one hand, too much privacy robs language of its public content; on the other, too much general content robs it of experience. This is much the same as saying that effective human language cannot be wholly participatory or wholly objective, but must find its place somewhere between, much as faith finds a place between private experience and public dogma, between the cross, let us say, and the resurrection which is its meaning. In keeping with this sense of the possibilities and limits of language, Paul's metaphors, which appeal to our emotions, also invite our understanding. Likewise, his clearly-stated binary opposites, which appeal first to our understanding, are means of stimulating desire. Images of milk and solid food (1 Cor. 3:2), foundations and building (1 Cor. 3:11), warfare and vineyards (1 Cor. 9:7), ploughing and running races (1 Cor. 9:24), death being swallowed (1 Cor. 15:54), veils and writing in stone (2 Cor. 3:7), clothing and nakedness (2 Cor. 5:3), armour and deception (2 Cor. 6:7–8), are deployed in a variety of contexts to communicate some felt sense of what is meant by participation in Christ's body, and to enable a deeper understanding of the distinction between spirit and the world, grace and law, separation and unity. As scholars have noticed, Paul's peculiar semi-technical terms ('flesh', 'body', 'spirit', 'heart', 'psyche')[27] hover provocatively between concept and metaphor. They are used in varying senses in different contexts, and, as we have seen with the word 'flesh', they evoke a quality of experience as well as demonstrate an anthropological theory.

I have now returned to a point not far removed from my opening discussion of *The Journey of the Magi*. True, Eliot's magus and St. Paul could not be confused for long, but Eliot's literary treatment of faith struggling for understanding provides a key for appreciating the literary distinction of Paul's Corinthian letters. As Eliot shows us, faith is at once participatory and objective. The participator's experience is limited, discontinuous, and emotionally complex. It is expressed through metaphor, typology, and intertextual devices, but is aimed at the plain truth which can be known and clarified. Just so, the Corinthian letters create the impress of a personal struggle to fix and define a powerful experience of the crucified and risen Christ. The texts are discontinuous yet interwoven, and metaphor, typology and the persuasive devices of rhetoric communicate the sense of personal involvement with an event Paul holds to be of overwhelming public significance, and which he struggles to fix and make clear. He remains careful, however, to prevent his discourse from escaping either into the perfect privacy of individual experience or the perfect remoteness of impersonal idea. Faith, like human language itself and like the Word made flesh, is tentative, committed to understanding and unity, yet patient of the contactual and contingent. The cross, which Paul preaches first of all, is its true sign, for faith suffers in the midst and death consumes our aspiration to the clear and full knowledge towards which faith tends. Yet, if we have eyes to see God present on the cross, we might look with hope to the resurrection which the cross might then also signify, and in that hope we might re-engage the world in all its cruel impermanence and opacity. Paul's correspondence especially gives us a sense of just such a re-engagement, with its human trials and frailties, disappointments and gratifications.

7

Hebrews: Blood on the Boundary

The central theme of Hebrews is the high priesthood of Christ, who is said to be like the Old Testament Melchizedek. In a brief episode recorded in Genesis 14:18–20, Melchizedek, 'priest of God most high' (14:18), appears as it seems from nowhere to bless Abraham, and then just as promptly disappears from the story. As Norman Perrin suggests,[1] Hebrews as a literary document bears some resemblance to this strange visitor without genealogy or descendants: scholars do not agree whether or not it is an epistle, for there is no opening formula such as an epistle requires; yet Hebrews ends like one, with personal notices, greetings and blessings. Not surprisingly, theories have been advanced claiming that it is an epistle but that the opening is missing, and, alternatively, that it is not an epistle and the ending is an interpolation. Again, there is a broad consensus today that despite its traditional attachment to St. Paul's name, Hebrews is not from Paul's hand: indeed, Origen's famous phrase, 'who wrote it, God knows' had already proposed in the second century an opinion which is all but universally established in the twentieth. Finally, the title 'to the Hebrews' appears for the first time in a third-century manuscript, and is most likely an inference based on extensive references throughout Hebrews to the sacrificial cult. But whether or not Hebrews was written expressly for converts from Judaism remains speculation.[2]

In short, nothing in the New Testament quite resembles Hebrews, and it seems best to regard it as a sermon, and, more specifically, as a midrash (that is, a freely-developed interpretation of a biblical text) on Psalm 110.[3] Like Hebrews, Psalm 110 refers to Melchizedek's priesthood ('You are a priest forever after the order of Melchizedek'); both documents emphasise the Lord's sitting at God's right hand; both deal with the day of wrath and with God's triumph.

The idea that Christ's priesthood is modelled on Melchizedek's is taken up by the author of Hebrews especially to present a radical criticism of the sacrificial cult performed by the Levitical priests whose descent is from Aaron. Jesus was from the tribe of Judah, and so had no official claim to priesthood, even though his sacrifice on the cross completes and makes perfect once and for all the expiation and atonement effected repeatedly by the sacrificial offerings of the official cult. Melchizedek likewise is without official priestly genealogy, but is 'a priest forever'. The fact that he blessed Abraham and received tribute from him suggests that his priesthood is superior to that of the Levitical line, which is descended from Abraham. In being a priest of the order of Melchizedek, and having 'neither beginning of days nor end of life' (7:3), Jesus thus transcends Levitical authority, and his sacrifice on the cross has an eternal significance and efficacy cancelling the need for repeated animal sacrifices.

As is quickly evident, Hebrews offers a subtle and complex interpretation of Jesus' death. Unlike the gospels, where the crucifixion narrative is a distinct part of the whole, Hebrews deals with the cross throughout, developing an interlocking set of themes and motifs to expound the meaning of Jesus' suffering on earth as our brother, and also as the means of our 'eternal salvation' (5:9). The rich and suggestive, interlocked structure of Hebrews is its main literary distinction, and I would like to suggest that this quality emerges especially from a set of motifs placed in tension with one another and then developed so that we discover a further set of tensions within the motifs themselves. The structure of Hebrews thereby continually keeps before us the symbol of the cross, the earthly altar for Jesus' high-priestly self-sacrifice.

The interlocked, binary structure of Hebrews can be clarified by a brief recapitulation of the main argument. First, we are reminded that God spoke in past times through prophets, but now the Son, image of God's person by whom God made the world, has purged our sins. The Son is higher than the angels (ch. 1), but he is made lower than the angels to suffer death, becoming like us, his brethren, by taking on flesh and blood in order to release people from the fear of death by subjecting himself to it. He is thus the high priest, making reconciliation for the people's sin (ch. 2). In order to enter into eternal rest, however, we must hold steadfast in faith (ch. 3) and continue to labour and endure, remembering that Christ also felt infirmities such as ours (ch. 4), for the Son is made perfect through suffering (ch. 5). In this he is like Melchizedek, who was without father, mother or descendant, and was therefore a high priest perpetually and unchangeably, unlike the sons of Levi. After Jesus' perfect high priesthood in which he offered himself, there is no more need for daily sacrifices. The gifts and offerings of the Levitical priests are shadows of heavenly things, like the tabernacle of

Moses, but now a new covenant is written in our hearts and minds (ch. 8). Just so, the blood sacrifices of the day of Atonement according to the old covenant are imperfect; Christ's tabernacle is not made with human hands, and the shedding of his blood brings eternal redemption (ch. 9). The law as a whole is a shadow of good things to come, but Jesus' perfect sacrifice causes the law to be rewritten within us. Therefore we must hold fast in faith (ch. 10), for, like the spiritual heroes of past times, we are strangers and pilgrims on the earth (ch. 11). Just as Jesus endured the cross in order to sit at God's right hand, so we must be patient in order to achieve the things that cannot be shaken (ch. 12). The bodies of sacrificial animals are burned outside the camp; likewise, Jesus suffered outside the gates, and we are to follow him, for on this earth there is no continuing city.

This brief summary will suffice to remind us of how insistent are the contrasts on the one hand between an enduring heavenly substance and the destructive work of time, and, on the other, between the imperfect foreshadowings of the old testament and the full significance of the new. There is, in short, a distinct tension between the vertical dimension whereby eternal things are opposed to temporal, and the horizontal whereby the imperfect foreshadowings of the old covenant are brought to light in the new. Thus, vertically the heavenly city is in contrast to our perpetually ruined earthly cities; the heavenly tabernacle to its earthly counterpart; the Son of God's right hand to the victim crucified outside the city gates. Horizontally, the daily animal sacrifices foreshadow Jesus' self-sacrifice; the spiritual heroes of past times are examples of a more fully self-conscious heroism of faith; the precepts of the written law anticipate a new law written in the heart.

Uniquely, Jesus combines these opposites in himself, joining in the knot of his incarnate life the very principle of creation (1:2) and the experience of human suffering in time. The comparison to Melchizedek helps to make clear how Jesus joins these two realms, for Melchizedek also appears in history, though maintaining a special connection to eternity. Interestingly, one of the Dead Sea Scrolls identifies Melchizedek with the kingly messiah, and Philo of Alexandria (to whose writings Hebrews is often compared) identifies him with the heavenly priest.[4] These similarities do not so much suggest specific interdependency among the documents as a generally circulating association between Melchizedek and the messiah, of which the author of Hebrews makes special use. Just as the priestly function is basically to mediate, so the comparison between Melchizedek and the messiah shows us how Jesus is our High Priest mediating the new covenant of redempttive and eternal life through his human nature born into time and suffering.

The main sign of Jesus' priestly mediation is the cross, in which the contraries again exist in tension, representing the trials of faith itself. For the cross is neither just a singular historical instance of atrocious suffering, nor merely a symbol of the tensions inherent in faith. On the one hand, the mind's relaxed indulgence of the symbolism breaks before the terrible fact of the public execution: a man was actually nailed out and hung up to die in unspeakable agony. On the other hand, the death calls out for meaning, and refuses to relapse into the mere anonymity which marks the equally cruel deaths of countless millions of innocents throughout history. Rather, the cross proclaims a message of eternal life through patient and faithful endurance, stating that this is God's way. The cross is thus a symbol which is itself a critique of symbolism; a sign showing us that signs will in the end fail us.[5] The cosmic Christ whose authority is higher than the angels is joined here to the brother who suffers alone, but among us. The cross both effects and represents the juncture of these two principles, and the striking originality of Hebrews is in making the cross, thus understood, the very principle of the book's structure. One result is that the significance of Jesus Christ emerges indirectly from the multiplicity of contraries reconciled in him.

As I have suggested, the main rhetorical oppositions in Hebrews can be described in terms of verticals and horizontals, and these dimensions themselves have positive and negative poles. Thus, on the positive side of the vertical we find descriptions of eternity, angels, and enduring substance. On the negative side are the fallen powers, and images suggesting the unmaking or dissolution of good. On the positive side of the horizontal dimension we find the process of perfection, and various foreshadowings of glory. On the negative side are mere repetition and the endless recurrence of death through time. The eternal rest to which Hebrews invites us is partly our reward in heaven for steadfast endurance on earth, but it is also the proper stance of faith, which is a kind of poise in the midst, the still point, as it were, at the intersection of the arms of the cross where contraries are in equilibrium. Hebrews is quite firm on the idea that such rest is a kind of vigilant self-giving and not just easy relaxation. This helps to explain the further, distinctive and paradoxical relationship throughout Hebrews between centre and circumference.

The true centre, it seems, is to be found at the boundary, at the point where we are open to all that challenges our security. This, again, is the position of faith, and at the conclusion Hebrews draws our attention to the fact that Christ was crucified outside the camp. We are to follow his way of the cross through faith, moving out from the established centres to the true centre, seeking the boundary between what we know and love and all that opposes our knowledge and love, thereby placing ourselves exactly at the point where we do not know our direction forward. This is the place of true sacrifice, and the fact that the Son of God offered himself in this manner for us is redemptive partly to the degree that we might follow him there without fear, through faith. The nexus of cross, faith, centre and circumference thus suggests the perilous equipoise and felt life of faith which abstract description alone could not achieve. Let us now consider some of these distinctive patterns in more detail.

A great deal has been made of similarities between the ideas and vocabulary of Hebrews and the allegorical treatment of the scriptures by the Jewish Platonist, Philo of Alexandria. In 1750, J. P. Carpzov found parallels to Philo in virtually every phrase of Hebrews, and in a well-known study published in 1952, C. Spicq confirmed an extensive indebtedness, concluding that the author of Hebrews was a Philonist converted to Christianity.[6] Certainly, there are tantalising similarities. As we have seen, Philo, like Hebrews, compares the messiah to Melchizedek; Jesus is referred to as the high priest in Hebrews, and Philo uses the same words to describe the logos; the Greek word *charakter* (image) occurs in the New Testament only in Hebrews 1:3, but is frequent in Philo and is used to describe the logos, as is also the case in Hebrews 1:3, and so on. Yet Ronald Williamson has recently brought under close scrutiny the whole idea that Hebrews is indebted to Platonism in general and Philo in particular, concluding that there is very little evidence that such is the case.[7] The distinction between an ideal, unchanging Reality and an ever-changing sense world which is an imperfect copy of the Real is fundamental to Platonist thinking, but Williamson finds that the outlook throughout Hebrews is opposed to it. Spicq's main problem is that he has concentrated on linguistic similarities, but ignored fundamental differences of outlook (9). Williamson claims that although the language of shadow and image is indeed Platonic, the author of Hebrews uses it predominantly to indicate the horizontal relationship between type and antitype rather than the vertical relationship between form and copy. Williamson concludes of the author of Hebrews that 'He almost certainly lived and moved in circles where, in broad, general terms, ideas such as those we meet in Philo's works were known and discussed; he drew upon the same fund of cultured Greek vocabulary upon which Philo drew. But this is as much as the evidence allows us to conclude' (493).

Williamson's careful study warns us to be cautious, and not to rush into uncritical assumptions. Yet it is hard to avoid the broad and fairly obvious effect throughout Hebrews, whereby a higher world is compared to the world of common experience in a manner inviting us to imagine the comparison vertically. Thus, God's throne in heaven 'is for ever and ever' (1:8). In heaven we have 'a better possession and an abiding one' (10:34). Christ, we are told, does not enter 'into a sanctuary made with hands, a copy of the true one, but into heaven itself' (9:24). The Son 'through whom also he [God] created the world' (1:2) has come down among us, and as the great high priest 'has passed through the heavens' (4:14). The heavens here are above us, and the contrast is clearly enough between high and low.

Various allusions to angels help to confirm the mind's vertical eye-view, so to speak. Admittedly, angels are traditionally God's messengers who deliver his word into history, and thus the words of angels can stand for the old covenant 'horizontally' foreshadowing the new. Yet the sense that angels are higher creatures than humans is also emphasised. Man, we learn, is made 'lower than the angels' (2:7). Jesus, who sits at 'the right hand of the Majesty on high' (1:3), and is 'much superior to angels' (1:4), has been 'made lower than the angels ... because of the suffering of death' (2:9). Superiority here is indicated by language suggesting elevation and debasement: the cosmic Christ comes down from his seat at God's right hand to share in our earthly suffering and fear, putting himself below the angels for this purpose.

Likewise, the description of a 'better possession and an abiding one' (10:34) in heaven confirms the sense of a higher power sustaining a lower creation, however much the author of Hebrews is aware of the dynamism of this lower creation being directed through history towards the kingdom (12:28). Thus also, the 'copies of the heavenly things' (that is, the earthly sanctuary) are purified by the cult sacrifices, but 'the heavenly things themselves' require 'better sacrifices' (9:23). Williamson is correct to say this does not mean there is a form-copy relationship between the animal sacrifices and Christ's, but the contrast between heaven itself and the earthly sanctuary, its copy, is 'vertical', and even Williamson admits that a Platonist kind of contrast between earthly and heavenly reality is evident in descriptions of the tabernacle.[8]

The 'vertical' imagery of Hebrews is further developed through the contrast between a higher, enduring substance and its negative analogue, the energy of unmaking which destroys the God-given, created identity of things, or causes restlessness and unease. Thus, the Lord remains, but his creation, the heavens, will be folded up like a garment (1:11); unbelievers will not enter into rest (3:18), but those who have faith can stop lions' mouths (11:33) and quench the violence of fire (11:34). We are warned against any 'root of bitterness' (12:15) because it will bring trouble and defilement, and when the things that are shaken are removed, 'what cannot be shaken may remain' (12:27). God is a consuming fire (12:29), and the thorns and briars will be burned (6:8), just as 'what is becoming obsolete and growing old' (8:13) will vanish away.

The imagery of fire and of old things being replaced by new is clearly enough eschatological, but it is too simple (and certainly unliterary) to conclude that because such language has a typological or 'horizontal' application it cannot also have a 'vertical' one, whereby the eternal, heavenly domain to which the Son is elevated at the resurrection stands in contrast to the restlessness and de-creative forces at work in the lower world.[9] The profoundest literary language is often multivalent, thereby breaking the over-confident thrust of merely linear thinking. Like the cross itself, the images and motifs of Hebrews characteristically undermine allegorical abstraction, while provoking us simultaneously to seek a higher and stable significance in which our agitations and fears can come to rest.

The horizontal dimension of the imagery in Hebrews is largely synonymous with the author's use of typology, and we are insistently reminded of how Old Testament history and rituals are imperfect types of truths revealed in Jesus. Thus, Jesus is worthy of more glory than Moses (3:3); the law is 'a shadow of the good things to come' (10:1); Jesus' blood 'speaks more graciously than the blood of Abel' (12:24); the high priest's sacrifice and the repeated Old Testament rituals (9:9, 19) are figures for the one perfect sacrifice of the eternal high priest which takes up into itself and clarifies the uncertain significance of cult practice. Such a reduction of the Jewish sacred scriptures, subordinating them to the meaning of Jesus' ignominious death, is a bold, even arrogant appropriation, but it is also an acknowledgement of the power and authority of those scriptures. The spectacle of defeat and humiliation at Calvary was so complete and devastating that only the most over-reaching and far-flung of claims would save the appearances. The author of Hebrews places such a claim before us: God's authority as the scriptures reveal it in all its majesty and power, tenderness and compassion, becomes our means of understanding Jesus' death. For

Jesus is the pre-existent logos, the cosmic Christ who came among us as our brother to suffer in time, thereby freeing us from the fear of death. Calvary is God's way, and the developing understanding by man of his own position in history, which the scriptures record, gives us a purchase, as it were, on the catastrophic public execution which would otherwise dissolve into anonymity with so much else subject to the decaying power of time. The idea of a covenant through which human history is bound to God, of sacrifice through which God is made near and expiation effected, of priesthood through which mediation is brought about between men and God: these are the categories, the language of sacred scripture through which we are enabled to understand and communicate the meaning of Jesus' death. Like all language, these terms and concepts have evolved through time, which itself thus becomes the context of our understanding. The horizontal imagery is not so much a rhetoric of persuasion (though it is also that) as the very means of making available a certain interpretation of Jesus' death.

The language of typology is closely associated throughout Hebrews with the idea of perfection (*teleiosis*), or achievement of an end.[10] As with many ideas in Hebrews, this one carries the resonance of Greek thinking whereby perfection is a higher state, spatially imagined on a higher plane. But the term is used with a deliberately horizontal application in Hebrews, to confirm the sense that the Old Testament types are fulfilled in the singular moment of the Lord's descent into historical time. Again, the intersection of the horizontal time line with the idea of vertical descent from eternity into the realm of imperfection reproduces the tension and paradox which the cross itself symbolises. Perfection, we are told, is not found through the Levitical priesthood, but by 'another priest' (7:11), Christ; the law 'made nothing perfect' (7:19), but Jesus offers us a 'better hope' (7:19); the Old Testament sacrifices 'cannot perfect the conscience of the worshiper' (9:9), but Christ the high priest offers a 'more perfect tent' (9:11); the repretitions of animal sacrifice 'continually offered year after year' (10:1) cannot 'make perfect those who draw near' (10:1), but Jesus' sacrifice, offered once for all on earth and then confirmed eternally in heaven, is perfect.

Once more, the vertical, transcendent dimension is offered to us conflated with the contingent and temporal horizontal to prevent our easy rationalising of the problematic, lived experience of faith. Not surprisingly, there has been a good deal of debate about the precise location of Christ's sacrifice. Is it temporal (on Calvary) or eternal (in heaven), and can we reconcile these alternatives?[11] Clearly, the death did take place in the flesh on Calvary, but we learn also that Christ offers his blood to the Father in heaven (9:14). As we have seen, the author of Hebrews insists that the heavenly sanctuary (9:24) is to be purified with blood on the model of the earthly sanctuary which is purified by the blood of animals. As is now generally acknowledged, the shedding and manipulation of sacrificial blood symbolises the offering of life itself, which was thought to reside in the blood. Hence, Christ's spilt blood is also the offering of his eternal life to God. As scholars point out, the author of Hebrews consistently uses the aorist to describe Jesus' sacrifice, whereas when dealing with the priestly sacrifices he uses the present.[12] The use of the aorist confirms that the sacrifice is complete, and implies that Jesus' high priesthood endures in heaven. Whether or not his sacrifice continues there, or in what sense we should understand such a transaction is not clear, but we are meant to understand that the sacrifice is not confined to the historical moment on Calvary. We are told rather that in heaven Jesus intercedes for us ('since he always lives to make intercession' [7:25]), and appears before God on our behalf ('now to appear in the presence of God on our behalf' [9:24]). This eternal intercession cannot be divorced from the earthly sacrifice, even though the connection between them remains opaque: the darkness of that compelling juncture of two worlds is also the darkness of the cross.

So far, we have seen the horizontal images in relation to typology and the process of perfection. But, as with the verticals, the horizontals have a negative dimension, for time is the bringer of death, and of the same deadly round of repetitive behaviour and ritual observance. The old covenant 'is ready to vanish away' (8:13) because it is subject to decay, like the creation itself, which will perish with passage of time (1:11). The 'dead works' of ritual observance (6:1) bind us to sacrifices 'continually offered year after year' (10:1); in the world of time we find 'no lasting city' (13:14); so in faith we are to follow Jesus beyond the boundary, to the place of rejection. Thus the process of perfection through time, and of an imperfect but true revelation anticipating Calvary, is offset by an acknowledgement of time's remorseless destruction and the deadly repetitiveness of human destinies committed to time's dictation. The horizontal images of Hebrews are not therefore simply in tension with the verticals, but, like the verticals, present us with a further series of internal tensions, themselves reproducing the dynamics of the cross, symbol of faith.

As now begins to become clear, the author of Hebrews reverts at every turn to his one compelling theme, that in Christ's high priesthood earthly suffering is the means by which the great creator reconciles us eternally to himself. There can be no substantiation or proof of this claim except through the powerful relevance which the event at Calvary and its explanations exert on our sense of the human condition and man's religious nature. The claim that the cross brings us to God, and that the layman, Jesus, mediates our reconciliation, boldly offers to make obsolete the ritual practices of religious observance, directing us instead to an inner steadfastness whereby we can face our own fear of death (2:15). Such an attitude is, in the end, a matter of faith, a leap outside the boundaries of prescribed order and religious observance, and not a conclusion deducible by any kind of straightforward 'linear' argument. Thus the author of Hebrews returns us repeatedly to various paradoxical junctures at which the eternal Christ and our brother suffering in history are identified. If God is not our compassionate fellow-sufferer, then Jesus indeed dies an ignominious and, ultimately, insignificant death. How God can abase himself, and how we are to understand the incarnation are matters which theologians might attempt systematically to conceive, and already one feels in Hebrews a strong theological bent. But that is not the book's most compelling claim to authority: rather the sinuous, elegant severity with which it places before us the perpetual conflict between our human fear and unquenchable hope, each tempering the other in the troubled knowledge which is faith.

The cross, then, is the main symbol of faith, and is one among a multiplicity of contraries with which Hebrews confronts us. Yet faith also is associated with rest: 'For we who have believed enter that rest' (4:3). We are advised to 'strive to enter that rest, that no one fall by the same sort of disobedience' (4:11). Faith, it seems, is a kind of endurance, a patient holding-fast (10:23) preceding the heavenly reward. Yet the author of Hebrews draws also on the familiar apocalyptic idea that events of the end time are already present in heaven,[13] so that the promised future is also present to those who can know it: 'For we who have believed do enter that rest ... although his works were finished from the foundation of the world' (4:3). As we have seen, Christ's sacrifice is eternally efficacious, thus making the perfect end already present. It follows that the steadfastness of faith is to some degree the experience itself of God's promised rest, and faith is thus a peculiar combination of strain and release. Faith is at once the imperfect knowledge reminding us of our transience as 'strangers and exiles on the earth' (11:13) (a condition which we share with our forebears, for, like them, we find 'no lasting city' [13:14] on this earth), and our assurance of eternal peace. It is our reminder that on this earth believers are perpetually thrust out beyond the bounds of institutions which make them secure, even while they are perpetually at rest in the knowledge of God's eternal assurance, mediated through his son's high priesthood.

This unsettling tension between now and then, promises effected and postponed, rest and labour, is further developed through an engaging but elusive interplay between the notions of centre and circumference. The place of rest – the centre where we might expect to find stability – is often displaced to the circumference, the perimeter where we are challenged and confronted, so that the condition of labour and patient endurance becomes the place where truth is most profoundly discovered. Chapter 1 describes how God himself sets the example. The Son, upholder of creation, dwells at the centre of all that is made. But the logos is called out from this secure habitation to the perimeter, to earthly time for 'the suffering of death' (2:9). Placing himself in a situation where he must suffer, paradoxically enables him to create a new centre for human consciousness through his perfect sacrifice whereby humankind is enabled to find rest in the midst of ceaseless labour and bondage. Likewise, the Lord's name is declared to the brethren 'in the midst of the congregation' (2:12), but this place in the midst where God's praises are sung (2:12) is the pilgrim church itself, invited to follow Jesus to perfection through suffering (2:10). Once more, the true centre turns out to be the place of testing and unrest. Through offering up his body to death in the place of rejection at the perimeter, Jesus puts a new law into our hearts and minds (10:16); that is, into the centre of us. Like the sacrificial beasts whose bodies are burned outside the camp, Jesus also is immolated 'outside the gate' (13:12), and the injunction to us is unremittingly plain: 'let us go forth to him outside the camp, bearing abuse for him' (13:13). For our adventure, the author of Hebrews prays that 'the God of peace' (13:20) equip us 'with everything good' (13:21). The centre and sustainer of our lives, the giver of rest now and eternally, is to be found in the radical displacement of ourselves, the opening of ourselves to alienation and otherness, to recrimination and rejection. The blood which saves us and brings perfect life and security is the real, terrible blood of the criminal cast outside the boundaries of civilized order. To see that demands faith; not to see it commits us afresh to the old, familiar terrors.

Jesus, then, is our suffering brother, and also the mediator who brings us rest in God: this is the single theme of Hebrews, to which imagery and diction are consistently and skilfully made subordinate.

Clearly, the author is everywhere concerned with human suffering, and Jesus the High Priest is above all compassionate, 'For he who sanctifies and those who are sanctified have all one origin. That is why he is not ashamed to call them brethren' (2:11). Jesus, in short, is especially relevant for those who are themselves suffering or outcast, and the cross, which in one sense puts an end to the efficacy of signs, also stands for the faith in which we are to endure our own suffering and death. Religious tradition, practice and observance do not save us from anxiety and alienation, the unmaking powers ('the power of death', we learn, 'is the devil' [2:4]). Only the knowledge that human degradation and suffering are somehow also God's, and the means of our true rest, can sustain us in the teeth of what the world makes all-too obvious: that death is the human lot, that we do not know why we suffer, that cruelty, horror and terror prevail in history, that there are no guarantees of absolute meaning but only promises and signs and the heart's desire.[14] Christ's cross is the most radical challenge to faith because it is either God's act fulfilling his promises, or it is yet another frightening instance of the blind terror of human existence and of the emptiness of everything that promises absolute assurance. Only an uncompassionate God would let his creatures suffer so, or no God at all: the rallying cry of all protest atheism is clearly before us here, and there is no avoiding it. Faced with a man on the cross, what theology remains?

Faced with God on the cross, there is at least room for faith that suffering might be significant, despite evidence to the contrary. From one point of view, the claim that God is on the cross is of course preposterous, and from the beginning, cultured opinion declared it so. But the author of Hebrews does not balk: he puts this claim in a strong form, for nothing else will serve. The elevated Jesus sits at God's right hand, bringer of rest to humanity in bondage to death. The cross is therefore associated with joy as well as with anguish, and Jesus 'for the joy that was set before him endured the cross' (12:2). In this knowledge, our brotherly love is to continue (13:1), and whatever rest in the world we achieve through faith is a perilous equipoise. It is at once our willingness to suffer and to share the fear of suffering but without the self-centred anxieties which cause us to harden ourselves in self-protection, or to expiate our suffering by thrusting it onto others. Such faith and such rest are neither to be sentimentalised nor cheapened, nor reduced to any kind of simple logic. Despite his excellent Greek and clear, objective exegesis, the author of Hebrews denies us easy solutions. As we have seen, his diction and images consistently represent the challenge of the cross through a multiplicity of contraries in tension, then opening upon further internal contraries so that his discourse is permeated to its depths with a rich sense of the compelling paradox of faith.

As is often noticed, however, Hebrews is also highly theological. Unlike Paul's letters, there is no sense here of passionate, first person involvement in one half of a dialogue, but rather of a clear, subtle intellect, however much capable of compassion and profundity. As I began by pointing out, Hebrews is a unique document in the New Testament. Indeed, it might remind us of Paul's letters up to a point, but its objectivity, its interest in judgement and in God's wrath, and its conception of the eternal city already present in the heavens, might remind us also of that other unique New Testament book, Revelation. In the development of the present study, Hebrews thus forms a bridge between the Pauline letters and the strange apocalyptic discourse with which the New Testament ends. Yet, as with all of the documents we have discussed, Hebrews presents us centrally with a faith which we can approach only with a certain trepidation. The cross enables us to take joy in the world and in one another: but what joy is there in a world where innocence is crucified, and where all our secure boundary-lines are marked with blood?

8

Revelation: the Two-Edged Sword

To turn from the gospels to Revelation is always a shock. We feel we are entering a different world, full of frightening spectacle, bizarre imagery and wholesale violence. Revelation, says D. H. Lawrence, is the Judas Iscariot of the New Testament,[1] and he is echoed by C. G. Jung, who sees it as an eruption into consciousness of pent-up negative feelings denied or repressed by Christians attempting to live according to the conviction that perfect love casts out fear.[2] Like Jung, commentators have often felt uneasy about the frightening excess of John's visions: Amos Wilder points to their 'archaic and acultural' character;[3] John Sweet is concerned about the 'lethal concentration' of negative elements found only 'in small deposits' elsewhere in the New Testament, and he worries lest Revelation should propagate vengefulness.[4]

Much of the power of Revelation indeed resides in its turbulent imagery. As Austin Farrer says, the book depicts 'a realm which has no shape at all but that which the images give it',[5] as they strive to uncover the spiritual principles at work within human history. Such principles are obscured by the deadening weight of familiar experience, which John's imagination in turn defamiliarises to have us detect anew how the perpetual, archetypal drama of good and evil is at work even in ordinary events. One result is that Revelation is also an encouragement to Christian martyrs: spiritually regarded, their perseverance and suffering are victory blows for the forces of good against the dragon and his beasts, despite the fact that from a worldly perspective martyrs seem only to suffer defeat and immolation. By the same token, we are warned against slackness and complacency: beneath the comfortable surfaces of life in the cities of this world, a spiritual warfare is in full tilt. By our behaviour we are aligned either with the forces of good or evil, and we will be called to account.

One way of helping to explain these striking characteristics of Revelation is to describe the book as an apocalypse. The word *apokalypsis* means 'revelation' or 'uncovering', and apocalyptic writing offers a vision of the world's end in which present suffering and alienation are overcome and God's elect will reign in a new paradise. Jewish apocalypses flourished especially under the domination of the Greeks and Romans between approximately 200 BC and AD 100. The main example is the Book of Daniel, which, like others of the kind, is pseudonymous and attributed to a prophet of an earlier age. In Daniel, an unknown author looks back to the heroic perseverance of Jewish exiles in Babylon six centuries before Christ, as a means of encouraging the second century Maccabean revolt against Antiochus Epiphanes (175–164 BC). There is a series of visions in which terrifying beasts from the sea represent the empires of this world, destroyed at last by the Son of Man. Angels offer advice on the course of events, and veiled allusions to second-century politics are delivered by means of a 'book of truth'. Other works like Daniel are Zechariah, Joel, the Ezra Apocalypses, Ehtiopian Enoch, and the Syriac Apocalypse of Baruch. There are also apocalyptic elements in St. Paul and the gospels, for instance I Thessalonians 4:13–5:11; II Thessalonians 2:1–12; I Corinthians 15:20–28, and the so-called 'synoptic apocalypse' in Mark 13 and its parallels. Indeed, there is good reason to see Christianity itself beginning as an apocalyptic sect, and the expectation of a new, transformed reality endures as a central element of Christian hope.[6]

Scholars have attempted to describe the main components of apocalyptic writing, but the debate is complex and intricate. J. Christiaan Beker, drawing on Vielhauer and Koch,[7] stresses three main ideas: '(1) historical dualism; (2) universal cosmic expectation; and (3) the imminent end of the world' (136). Beker insists that 'historical dualism' is not to be confused with utopian fantasy: an Apocalypse is 'not to be understood without the existential realities of martyrdom, persecution, moral fibre, and encouragement and the longing for a final theodicy' (137).

Revelation conforms well to these broad criteria, and scholars have charted a dense tissue of allusions, especially to Daniel, Ezekiel, the synoptic apocalypse, and also to a widening spectrum of scriptural and rabbinic sources with apocalyptic leanings.[8] Revelation should therefore be understood not as a grotesque anomaly in the New Testament, but as an example of a literary type. John of Patmos adapts a set of well-tried conventions to declare Christ's victory at the end of history as the slain and triumphant lamb, and to encourage Christian hope and perseverance in the present when evil and complacency seem ascendent, and God's purposes obscure. However, Revelation differs from other examples of the kind in not being pseudonymous.[9]

Still, John's peculiar power and originality are not diminished by knowledge of his sources. The wrathful lamb, the multi-horned, multi-headed beasts, the sinister horsemen, the cosmic woman with her mysterious child, the alpha and omega, the figure like the Son of Man with hair as white as snow and eyes like flame, the vials of pestilence, horses up to their bridles in blood, the caustic lament for a lurid, thriving Babylon, the hideously improvised locusts, the fiercely bejewelled New Jerusalem without a temple: all this and a great deal else comes upon us in a cataract, with the power of nightmare engendering bewilderment, fright, and fascination. Knowledge of the aims and conventions of apocalypses in general and the painstaking search for analogues and sources merely throw into sharper relief the strange, unique vigour of this particular example. The many books to which Revelation can be compared show that no book is quite like it.

My point is familiar to literary critics: great literature uses conventions in a special way, and genre is a schematic notion calling up in the reader a broad set of expectations which then exist in tension with a particular voice, an individual mode of expression. And yet, a critical reading of Revelation is difficult, partly because there are so many problems with interpreting even the individual mode of expression, the surface meaning. Is there a progression of events? How do elements of the vision belong together? Often we have to struggle so energetically to find our feet amidst the bewildering power of the spectacle that generic characteristics become uncertain. For instance, as Austin Farrer says, the book has many elements suggesting a framework which no one can miss,[10] 'Yet, as we advance, it does not appear to us that the promise is fulfilled.' Consequently, 'we are left unable to reconcile ourselves either to the hypothesis of formal order or to the hypothesis of its absence' (36). These words no doubt reflect the experience of many readers who have responded to the book's suggestions of pattern and structure, but who have then become lost in the welter of details calling to be fitted securely.

Farrer's own account of the framework about which he appears to be so tentative is, however, among the most thoroughgoing and painstaking in existence. He suggests that there are six visions, each of seven parts (that is, six working days and a sabbath), and that the book ends with a final sabbath eve (58, 65). Inconsistencies are worked out by a theory of 'intrusive visions' and deliberately cancelled conclusions whereby we are invited to check our expectations and restructure events retrospectively. Farrer then develops his outline in terms of astrological symbolism whereby the order of days corresponds to the twelve zodiac signs, which in turn correspond to the tribes of Israel and the principal feasts and rituals of the Jewish liturgical calendar. Finally, he produces a four-cornered diagram representing heaven and earth, the four cardinal points, four elements, and four seasons of the year, into which all the details of the larger scheme are seen to fit. He claims that John must have worked from some such diagram, for the elaborately interwomen motifs cannot be explained otherwise.

Farrer is quite aware of the difficulties his argument presents. He admits that a structure this subtle is not really successful as literature because it has baffled virtually all its readers (36). Still, he claims we are in a better position today to understand the Judaeo-Christian mind of John's time than at any period since the second century, and so the investigation might not be unrewarding (36). Indeed, Farrer offers much interesting interpretation and brilliant analysis, but he remains wryly aware of his necessary ingenuities. On the zodiac symbolism, for instance, he coyly concedes, 'you may not wish to assume that he [John] did anything so elaborate' (216), and after a subtle interpretation of the 1600 furlongs of Rev. 14, he says: 'That is the best we can do with the 1,600. Let us hope someone will soon do better' (255). The main difficulty is that John's inconsistencies must be interpreted as some kind of 'ingenious variation on a theme', and such ingenuity threatens to become an end in itself. Exegesis then turns into an act of imagination as obscure and entangled as the text it offers to explain.

Some interpretations attempt to negotiate these difficulties by claiming that Revelation is made up of a number of documents. Such is the position of M.-E. Boismard,[11] who argues from John's use of doublets to the conclusion that the text consists of three units: two apocalypses written by John, and the group of seven letters. Plenty of other schemes are available: J. W. Boman[12] argues for a drama in seven acts; A. Feuillet[13] suggests a two-part structure in which chapters 4–11 deal with God's judgement of Israel and chapters 12–20 with the church and the world; C. E. Douglas[14] points to the four-times repeated 'in the Spirit' as indicating the principal divisions, and stresses a contrast between settings in heaven and on earth.

None of these interesting schemes is wholly satisfactory: those who favour multi-documentary hypotheses to some degree fail to acknowledge John's synthesising activity; those who stress imaginative distinction fail fully to explain the relationship of parts to the whole. Yet Farrer's basic tenet remains everywhere in force: Revelation so strongly suggests formal order that we cannot do without it, even though we cannot fully identify it. The patterns of 7 (seals, trumpets, plagues) and of 4 (beasts, horsemen, elements), the repeated motif of plagues from Exodus, the counterpointing of Babylon and Jerusalem, the indications of progress towards a millennium, the constant promises and reassurances, and a highly conspicuous numerology (144 000 elect, 24 Elders, 1260 days, and so on), all suggest careful design. Yet in the avalanche of grotesque beauty and sheer peculiarity of detail, the cool lineaments of order are taken up and melted into a persistently elusive strangeness.

My own suggestion here is simple, but it has two sides. On the one hand, Revelation is indeed a Christian apocalypse, loosely structured on a central plan of four divisions of seven elements, with an introduction and conclusion. Here I follow the broad arrangement set out by John Sweet.[15] The four main divisions are the seven letters, seven seals, seven trumpets, and seven vials, and they are a kind of central massif about which are gathered a body of heterogeneous details and transitional materials. Also, throughout Revelation is a counterpoint between the earthly and heavenly cities and their powers, and the author might well have had before him some kind of diagram, such as Farrer suggests, to guide his complex and imaginative fusion of images, which could be partly astrological.

On the other hand, I would suggest that our very failure to find a satisfactory pattern despite strong intimations of its presence is part of the book's lesson, expressing the trials of faith. It is as if John had written Revelation on Paul's prescription that in this life we see through a mirror dimly. The book's images, like all images in poetry, are this-worldly and opaque, even though the heat of visionary experience opens them towards an awful transcendence. So also, the structure of Revelation thematises the conflict between human desire for secure knowledge and the fact that such security is always denied to particular experience. A warning against naive apocalypticism is therefore implicit in the book's structure. We approach the end times in fear and trembling, for despite assurances of reward for perseverance, we cannot see God's design clearly enough to be certain that it favours us. While insisting on righteousness, Revelation clearly warns its readers against too much assurance about what is going to happen, and even divine assurances have a tendency to pass into unsettling ambivalence reminding us of our human insecurity.

'The time is near' (1:3; 2:20), we learn, or 'I am coming soon' (22:7; 22:20), or 'Lo, I am coming like a thief' (16:15). These statements are partly answers to prayer, but they are also warnings: 'I am coming like a thief' is directly followed by 'Blessed is he who is awake' (16:15); 'I am coming soon' by 'Blessed is he who keeps the words' (22:7), and 'the time is near' of chapter 1 is counterpointed by the concluding chapter: 'Let the evildoer still do evil' (22:11). The cries of 'How long?' among the persecuted are here stirringly answered, but not without ambiguity. Who knows who will be taken unawares? Do not be entirely sure that you will be sufficiently watchful, John implies, or that you will keep the sayings and not be taken by surprise.

In the seven letters to the churches, 'I am coming soon' is often used in this threatening manner in contexts which at first seem comforting. The labour and patience of the church at Ephesus are praised (2:2), but the church is then accused of having left 'the love you had at first' (2:4), and is told to repent: If not, I will come to you and remove your lampstand from its place' (2:5). The church at Pergamos is praised for holding fast and not denying the faith, but is accused also of fornication and told to repent, or else 'I will come to you soon' (2:16). The church at Sardis is told that if it is not watchful 'I will come like a thief, and you will not know at what hour I will come upon you' (3:3). And the Philadelphian church is told, 'I am coming soon: hold fast what you have, so that no one may seize your crown' (3:11). In these examples, the Lord's promise is uncertainly poised between assurance and threat, and a reader might well wonder how he would find the Lord should the Lord choose to find him out on the instant.

In other ways, the seven letters continue to stress the present moment's uncertainty for which we are nonetheless responsible. Images of doors are especially telling. The carrier of David's key 'opens and no one shall shut ... shuts and no one opens' (3:7); an open door is set before us 'which no one is able to shut' (3:8), yet the Lord knocks on a door and 'if any one hears my voice, and opens the door, I will come in to him' (3:20). These contrary instructions about opening and shutting suggest a mixture of power and powerlessness, activity and passivity connected with the crossing of a threshold either by entering into a sacred place of our own initiative, or being allowed to enter it, or allowing it to enter us. The simple reassurance of an open door is confounded in the ambiguity of the conditions under which it would be certainly open for us. Also, we might notice how the image of a door leads us out of the letters section by introducing the next main section of trumpets. The transitional verse is: 'After this I looked, and lo, in heaven an open door' (4:1). Passing through this door, however, does not lead to a final destination in heaven as the verse suggests, but to a further set of visions, and this is consistent (as I will soon show) with John's refusal of a satisfying closure to any of his main seven-fold parts.

The two-edged sword in the letters section is also analogous to the imagery of doors in that both have two sides and effect a division. For instance, the church at Pergamos is warned of the Lord's 'sharp two-edged sword' (2:12), which is 'the sword of my mouth' (2:16), and it is clear from other references (1:16; 19:15; 19:21) that the two-edged sword is God's word. But, as with the door, it provides uncertain reassurance. The sword of his word is God's weapon against evil, but when the Lord comes like a thief, will the sword cut for us, or at us? The Laodiceans are told they are lukewarm, 'neither cold nor hot' (3:15), and for that reason 'I will spue you out of my mouth' (3:16). In this they are like most of us, unsure about our spiritual fervor and of how deserving we are to be rejected because of our half-heartedness.

The letters section is also broadly linked to the introductory materials describing seven spirits before God's throne (1:4). Because the number seven indicates completeness, as in seven days of the week, the seven spirits represent the full Holy Spirit just as the seven churches (which are disposed roughly in a circle if we look at the map) represent the whole church. Despite these suggestions of wholeness, however, the letters are heralded by the frightening figure 'like a son of man' (1:13), with hair white as snow, eyes of flame and feet of brass as if fired in a furnace, with a voice that sounds like water, and seven stars in his right hand. Again, a 'sharp two-edged sword' (1:16) comes out of his mouth, and, not surprisingly, John falls down in fear. The figure then reassures him: 'I am the first and the last' (1:17), he says, echoing the 'I am the Alpha and the Omega' of 1:8. Yet this consoling voice also claims to have 'the keys of Death and Hades' (1:18), so that comfort once more is tempered by fear as the images of sword and door combine with the powerful, anomalous figure to suggest danger as well as sustaining strength. Like so much else in Revelation, then, John's introduction records a powerful sense of divine order while simultaneously reminding us of how uncertain we are about where we belong in that order. His further technique of breaking the narrative design at key points contrary to our expectations, and his use of numerology which is both specific and vague, re-enforce the effect of unsettling doubleness.[16]

For instance, the second main group describes the seven seals, each having a frightening portent as the four horsemen venture into the world to conquer (6:2), to slay with the sword (6:4) and with famine (6:6), and to let loose death and hell (6:8) signalling the wrath of the lamb (6:16–17). After the first six seals are opened there is an extended interruption. Four angels hold the winds in abeyance (7:1ff.) and another calls for a stay of proceedings until God's servants are marked on their foreheads. There follows a list of the twelve tribes, and an innumerable multitude stands before the throne. These have made their robes white in the blood of the lamb (7:14), which will lead them to fountains of water and comfort them (7:17). The seventh seal is then opened, and 'there was silence in heaven for about half an hour' (8:1). We then pass immediately to the seven angels with seven trumpets (8:2).

John's procedure here is the kind of thing that gives headaches to structural analysts. The pattern is interrupted, and when the seventh seal is finally opened, the delayed event is so muted as to be distinctly anti-climactic, passing off quietly into the new sevenfold series of trumpets. Farrer is correct to suggest that the interruption is a sabbatical pause after the sixfold work of opening the seals, and he equates the half-hour silence with the incense ritual of the Temple ceremonies. He also points out how each main group of seven almost is a complete little apocalypse, but that John consistently prevents satisfactory closure, forcing us instead to look for other developments, and eventually for the grand consummation when heaven and earth as we know them will pass away.[17] We have already seen an example of this deferred closure in the seven letters, where the door opened in heaven in fact leads to a further set of visions. The same technique is evident now with the trumpets. The first six herald a series of plagues and scourges, increasingly terrifying. An angel descends (10:1) and we expect the seventh trumpet, but instead there are 'seven thunders' (10:3). The angel then commands John to 'Seal up what the seven thunders have said, and do not write it down' (10:4), announcing 'that there should be no more delay' (10:6). John then must eat a little bittersweet book before measuring the Temple with a reed. There follows a prophecy about two witnesses who are killed by the power of the beast but revive again and are raised up to heaven, to the consternation of their enemies. The seventh trumpet is at last introduced, but, as with the seven seals, it announces a heavenly liturgy in which God is worshipped, and prepares for the section on the woman clothed with the sun. Again, our expectation is primed only to be disappointed: the seventh angel turns out to be a trumpet angel, and announces that John has recorded enough sevenfold patterns. The thunders are cancelled, and John must get to the point: the 'little scroll' (10:19) contains a call to prophesy, and he is to eat it (that is, read or assimilate it), and measure the temple with a reed (perhaps, record the message of the kingdom in writing).[18] The story of the persecution, revival and glorification of the witnesses[19] duplicates the main motifs of Revelation as a whole by alluding to the holy city, the beast, martyrdom, and divine vengeance heralded by earthquakes (11:13). The seventh trumpet, with its heavenly liturgy, then functions as a sabbath completing the process described by the 'little scroll' and the story of the witnesses.

Once more, closure is incomplete because the seventh trumpet does not really round off the series, but completes the usurping sub-section. Also the pattern has been disturbed already in the description of the fifth angel. He introduces three woes, and we learn that 'The first woe has passed; behold, two woes are still to come' (9:12). The second woe is then named at the end of the section on the witnesses, and we are told: 'The second woe is past; behold, the third is soon to come' (11:14). The seventh trumpet, however, is not a 'woe', but an interlude followed by the story of the woman and her persecution by the dragon. Although the third woe is not specifically mentioned, it must belong in this story of persecution, therefore again breaking the self-containedness of the trumpets section which in any case, as we see, was already broken by the account of the 'little scroll'.[20]

The development of the seventh trumpet into the persecution of the woman and war against the dragon prepares for the final main group of seven plagues. The first four plague-angels pour pestilence upon the earth (16:2), sea (16:3), rivers (16:4) and sun (16:8). The fifth infects the beast's throne (16:10), the sixth poisons the Euphrates (Israel's frontier with invaders from the east), and the seventh pours his vial on the air, the element of Satan's power as St. Paul says (Ephesians 2:2). Again there are earthquakes and catastrophes, and Babylon is divided. An angel offers to show how judgement falls on the great whore, Babylon; yet what follows is not quite a judgement, but a symbolic description of the earthly city, with contemporary political allusions (17:9ff.) and a rather splendid account of 'the merchants of the earth' (18:11). At last the destruction of Babylon is foretold (18:21), preparing us for the defeat of the beasts and the dragon, the millennial rule of saints, and marriage of the lamb.

Unlike the seals and trumpets, the sequence of seven vials is uninterrupted[21] and is introduced by an assurance that these 'seven plagues ... are the last' (15:1). They occur swiftly, and when the seventh is poured, a voice from the throne says 'It is done' (16:17). Finally, we seem to have a series intact within itself, except that one angel returns to develop the judgement of Babylon which is carried forward in an unexpected, open-ended manner. Also, the sixth vial contains a deliberate allusion to the seven letters to the churches: 'Lo, I am coming like a thief. Blessed is he who is awake' (16:15). These words warn again against complacency, and the echo cautions readers against thinking the plan complete.[22] The judgement of Babylon is really about the earthly city where we all dwell, and where we are not safe enough to be complacent.

The four groups of seven are clearly a groundplan for Revelation, though the linking material, interruptions and asymmetries offer endless puzzles for interpreters, and John seems concerned to prevent our acquiescing in any secure sense of pattern. The doorway to heaven opens surprisingly upon a further set of visions; the seven seals are interrupted from within and pass into the seven trumpets; these in turn are interrupted after the sixth episode, and the delayed seventh both concludes the interpolated material and introduces a further section; finally, the seven plagues are extended asymmetrically into the judgement of Babylon. We thus encounter consistently the effect of the two-edged sword as I have described it earlier, and John's assurances of order do not free us from anxiety.

At this point I should add a brief comment on the conclusion to Revelation and the thousand-year rule of the saints. When the armies of God assemble after the fall of Babylon is predicted, once more the sharp sword goes out of the Lord's mouth (19:15) and terrible carnage follows. The two beasts (19:20) are cast into a lake of fire, and the dragon is bound for a thousand years, during which time the martyrs rule on earth. Then the dragon is 'loosed from his prison' (20:10) to the confusion of the nations, until he is finally defeated, at which time the last judgement of all the dead occurs.

Numerous theories have been offered to account for the millennial rule.[23] The broadest of these notices two traditions in apocalyptic writing, the first stressing renewal in this world, and the second renewal in heaven. John, it seems, incorporates both by having a temporary rule of the saints on earth before the final passing of heaven and earth and the establishment of the New Jerusalem. This explanation, however, does not dispel the fact that the millennial episode comes upon us as a surprise, for nothing in the preceding chapters prepares us for it. Another theory seeks a clue in the fact that the Bible elsewhere depicts each day of creation as a thousand years (Psalm 90:4); in that case, the rule of the saints could be interpreted as a sabbatical rest. This sabbath is preceded by the dominion of antichrist (whose number, as we shall see, is based on six), and followed by the coming of Christ, whose number is eight. Again we are invited to detect a plan here, but we are simultaneously warned that during the millennium only those rule who 'had been beheaded for their testimony to Jesus and for the word of God' (20:4). The word is associated once more with the sword (the *ius gladii* which exacts punishment by beheading), but only those who suffer under the swords of this world will triumph during the millennium. The promise of a rule of the saints is therefore also a warning against complacency.

The conclusion to Revelation is, in a way, a conclusion in which nothing is concluded, for we are brought round again to the beginning, with the same over-arching sense of completeness – 'I am the Alpha and the Omega' (22:13) – and the same combined promise and threat – 'Behold, I am coming soon, bringing my recompense, to repay every one for what he has done' (22:12). The image of the door is now a gate, and we are invited to enter, but only if we have kept the commandments (22:14): on the wrong side of the gate is a society of criminals (22:15) with whom, otherwise, we belong. Jesus' voice then warns in no uncertain terms against tampering with the words in John's book: 'If any one adds to them, God will add to him the plagues described in this book, and if any one takes away from the words of the book of this prophecy, God will take away his share in the tree of life and in the holy city, which are described in this book' (22:19).

This warning to over-eager editors might seem, as indeed it is, a prudent way for John to keep his text intact. But it takes on another dimension when we read it in context of all the preceding warnings about imminent judgements. Jesus' words confirm the alarming sense of our contingency and insecurity if we take them to mean, not just 'Do not tamper with the text', but 'Do not depart from the behaviour prescribed by this book; follow its meaning exactly.' The warning is now integrated theologically in a way that makes sense out of the threat to blot the offender's name from the book of life, for we are now instructed about how we should live: aware, that is, of divine providence, but without assuming that we understand its intricate design. By such combinations of imagery and structure, Revelation at the end therefore assures us once more that we are neither to seek securities inappropriate to our state, nor to ignore the signs of God's plan made available to us. We must proceed betwixt and between, according to our half-lights.

The pervasive use of numerology in Revelation is also relevant here.[24] As with the book as a whole, it is impossible not to feel that John's symbolic numbers indicate some kind of order, and yet because they are symbolic they do not provide exact information, and shade off into dark predictions and suggestive intimations. As with almost everything else in Revelation, there is much debate on this subject, but there is also a fair degree of consensus on the general principles. For instance, the number seven indicates perfection of the divine creation. Six represents a falling off from perfection, and is especially associated with evil and antichrist. Eight, the first of a new beginning or new week, is Christ's number. Four is the number of natural perfection (four corners of the earth, four seasons), and three is God's number (the Father, Son and Spirit). Twelve also represents perfection, partly because it is the product of four multiplied by three, and because there are twelve months in a year, twelve zodiac signs, twelve tribes of Israel, and twelve apostles. Five and ten are natural numbers and indicate a certain round sum. A thousand and its multiples indicate a very large number. There are also the curious permutations of three-and-a-half, which are based on the reference to 'a time, two times, and half a time' in Daniel (7:25), indicating the duration of persecution. Three-and-a-half is half a week, and can appear as three-and-a-half years, or forty-two months, or 1260 days. These numbers always symbolise the temporary nature of persecution and suffering.

Multiplication intensifies, and this is the basis for grasping the meaning, for instance, of the 144 000 elect. It is 12×12 (perhaps representing Israel and the apostles, but certainly suggesting the idea of perfection intensified), multiplied by 1000, or a very large number. Likewise, the dimensions of Jerusalem (21:15) are best understood as combinations of 12 and 1000. The much-debated number of the beast, 666, is perhaps simply an intensification of imperfection represented by six, despite the intriguing explanations through gematria, suggesting that the number is a code for Nero's name.[25] Destruction by thirds and quarters perhaps indicates whether a divine or natural agency is responsible for an action, though sometimes natural forces parody the divine, and it is difficult to be sure. Indeed, the dragon and his minions consistently parody the forces of good, and we must be aware of deliberate misappropriations of symbolic numbers, as is the case, for instance, with the whore of Babylon's seven-headed beast (17:3, 9–10).

My point here is not so much to provide a guide to John's numerology as to show how consistent it is with his structure and imagery. In general, the numbers suggest design, but they cannot be taken literally. Indeed, John seems to exploit the difference between these two levels of information. For instance, we are told that the number of the sealed is 144 000 'out of every tribe of the sons of Israel' (7:4); the twelve tribes are then listed, and in each the number of the sealed is 12 000. John hears this information from an angel, but then sees 'a great multitude which no man could number, from every nation, from all tribes and peoples, and tongues' (7:9). The twelve tribes in this account symbolise the true Israel, and the figure of 144 000 combines ideal perfection (12 × 12) and completeness (1000). From God's point of view, that is, the plan is meticulous and well-ordered. Yet John sees merely a horde of people, variegated and indiscriminate, which 'no man could number'. The literal experience from the human point of view is perplexing and inexact, and our attention is drawn to the difference between symbolism and actual counting, numerology and arithmetic, divine plan and human experience.

Another example is the measurement of Jerusalem, on whose twelve gates are inscribed the names of the twelve tribes. The city is 'foursquare' (21:16), symbolising perfection which is then intensified by a third dimension making a cube (21:16), even though a cube-shaped city is hard to imagine. John measures this structure and finds it to be 12 000 stadia on each side. Again, the number is symbolic, and corresponds to the 12 000 sealed in each tribe. The city wall is also said to be 144 cubits, which, again, is a multiple of twelve and indicates perfect design. Taken literally, however, 144 cubits is about 216 feet, and if this figure indicates breadth, it is entirely out of proportion to the other dimensions. It is sometimes suggested that this is the height of a wall erected for defense, and it is conspicuously low to indicate that defence of a city like this is scarcely necessary. Such literalism, however, is surely wrongheaded however much the text seems to invite it, and indeed we only discover our mistake by recognising the absurd consequences. The dimensions, as it were, compel us to make a mental picture, and then to revise our opinion, as we come to recognise that the dimensions symbolise a design beyond our imaginations: we faintly grasp the idea, but cannot see it, exactly. Here again John exploits the difference between literal and symbolic numbers in a manner consistent with his use of genre, images and structure to express the human struggle for faith against complacency or in difficult times when God seems far removed. In relation to this series of elements, I would like now to turn to John's use of typology.

Roughly speaking, typology is the relation an event bears to a later event which seems to complete or fulfil its significance. Typological thinking is at the heart of New Testament interpretations of the Hebrew Bible, which becomes known as the Old Testament mainly because the earlier events of Israel's history are held to be fulfilled in the story of Jesus Christ. As A. C. Charity points out, however, discussions of typological thinking are too often descriptive, and do not sufficiently stress the radical challenge the whole notion presents to faith,[26] for typology depends on a perpetual introduction into history of some radically new thing (23). Sacred history is the record both of God's steadfastness (he has always shown Israel the way), and of his unpredictable newness (26ff.). Thus, in times of stress we believe despite our knowledge that the way out is impossible. The record of divine steadfastness in the past does not tell us what to do in a present crisis, except to await in faith some event we would not have anticipated, some surprising thing which will again show us the way and thereby become part of history (33). Appropriately, the exodus story is the basic model for Biblical typology and it keeps happening through Israel's history (38). There is always an impasse, always a perilous journey, always a surprise.

Such is the case also with Revelation, for it asks about the way out of history itself, and tells us yet again to await some surprising newness which comes when we least expect and in a manner undescribable in advance. 'Behold,' says the Lord from the throne, 'I make all things new' (21:5), and his words are not only a promise of steadfast design, but a challenge to faith. Can we believe in God's new exodus in the midst of so much apparent nerveless complacency among so many held in thrall to Babylonian worldliness? As usual, typology confronts us, and as A. C. Charity says, neutrality is impossible (153).

The typological intricacies of Revelation are often complex, but John alludes consistently to the exodus story, and especially to the plagues which hardened Pharaoh's heart and prepared the way for Moses to escape. The seven seals, trumpets and vials all interpret the plagues of Egypt as a consequence of our resisting the heavenly Jerusalem. The Jesus of history resurrected and come again in glory shows us the last exodus from history itself, and Revelation invites us to believe in a heavenly city where the promises of the historical Jerusalem are eternally fulfilled. Whether or not we accept these promises is a matter of faith, but in the terms in which the choice is offered to us, not to be of Jerusalem is to be of Babylon, not to choose the bride is to choose the harlot.

We are thus confronted not only by a typology of event and fulfilment, but also of salvation and rejection. To complicate the matter, these opposites are not entirely distinct, for evil parodies the good, and yet the parody itself becomes evident only if we recognise the true types in the first place. Because of our commitment to a New Jerusalem, the iniquity of Babylon becomes identifiable as a serious problem. Because the woman clothed with the sun, with her stars and her child, suggests the new Israel in the form of a cosmic, redemptive *magna mater*,[27] we can identify her evil opposite in the scarlet woman, 'the mother of harlots and of earth's abominations' (17:5). Because there is God, Christ, and Holy Spirit, we can recognise the dragon and the two beasts as a demonic parody of the threefold divine agency. Thus the great red dragon, 'that ancient serpent, who is called the Devil and Satan' (12:9), in parody of the divine creation destroys one third of the stars and seeks to devour the newborn child. Thus the first beast, a chaos monster from the sea, has seven heads and ten horns like his master the devil, and these are an asymmetrical parody of the seven spirits (1:4) and the lamb's horns of divine power. The fact that one of the heads had been wounded but revived parodies Christ's resurrection (13:3). Likewise, the second beast, which comes from the earth to make people worship the first beast, speaks like a dragon but has 'two horns like a lamb' (13:11).[28] This beast is a false prophet: it performs miracles (13:13) to promote the message of the beast which was wounded (13:14), and it seals many whom it has deceived with its name or symbolic number. Its work is clearly enough a demonic parody of Spirit in the world. Such work, however, appears demonic only to those whose belief in God, Christ and Spirit permits them to take seriously this particular evil dynamism.

In Revelation, therefore, we are not asked just to choose between good and evil, but to accept an entire interpretation of good-and-evil. Our non-acceptance makes us complicitous with the evil which we do not recognise, partly indeed *because* we do not recognise it. The main challenge is not so much to choose between the alternatives described in the book, as to choose the book itself. And when that has been done and the hope of newness accepted, the book will then describe how evil derives from good and frequently parodies it, so that even as believers we might not have an easy time seeing the differences between them. Like the original exodus, our enterprise remains perilous on whatever level we engage it.

The impersonality with which Revelation presents all this is frequently noticed. The loving Jesus of the gospels is hardly evident here, and instead we are faced with the grotesque prospect of a wrathful lamb. Combined with John's heavy emphasis on the inanimate world (glass, precious stones, mountains, walls, brass, and so on), and on monstrous animals, this depiction of our meek redeemer turned theriomorphic avenger is frightening. Jung is correct to say that Revelation puts the fear of God into its readers, for God is indeed terrible and dark too, and we must not forget it.[29] Impersonality and fear combine especially in the cosmic war featuring the nourishing and destructive aspects of the archetypal great mother, dragons and heroes, chaos and a perfectly symmetrical city of heaven. This is a world with beasts full of eyes and wings (4:8), a seven-eyed, seven-horned lamb (5:6), locusts like horses with men's faces, women's hair, lions' teeth and tails like scorpions (9:8), a monster with seven heads and ten horns, shaped like a leopard and with bear's feet and a lion's mouth (13:2), and a grotesque dragon (12:3) out of whose mouth come spirits like frogs (16:13). It is a world of avenging angels who pour pestilence on the earth and turn the sea into dead men's blood (16:3), and of mysterious horsemen bringing famine and the sword (6:4–5). It is a world where the sun turns black and the moon to blood, where stars fall from the sky (6:12–13) where hail and fire are mingled with blood (8:7) and the bottomless pit is opened, darkening the sun with its smoke (9:2).

One of course recoils immediately to explain these lurid composite images by assessing the symbolic meaning of their individual elements, and linking them to types in the Old Testament. Yet the disturbing impact of the imagery is attested by the very energy taken to pin it down more securely by discovering its sources. The unsettling power remains, and we remind ourselves that it belongs not only to the depiction of evil, but also to the forces of good – to the plague-pouring angels, the blood-thirsty lamb with the two-edged sword and the snowy-haired, red-eyed ancient of days. All of which brings us to the difficult question of how we are to regard such a fervent display of divine violence, terror, and wrath.[30] As the martyrs cry out, 'How long?' (6:10), the pool of holy fury builds, for God is angry (15:7; 16:19). In the winepress of his wrath his enemies are trodden until blood rises to the horses' bridles (14:20), and there is much worse, as Revelation goes on to disclose its orgy of revenge.

The danger of such writing is of course that it comes perilously close to inciting violence in God's name, the worst kind of violence. However, the images might also depict the spiritual consequences brought upon their own heads by the evil powers. Violent action against these powers is the same thing as their departure from good, for self-destruction follows upon their turning from God. The powers of good do not therefore set out after the forces of evil to hunt them down: the destruction of evil is the self-cancellation of its own nature when we see it through the light of our belief in God, or when it sees itself before God. Such an interpretation helps us to make sense also out of the rule of the saints and the martyrs' victory. By suffering violent death in the physical world, the martyrs in fact strike a spiritual blow at evil, bringing it closer to destruction because good reveals to evil its separateness, pain, futility and self-hatred. John does not deny that this process is terrible and frightening, for evil unleashed by freedom abused among created spirits makes the cosmos shudder to its foundations. Yet the two-edged sword of retribution clearly is God's *word*, and not the kind of metal blade used to decapitate the persecuted saints on earth. As Hanson suggests, John's use of the word *hromphaia* for sword as distinct from *machaira*, indicates that we are not to take the divine sword literally.[31] Indeed, part of the ambivalence or two-edgedness of the sword image is that we might mistake the first kind of sword for the second and merely take up the weapons of the world against the world. Just so, we must look discerningly at the paradoxical images of the wrathful lamb and the child ruling with a rod of iron. The lamb is at once the meek saviour who has endured the cross, and simultaneously the judgement upon themselves by those who have imposed the cross. Likewise, the child is the vulnerable and trusting saviour whose persecutors condemn themselves to the iron tyranny of their own desire to destroy him.

Admittedly, this is an intellectual way to interpret the graphic vengefulness of Revelation, and there seems little doubt that the book also provides rather simpler, coarser gratification: you might be humiliated now, John of Patmos seems to say, but soon you will get satisfaction. Commentators have struggled to ease the moral discomfort of this: for instance, A. T. Hanson[32] carefully establishes that John's words for wrath 'invariably refer ... to wrath worked out in the events of history' as a result of the crucifixion. Christ's victory is his suffering on the cross (165), and God's wrath is identical with the negative consequences which follow, 'stretching from the cross to the Parousia' (170). This argument is compelling, but again it is predominantly intellectual, and Hanson admits that many professional scholars have been 'misled' (161) into imagining that God's wrath is 'personal and direct'. Hanson himself even finds 22:18–19 so 'utterly incongruous with the extremely profound conception of wrath' (178) for which he has argued, that he concludes John was not the author of these verses. Likewise, Martin Hengel[33] sees an invitation to violence everywhere surrounding apocalypticism, including Jesus' teaching about the kingdom, but maintains that Jesus is against violence (36ff., 68ff.), though there is an 'insoluble conflict' (91). T. F. Torrance[34] tries to avoid such conflict by sanitising the wrath (it is, he says, 'a pure and sinless wrath, priestly in its function and golden in its integrity, quite unlike the wrath of man'), but he ends up with an even more heartless spectacle of divinely surgical terror. Adela Yarbro Collins[35] brings to bear an admirably clear sense of the ambiguities, acknowledging that 'aggressive feeling and violence can be destructive as well as constructive' (172), and interpreters must be aware of the dangers. At best, Revelation transposes aggressive feelings 'into imagined aggressive acts in the future' (517), or contains aggression by internalising it. But she admits that the violent imagery is inflammatory (171), and concludes that Revelation is a 'broken myth'. We must read it as 'a partial, imperfect vision that can still speak to our broken human condition' (172). I have every sympathy with this sensitive assessment, but all great literature could be described as a 'partial, imperfect vision' and we must be careful (as Collins is) not to explain literary weakness by saying that human nature is also weak: for instance, violent pornography is often defended on grounds that it expresses one potential of our flawed human nature.

The virtue of Revelation lies rather in its perilous balance. Indeed the instinct for revenge runs deep in human beings, often uncomfortably confused with zeal for justice. Against the enormities of the persecutors who seem to walk off untouched or who are even amused by the impotency of their victims, against them the blood itself of anguished parents or loved ones rises in a revolt full of dark vengeance and wild imaginings. No human being is certain proof against such disturbing reactions, against the sense of outrage forming the awful phantasms of retribution. St. John affirms the vigour and power of just this kind of atavistic fantasy, but without legitimising its translation into action. For as we have seen, endurance in patience itself exacts the completest vengeance on a deeper level than that of ordinary manifestation. We are assured that it is not inhuman to imagine revenge but it is dehumanising to exact it. As the entire rhetoric of Revelation informs us, we are not secure enough, and we do not see the fullness of God's plan: the two-edged sword, after all, might fall on us.

The literary structure of Revelation thus works consistently to make us feel the challenge of faith by confronting us with our own insecurity, especially in face of the great conundrums of death and the meaning of history. Assurances of God's steadfastness are presented through various kinds of pattern: in genre, structure, repeated formulae, numerology, typology, parody, and the self-reflexive dynamics of evil. But John's originality outreaches his generic formulae: structure is undermined by cancelled expectations, asymmetrical development, discontinuities and extended appendices; reassurances have a way of turning towards threat when we apply them to ourselves; numerology shades off into dark prediction and ominous inexactitude; typology presents us with the choices of fulfillment and rejection, and with a series of parodies wherein the opposites become confusingly interdependent; the intellectual interpretation of evil is in tense, uncertain balance with our own capacity for regressive atavism. This entire vision calls finally upon our assent or denial, confronting us imaginatively with the position of faith in the world, hounded by the grandeur of death, and calling for vindication of the suffering innocent.

At the centre of this vision, Revelation tells us that saving faith depends on us deliberately reversing the most palpably disturbing and frightening things about human history: the cross we are to see as in fact God's victory, and the deaths of martyrs (indeed of all the suffering innocent) are a liberating triumph of righteousness in action, despite appearances. Such an interpretation of the meek and innocent victims, seeing them as in fact spiritual marauders up to their eyes in apocalyptic blood, must seem to the unbeliever a most transparent example of compensatory imagination. Moreover, it is precisely the kind of delusion which might cause people to have themselves killed and call it martyrdom (think of how many thousands of young Iranians); even worse, it might provoke to violence those so convinced of their own righteousness and of God's will that they take up physical weapons to fight their holy wars.

As a work of literature, then, Revelation powerfully calls our attention to how imagination's wishful designs help us to compensate for life's cruelties; also, it draws attention to our propensity for violence, which imagination and fear too easily feed. Yet the challenge of faith remains, for Revelation makes an urgent claim on us which is not finally different from that in the gospels. The crucified one, we are told, is God. If that is not true, then the narrative is indeed a fiction expressing our desire that all manner of things will be well. If it is true, then suffering on earth is God's way, and apparently is to be our path to the New Jerusalem. There might be comfort for believers here, but it is modified by the consistent warnings against self-righteousness and complacency: we can never know certainly how much we are the imposers of suffering on others, unmakers of good, and whether or not the terrifying God of judgement chooses us among his elect. Seeing it all as an escapist device to help us avoid being numbed by a hard world might indeed be the more consoling interpretation.

9

Coda

Christian faith centres on the crucified and risen Christ. The cross was a scandal, an ignominious end to a preaching ministry which must have seemed thoroughly defeated by the public execution of its leader and the scattering of his followers. The Christian explanation of this debacle lay in the astounding claim that the crucified Jesus is God. We must decide whether Jesus' death makes nonsense of this claim, or whether God reassures us that even extreme suffering has meaning in which he also shares, and which he permits for reasons unknown to us. Christianity thus isolates the question on which theodicies founder, and places it at the centre: faced with suffering innocence, can we affirm God?

The centrality of the cross to Christianity offers a radical critique of religious institutions and practice. Jesus is alone outside the boundary; just so, there is no consolation for those who seek to escape death, pain and the problem of evil through the comfortable orthodoxies of religious practice. God himself shows us this. The written presentation of such an idea of course blunts it, and the documents frequently draw our attention to this fact. Yet, through metaphor and symbol, story and image, the literature informs and moves us to acknowledge our desire for health and wholeness, forgiveness and reconciliation, meaning and absolute assurance. We are asked to believe that God desires and affirms these things too. So, on the one hand, Christianity is life-affirming and world-embracing; on the other, it asks us to accept that God sanctions innocent suffering. Christian faith depends on us accepting both points.

The expression of such faith in the New Testament is often imaginative and complex, but the documents also make an extra-literary claim on us. If Jesus is not God, then they are in the end fictive. Either they tell a complex and imaginatively-compelling story offering us an escapist, wish-fulfilling conclusion, or the central claim is true. In the foregoing chapters I have attempted to show how such a vision of faith is expressed in the documents under consideration.

In the gospel according to Mark, the indeterminacy of signs is a central theme. Mark's Jesus especially overthrows our expectations, and the signs he offers, or refuses to offer, bring home to us some difficulties of following him in a straightforward way. Mark's story is full of fear and amazement, strange secrecy and fierce ambivalence. It highlights our vulnerability and incurable equivocations, and through images of casting down and raising up it brings home to us the instability of our plans and expectations. The cross in Mark is especially a sign of the failure of signs alone to deliver certain knowledge, and yet Jesus offers tokens of joy, grace and beauty confirming our desire for health and the overcoming of alienation.

The anointing at Bethany is a striking example of how elusive is the relationship between grace and understanding, as Mark deploys interwoven points of view to suggest various levels of awareness among the participants. The anointing can be read even as a token of art itself in the service of religion, or of the efficacy of signs as Mark deploys them, whereby material things are raised to express a transcendence which they promise but do not encompass. The signs Jesus offers convey the good news of salvation, and yet without the cross these signs are all too easily misunderstood. Mark's characteristically apocalyptic mood helps to confirm the message of the cross that for Jesus' followers there is no easy consolation, no finally secure interpretation of faith.

Matthew's catechetical emphasis helps to explain the arrangement of his material in large sections with frequent formal antitheses and binary structures. Matthew's Jesus is striking for his solemn power and messianic serenity, and his miracles, parables and preaching relate these qualities especially to a developing institutional church. Yet the inbreaking of Christ's power entails a radical upheaval of familiar order, and Matthew's special use of the word *seismos* is an example of his deployment of rhetorical strategies to express the shattering invasion of Christ's proclamation and the experience of faith it entails. However well-organised our institutions, or carefully structured our knowledge, or pleasingly classified our doctrines, faith is disruptive and disorienting. The institutions of course remain necessary for transmitting knowledge and guarding against false teaching, but only when the foundations are shaken do we stand in that perilous darkness where believers tell us the Spirit is also discovered.

Descriptions of journeys are central to the two volumes of Luke-Acts, highlighting Jesus' voyage to Jerusalem and Paul's missionary travels. These journeys complement one another, for Jesus is rejected at Jerusalem and thereby prepares the way for a missionary outreach to the gentile world, whereas Paul travels to the gentile world but constantly returns to Jerusalem. Both journeys are also to some degree paradoxical. In the gospel there is much travelling but surprisingly little geographical progress: the various journeys within the main journey are carefully patterned to suggest that spiritual decisions to 'take a direction' are more important than geographical location, even though place and time are also necessary for decision-making. In Acts, itineraries are provocatively obscure to suggest how spiritual directions are often found by indirection. Likewise, both volumes resort to similar kinds of irony to suggest how peculiar are the ways in which we seek in order to be found, and how mysterious are decisions which change the directions of a life. The ironic descriptions of voyages away and back, of things lost and found, of crossing over, of motivation and counter-motivation and so on, confirm that in the way of faith we are all ironic travellers, perennially perplexed, yet able to be taken by surprise. Throughout Luke-Acts, the event of the cross is thus conflated with the idea that we must follow the way of the cross, and our travelling through this world itself should be in imitation of Jesus' renunciation and sacrifice. Paradoxically, the very token of our positive engagement with the world as we journey through it, might well be the world's rejection.

Of the four gospels, John's is most explicitly governed by the dialectic of belief and unbelief, and presents the difference between them in the starkest terms. Yet John presents us also with a full sense of the variety and openendedness of the human search for God. Although he alludes repeatedly to seeing and hearing to describe belief, John's rhetoric is complicated by the shades of meaning these words convey. In the episode of the woman taken in adultery, seeing and hearing in literal and spiritual senses combine with words written and spoken, and with contrasts between external and internal experience to show how the accusers' accusations turn against themselves, and how indirectly they come to insight. Analogously, John's book as a written text presents us with visible words which we are to hear according to our circumstances and condition, as we both discover and decide whether we are believers or unbelievers, at once chosen by the omniscient Christ, and responsible for recognising the truth in him. For John's Jesus is also the pre-existent logos, whose crucifixion is likened to an enthronement: the terrible prospect of an omniscient divine figure coming among us and allowing himself to be killed creates an unsettling sense that our belief or unbelief, our choosing the light or dark, is as much a matter of him choosing us as us choosing him. The very insistence in the fourth gospel on Jesus' direct declaration of the Father's will serves also to show how indirectly we might come to faith, and how unpredictable is the relationship between evidence and insight.

Paul's letters bear witness to his experience of the living Christ, the crucified and resurrected Lord whom he struggles to understand. Paul holds that Christ is the supreme reality in whom death, suffering, separation and egotism are overcome, and in whom the heart's desires are gratified. Yet the epistles recreate also Paul's suffering experience in the midst, seeing through a glass darkly. The Corinthian correspondence is full of a complex, felt sense of love and suffering which Paul does not falsify, despite his over-riding desire for doctrinal clarity. The Corinthian letters present faith struggling for meaning between fragments and unity, plain speech and rhetoric, concept and image, vision and glossalalia, objective truth and subjective engagement.

Hebrews is an oddity among the New Testament documents, and we have regarded it as a sermon taking the form of a midrash on Psalm 110. From another point of view, Hebrews is a kind of bridge between Paul's letters and Revelation. It has some characteristics of an epistle and has traditionally been associated with Paul's name, but it is stylistically different and is without the first-person involvement which contributes so distinctively to Paul's literary discourse. Hebrews is more objective than Paul's letters, and this quality, together with a marked interest in God's fiery wrath, judgement, and the abiding heavenly city, recalls Revelation.

The main subject of Hebrews is Christ's high priesthood: that is, the means by which the blood sacrifice on Calvary is also the eternally significant means of our reconciliation to God. Christ's cross is the dominating theme, and the challenge of faith which it entails is investigated with toughness and compassion. The cross represents for faith the juncture of two worlds: the vertical, stable and eternal heaven where Christ reigns at God's right hand, and the horizontal of time and death where Jesus suffers as our brother. As a layman without official priestly lineage, as an outcast executed as a common criminal, Jesus radically challenges the securities offered by religion and civilized order. The cross is the sign of our necessary human insecurity, of the fact that faith is 'evidence of things not seen', and of the fact that if the way of human suffering is not also God's suffering, then Jesus' death merely reconfirms the tyranny of anxiety about time and death to which we are all subject, and which no cult practice will assuage. For the author of Hebrews, the meaning of the eternal Christ is the significance of Jesus' historical death, and this paradox is kept before us by a series of rhetorical developments which enrich and deepen our perception. The main tension between verticals and horizontals opens up to a further series of internal tensions and oppositions through which we come to see how Jesus' significance is in part measured by the multiplicity of contraries which he reconciles in himself. The texture elucidating the conjunction of eternal and temporal, cosmic and human elements in Jesus' sacrifice, and keeping before us the terrible challenge and lived intensities of faith, marks a distinctive literary achievement. The cross, we are told, enables us to serve one another in joy, while teaching us also to follow Jesus outside the boundary to the place of rejection where innocence is crucified. We are promised rest, but assured of suffering: faith takes its place at the point of scarcely bearable tension where these contraries might somehow be reconciled.

The power of Revelation derives largely from its images, and the fact that the book belongs within the apocalyptic genre throws into relief its strange, disturbing originality. Similarly, the structure of Revelation suggests careful design, but the book resists our finding a wholly coherent pattern, and the effect of strangeness persists in a series of cancelled sequences and disturbing intrusions. The effect is to have us feel something of our human insecurity even while we are impressed by the awful power and majesty of God's over-arching plan, encompassing the end of history itself. We are warned against naive apocalypticism and self-righteousness, for although God's enemies will be undone, we do not know enough to be sure that we will not be among them. Even divine reassurance can be unsettling and two-sided, like the imagery of doors and swords, confirming the ambivalence of our human estate. So also, John's use of numerology, typology and parody presents us with a vision of the Good triumphant, but these devices are deployed also to communicate a sense of the problems of belief when complacency reigns in the world and God seems remote. Indeed we are encouraged to look forward to a consummation devoutly to be wished, but only while allowing that its newness exceeds the poet's images and will take us by surprise. For God's victories often are won by unpredictable means, and part of his strength lies in what might appear to be weakness. Consequently, we are not to wreak vengeance on his enemies, however strongly we imagine the righteousness of doing so, for our perspective is limited, and our patient endurance is also his glory and power. However fervent with love and desire, faith under such conditions is not without fear and trembling.

As I have pointed out in the Introduction, these readings of the New Testament's depiction of faith are partly prompted by a certain rapprochement between recent literary criticism and Biblical scholarship. Modern developments in literary theory and critical practice have raised radical questions about hermeneutics and imagination in such a manner that a literary humanist might be encouraged to give attention in a modest way to the sacred texts. But there is also another reason. Today, more and more people are encountering the New Testament not first as believers but as critical readers. These people might well be expected to cherish the hard-won right not to believe, and to be well aware of the savage record history preserves of the imposition of belief on others, of persecutions and wars conducted under the sign of the cross. It might therefore be worth pointing out afresh that the faith described in the New Testament is neither cheap nor simple, but an elusive kind of knowledge which is strongly critical of easy institutional answers and attitudes. In rejecting what is wrong in Christian history, we ought to be careful lest we cast away the wounded baby with the bloodied bath water. Aspirations to wholeness, life and love through selfless care of others, and the vision of healing power which would bring about the Reign of God remain desirable. Nor are these ideals presented for the benefit of the extraordinary, the peculiarly gifted, or the powerful. Rather, they are the fruition of ordinary consciousness and the common experience of people in the world, in contact with things of the world, which we are asked to affirm and engage. But we are asked also to acknowledge the cross, and to see it as God's way. To be able to do so is the key test of faith, for the root challenge to any belief in God lies in the fact of innocent suffering. Part of the genius of the New Testament is to thematise this critical question with such clarity. To those who feel it is absurd to claim that the crucified Jesus is God, the resurrection stories will seem a fiction. For those who feel otherwise, the stories will be true, for in the last resort, and despite its imaginative richness, the New Testament is intolerant of the merely fictive imagination. Yet the ways in which we are drawn through the literature towards the extra-literary remain to engage and compel us by means of a powerfully relevant narrative and the explanations of our condition which it offers.

Notes

CHAPTER 1: INTRODUCTION

1. See Charles H. Talbert, *What is a Gospel?: the Genre of the Canonical Gospels* (Philadelphia: Fortress Press, 1977); 'The Gospel and the Gospels', ed. James Luther Mays, *Interpreting the Gospels* (Philadelphia: Fortress Press, 1981) pp. 14–26; Norman Perrin and Dennis C. Duling, *The New Testament: an Introduction*, 2nd edn (New York: Harcourt, Brace, Jovanovich, 1982) p. 40: 'though the issue is debated, our view is that the written type, or genre, called gospel is the unique literary creation of Mark. In short, the "gospel" has no precise literary prototype'; Ralph P. Martin, *Mark: Evangelist and Theologian* (Exeter: Paternoster Press, 1972) pp. 17ff., and on verbs of speaking and responding, p. 23.

2. The debate on letters and epistles is dealt with in chapter 6, Acts in chapter 4, and the genre of Revelation in chapter 8 of the present study, where the footnotes deal with issues raised in this paragraph.

3. Amos Wilder, *Early Christian Rhetoric* (Cambridge, Mass.: Harvard University Press, 1971; 1st edn 1964) p. 36.

4. C. S. Lewis, 'Modern Translations of the Bible', ed. Walter Hooper, *First and Second Things: Essays on Theology and Ethics* (London: Collins, 1986) p. 86; 'Fern Seed and Elephants', ed. Walter Hooper, *Fern Seed and Elephants and Other Essays on Christianity* (London: Collins, 1975) p. 108: 'I have been reading poems, romances, vision-literature, legends, myths all my life. I know what they are like. I know that not one of them is like this'; Helen Gardner, *The Business of Criticism* (Oxford: Clarendon Press, 1959) pp. 101, 121ff.

5. See Edward Schillebeeckx, *Jesus. An Experiment in Christology*, trans. Hubert Hoskins (London: Collins, 1983) p. 192.

6. Jürgen Moltmann, *The Crucified God: the Cross of Christ as the Foundation and Criticism of Christian Theology*, trans. R. A. Wilson and John Bowden (London: SCM Press, 1974) pp. 7ff.

7. James P. Mackey, *Jesus the Man and the Myth: a Contemporary Christology* (New York: Paulist Press, 1979) pp. 10ff., *et passim*, on the nineteenth-century search for the historical Jesus, and on the relevance of a revitalised modern sense of the relationship of myth to history.

8. For a full account of this, see M. H. Abrams, *Natural Supernaturalism. Tradition and Revolution in Romantic Literature* (New York: Norton, 1971).

9. Owen Barfield, *Romanticism Comes of Age* (Connecticut: Wesleyan University Press, 1967; 1st edn 1944).

10. Two notable recent contributions to this endeavour, drawing upon contributors from various fields, are Michael Wadsworth (ed.), *Ways of Reading the Bible* (Sussex: Harvester Press, 1981), and James P. Mackey (ed.), *Religious Imagination* (Edinburgh University Press, 1986).

11. Frank Kermode, *The Genesis of Secrecy: on the Interpretation of*

Narrative (Cambridge, Mass.: Harvard University Press, 1979) p. 136: 'but it is astonishing how much less there is of genuine literary criticism on the secular model than there ought to be'.

12. S. T. Coleridge, *Biographia Litteraria*, ch. XIV.

13. This complex phenomenon, with which I now deal sketchily, is admirably summarised by the following books, to which I am indebted: Frank Lentricchia, *After the New Criticism* (London: Athlone Press, 1980); Christopher Norris, *Deconstruction: Theory and Practice* (London: Methuen, 1982); Terry Eagleton, *Literary Theory: an Introduction* (Oxford: Basil Blackwell, 1983).

14. See Northrop Frye, *The Great Code: the Bible and Literature* (Toronto: Academic Press Canada, 1982) p. xix.

15. Daniel Patte, *Paul's Faith and the Power of the Gospel* (Philadelphia: Fortress Press, 1983).

16. Biblical scholarship has of course tended in the direction of literary studies under the influence of Redaction criticism. (The dissecting efforts of the Form critics were countered by Redaction Criticism which stressed the purpose and point of view of the final redactor of a text, whose synthesising efforts unify his received materials. See N. Perrin, *What is Redaction Criticism?* [London: SPCK, 1970]). It is also worth noticing that the term 'literary criticism' is used by some biblical scholars in a manner unfamiliar to secular critics, as, for instance, by Klaus Koch, *The Growth of the Biblical Tradition* (New York: Charles Scribners Sons, 1969) pp. 69–70: 'The literary critic ... attempts to discover the original writings, to determine exactly their date of origin. . . . Literary criticism is the analysis of biblical books from the standpoint of lack of continuity, duplications, inconsistencies and different linguistic usage, with the object of discovering what the individual writers and redactors contributed to the text, and also its time and place of origin.' There have been, of course, many books presenting the bible 'as literature', in the sense of making it available to the common reader, or reading it as a literary narrative in the manner of Mary Ellen Chase, *The Bible and the Common Reader* (New York: Macmillan, 1944), or J. H. Gardiner, *The Bible as English Literature* (New York: Charles Scribners Sons, 1906), among others. Yet serious engagement with the critical issues by the secular literary humanists has been surprisingly intermittent, as Kermode says (see note 11), especially considering the concentrated development of literary studies in this century. Besides Frye and Kermode (who also draws upon Ricoeur and Gadamer – see *The Genesis of Secrecy*, pp. 39ff.), one might mention Robert Alter, *The Art of Biblical Narrative* (New York: Basic Books, 1981); T. R. Henn, *The Bible as Literature* (London: Lutterworth Press, 1970); Helen Gardner, *The Business of Criticism* (Oxford: Clarendon Press, 1959), especially pp. 101ff., and several essays in Michael Wadsworth (ed.), *Ways of Reading the Bible*, but an extensive bibliography is beyond the scope of this chapter. There is also the fascinating broad area where Biblical and secular critics are increasingly invited to meet. The journal *Semeia*, for instance, is concerned with structuralist criticism of Biblical texts, and one might cite R. W. Funk (ed.), *Literary Critical Studies of Biblical Texts*,

Semeia 8 (Missoula: Scholars Press, 1977). See also Paul Ricoeur, *Essays on Biblical Interpretation* (Philadelphia: Fortress Press, 1980); R. Barthes *et al.*, *Structural Analysis and Biblical Exegesis: Interpretational Essays* (Pittsburg: Pickwick Press, 1974); Alfred M. Johnson, Jr. (ed.), *Structuralism and Biblical Hermeneutics* (Pennsylvania: Pickwick Press, 1979); Edgar V. McKnight, *Meaning in Texts. The Historical Shaping of a Narrative Hermeneutics* (Philadelphia: Fortress Press, 1978).

17. See Edward Schillebeeckx, *Jesus*, p. 158: 'Jesus himself . . . his person, his stories and his actions . . . is a parable.'

18. Mary Warnock, *Imagination* (London: Faber & Faber, 1976).

19. See Schillebeeckx, *Jesus*, p. 588: 'if a transcendent reality is truly given in Jesus, it is not a bogus, mystifying transcendence but one that will manifest itself via our normal structures of human consciousness'.

20. The force of this paradox was brought home to me in a conversation with Terry Eagleton. I do not know if he has written anything on the subject, but I would like to acknowledge the conversation.

CHAPTER 2: MARK: THE ANOINTING AT BETHANY

1. See further, Monica D. Hooker, *The Son of Man in Mark* (London: SPCK, 1967) pp. 148ff., on the 'confusion' of historical and supernatural events; O. Linton, 'The Demand for A Sign from Heaven', *Studia Theologia* 19 (1965) pp. 112–29.

2. D. E. Nineham, *The Gospel of St. Mark* (London: Adam and Charles Black, 1963, rev. 1968) p. 346, suggests that the best commentary here is 2 Thessalonians, especially ch. 2, which shows that some Christians had been persuaded by events that the end had arrived: 'The aim of 2 Thess. is to persuade such people that *the end* is not yet.'

3. See B. W. Bacon, *The Gospel of Mark: Its Composition and Date* (London: Oxford University Press, 1925) pp. 120ff.; W. Kelber, *The Kingdom in Mark* (Philadelphia: Fortress Press, 1974) pp. 113–16, on 'parousia pretenders' in Mark's community.

4. D. E. Nineham, *The Gospel of St. Mark*, p. 351. The following account summarises Nineham's commentary on the 'desolating sacrilege'.

5. Ambrose, *De Fide*, V, 16; Cyril of Alexandria, *Adv. Anthr.*, xiv, cited by Ralph P. Martin, *Mark: Evangelist and Theologian* (Exeter: Paternoster Press, 1972) p. 125.

6. See Rudolf Bultmann, *Jesus Christ and Mythology* (New York: Charles Scribners and Sons, 1958) pp. 16–17; Hugh Anderson, *The Gospel of Mark* (London: Oliphants, 1976) p. 301; Eduard Schweizer, *The Good News According to Mark*, trans. Donald H. Madvig (Atlanta: John Knox Press, 1970) p. 279.

7. See for instance Sherman E. Johnson, *A Commentary on the Gospel According to St. Mark* (London: Adam and Charles Black, 2nd edn, 1972) p. 219.

8. Edward J. Mally, *The Gospel According to Mark*, eds. Raymond E. Brown, Joseph A. Fitzmyer, Roland E. Murphy, *The Jerome Biblical Commentary*, 2 vols (New Jersey: Prentice Hall, 1968), II, 39.

9.   William Wrede, *The Messianic Secret*, trans. J. C. G. Greig (London: James Clarke, 1971; 1st edn 1901).

10.   See Eduard Schweizer, *The Good News According to Mark*, p. 55; G. Minette de Tilesse, *Le secret messianique dans l'Evangile de Marc* (Paris: Beernem, 1968) pp. 26ff.; T. A. Burkill, *Mysterious Revelation: An Examination of the Philosophy of St. Mark's Gospel* (Ithaca, N.Y.: University Press, 1963).

11.   Ulrich Luz, 'The Secrecy Motif and the Marcan Christology', trans. R. Morgan, ed. Christopher Tuckett, *The Messianic Secret* (London: SPCK, 1983) pp. 75–96. Frank Kermode, *The Genesis of Secrecy* (Cambridge, Mass.: Harvard University Press, 1979), deals with secrecy in terms of a broad theory of interpretation whereby the 'secrets' of valued literary texts continually outstrip the interpreters.

12.   This is a cliché of modern criticism, and is connected to the idea that composition proceeded backwards from the passion narrative. See for instance A. E. J. Rawlinson, *The Gospel According to St. Mark* (London: Methuen, 1925) pp. 260–1; Martin Kahler, *The So-called Historical Jesus and the Historic Biblical Christ*, trans. C. E. Braaten (Philadelphia: Fortress Press, 1964); W. Marxsen, *Introduction to the New Testament*, trans. G. Buswell (Oxford: Basil Blackwell, 1968), and *Mark the Evangelist*, trans. R. A. Harrisville (New York: Abingdon Press, 1969).

13.   See T. J. Weeden, 'The Heresy that Necessitated Mark's Gospel', *Zeitschrift für die neutestamentliche Wissenschaft* 59 (1968) pp. 145–58, and *Mark, Traditions in Conflict* (Philadelphia: Fortress Press, 1971); H. D. Betz, 'Jesus as Divine Man' in *Jesus and the Historian*, ed. F. Thomas Trotter, festschrift E. C. Colwell (Philadelphia: Westminster Press, 1968) pp. 114–30. Discussion has continued beyond Weeden, whose main thesis is now often questioned. See D. L. Tiede, *The Charismatic Figure as Miracle Worker* (Missoula, Montana: Society of Biblical Literature, 1972).

14.   J. Jeremias, *New Testament Theology: the Procalamation of Jesus*, trans. John Bowden (London: SCM Press, 1971) I, 284.

15.   For a selection of opinions on these issues, see Hugh Anderson, *The Gospel of Mark*, p. 306; E. Schweizer, *The Good News According to Mark*, p. 291; D. E. Nineham, *The Gospel of St. Mark*, p. 372.

16.   See for instance Sherman E. Johnson, *A Commentary on the Gospel According to St. Mark*, p. 224, 'the woman was an enthusiast who hoped Jesus would rule over the nation', and Edward J. Mally, *The Gospel According to Mark*, Jerome Biblical Commentary, II, 53.

17.   See D. E. Nineham, *The Gospel of St. Mark*, p. 374. David Daube, 'The Anointing at Bethany and Jesus' Burial', *Anglican Theological Review* 22 (1950) pp. 186–99, argues that Mark wanted his reader to know that a burial rite had been performed, and so goes out of his way to emphasise how the anointing is for Jesus' death. Sherman E. Johnson, *A Commentary on the Gospel According to St. Mark* (London: Adam and Charles Black, 1972) p. 224, writes: 'This was a secret anointing for kingship, as in 2 Kings 9:1–3; 1 Kings 1:38–40; the woman was an enthusiast who hoped that Jesus would rule over the nation.'

18.   See Hugh Anderson, *The Gospel of Mark*, pp. 17, 45, 51, on the notion that this is 'unquestionably a dominant motif in the Gospel'; D. E. Nineham,

The Gospel of St. Mark, pp. 31–2 on the 'almost incredible obtuseness' of the disciples; Morna D. Hooker, The Son of Man in Mark, pp. 136, 139–40; Frank Kermode, The Genesis of Secrecy, pp. 33–4.

19.   For the emphasis on promises, see Ralph P. Martin, Mark: Evangelist and Theologian, pp. 68, 114; Louis Marin, 'Les femmes au tombeau. Essai d'analyse structurale d'un texte évangélique', ed. C. Chabrol and L. Marin, Sémiotique narrative: récits bibliques (Paris: Didier-Larousse, 1971) pp. 39–50, suggests that the desire for a concrete discovery is replaced by a message promising future gratification.

20.   On the empty tomb, see for instance James P. Mackey, Jesus the Man and the Myth (New York: Paulist Press, 1979) pp. 107ff. Austin Farrer, A Study in St. Mark (Westminster: Dacre Press, 1951) p. 130, connects the empty tomb and the anointing, and points out that the woman who anoints for glory anoints for burial, and the women who come to anoint for burial encounter Christ's glory.

21.   See note 19.

22.   The Homilies of S. John Chrysostom on the Gospel of Matthew, part III, A Library of the Fathers (Oxford: John Henry Parker, 1851), Homily LXXX, 2, p. 1060.

23.   Thomas Aquinas, Opera (Venice: Simon Occhi, 1775), III, 305, In Matthaeum Evangelistum Expositio, caput XXVI.

24.   Augustine of Hippo, On Psalm 12, Exposition 2, Expositions on the Book of Psalms (Oxford: John Henry Parker, 1847) I, 150: 'Who was the woman who came in with the ointment? Of what was she the type? Was she not of the church?'

25.   On Christian Doctrine, II, 7, 3, trans. D. W. Robertson (New York: Bobbs-Merrill, 1958).

26.   Jacques Maritain, Art and Scholasticism. With Other Essays, trans. J. F. Scanlon (London: Sheed & Ward, 1930).

27.   For a concise criticism of the excesses of Deconstructionist theory and its opposition to the 'logocentric', see John R. Searle, 'The World Turned Upside Down', a review of Jonathan Culler, On Deconstruction: Theory and Criticism after Structuralism, in New York Review of Books (27 Oct. 1983), pp. 74ff.

28.   Paul de Man, Blindness and Insight. Essays in the Rhetoric of Contemporary Criticism (New York: Oxford University Press, 1971) p. 17.

29.   See especially The Degrees of Knowledge, trans. Bernard Wall and Margot K. Adamson (London: Geoffrey Bles, 1937).

30.   Blindness and Insight, p. 32.

31.   Although Mark opens up perspectives of bleakness and insecurity, he asks us also to acknowledge the experience of joy. It comes in unlikely circumstances and to unpredictable people – the sort Frank Kermode describes as 'outsiders'. The privileged 'insiders' often stumble about in various degrees of confusion; the rejected or deprived – demoniacs, foreigners, women, children, the blind – recognise the living truth and are cured.

CHAPTER 3: MATTHEW: THE CENTURION'S EARTHQUAKE

1. See Günther Bornkamm, 'End Expectation and Church in Matthew' in Günther Bornkamm, Gerhard Barth, Heinz Joachim Held, *Tradition and Interpretation in Matthew*, trans. Percy Scott (London: SCM Press, 1971) p. 38: 'No other Gospel is so shaped by the thought of the Church as Matthew's, so constructed for use by the Church; for this reason it has exercised, as no other, a normative influence in the later Church.' John P. Meier, *The Vision of Matthew. Christ, Church and Morality in the First Gospel* (New York: Paulist Press, 1979) p. 14, says that Matthew's gospel 'is meant to be a public lectionary, catechism, and manual of order to be proclaimed in and read by his entire church'. See also Eduard Schweizer, *The Good News According to Matthew*, trans. David E. Green (Atlanta: John Knox Press, 1975) p. 13.
2. Edward Massaux, *Influence de l'Evangile de saint Matthieu sur la littérature chrétienne avant saint Irénée* (Lowen: Diss. Theol. II, 42, 1950).
3. A strong tendency towards consensus rests on a great amount of detailed argument, but the question is by no means closed. See for instance John M. Rist, *On the Independence of Matthew and Mark* (Cambridge University Press, 1978).
4. Most commentators point this out. See for instance Norman Perrin and Dennis C. Duling, *The New Testament. An Introduction* (New York: Harcourt, Brace, Jovanovich, 2nd edn, 1982) p. 288: 'Matthew diverges from that structure [Mark's] by making additions and insertions, or by rearranging related material, such as teaching or miracles, into large blocks.'
5. See B. W. Bacon, *Studies in Matthew* (London: Constable, 1930), whose scheme is still widely followed. For a summary, see J. D. Kingsbury, 'The Structure of Matthew's Gospel and His Concept of Salvation-History', *Catholic Biblical Quarterly* 35 (1973) p. 451, note 3. Kingsbury suggests an alternative three-fold view. Dan O. Via, Jr., in 'Structure, Christology and Ethics in Matthew', ed. Richard A. Spencer, *Orientation by Disorientation: Studies on Literary Criticism and Biblical Literary Criticism Presented in Honor of William A. Beardslee* (Pittsburg: Pickwick Press, 1980) pp. 199–201, argues for a tension between the fivefold pentateuchal structure and the threefold Christological one.
6. Eduard Schweizer, *The Good News According to Matthew*, p. 27, notices that there are twelve 'reflective quotations' (that is, reflecting on the fulfilment of the Old Testament in Jesus). Matthew has more of these than the other gospels combined.
7. Augustine of Hippo, *Concerning the Agreement of the Evangelists*, I, 2, 4.
8. As Eduard Schweizer among others, points out. See *The Good News According to Matthew*, p. 11: 'most of the stories that also occur in Mark are recounted much more briefly in Matthew'. Se also p. 210: 'He reduces the miracle stories as a whole to about 55% of their compass in Mark, while shortening the narratives that display Jesus as the Christ by only about 10% and the narratives associated with the controversies by 20% on the average.'

9. Johannes Weiss, *Dasälteste Evangelium* (Gottingen, 1903) p. 156, cited by
    Heinz Joachim Held, 'Matthew as Interpreter of the Miracle Stories', in
    Günther Bornkamm *et al.*, *Tradition and Interpretation in Matthew*,
    p. 175.
10. Frank Kermode, *The Genesis of Secrecy: on the Interpretation of
    Narrative* (Cambridge, Mass.: Harvard University Press, 1979) p. 133.
    Kermode points out that Mark's statement about eating indicates the
    girl's restoration to society.
11. See for instance Gen. 22:18, 'and by your descendants shall all the
    nations of the earth bless themselves'. See further, Raymond E. Brown,
    The Birth of the Messiah (New York: Doubleday, 1977) p. 68, for a full
    account of this. I am indebted to this study for the following remarks on
    the infancy narratives.
12. John L. McKenzie, 'The Gospel According to Matthew', ed. Raymond E.
    Brown *et al.*, *Jerome Biblical Commentary*, II, 112: 'It is only in the passion
    narratives and the infancy narratives of Matthew and Luke that the
    theme of kingship appears in the Syn.'
13. See M. D. Goulder, 'Characteristics of the Parables in the Several
    Gospels', *Journal of Theological Studies*, N.S. 19 (1968) p. 57: 'In Matthew
    all is stylised. People are either good or bad, wise or foolish, obedient or
    disobedient, merciful or merciless. His Two Builders is typical.... His
    Two Sons is more stark than most of his parables, but it reveals the
    essential Matthean technique.'
14. Rudolf Bultmann refers to Matthew's 'scenic twofoldness'. See *The
    History of the Synoptic Tradition*, trans. John Marsh (Oxford: Basil
    Blackwell, 1963) pp. 307ff.
15. See Günther Bornkamm, 'End Expectation in the Church of Matthew',
    and Gerhard Barth, 'Matthew's Understanding of the Law. (1).
    Expectation of the Judgment and Exhortation to do the Will of God' in
    Tradition and Interpretation in Matthew, pp. 15ff.; 58ff.
16. As Northrop Frye remarks, discussing the Sermon on the Mount, 'the
    standards of the highly integrated individual are far more rigorous than
    those that apply to society in general, hence the gospel made into a new
    social law would again be the most frightful tyranny', *The Great Code:
    the Bible and Literature* (Toronto: Academic Press, 1982) p. 132.
17. Matt. 8:24; 21:10; 24:7; 27:51; 27:54; 28:2; 28:4.
18. Rev. 6:12; 6:13; 8:5; 11:13 (twice); 16:18 (twice).
19. Matthew attacks antinomianism as well as legalism, and uses the word
    anomia at 13:41; 23:28; 24:12.
20. Raymond E. Brown, *The Birth of the Messiah*, pp. 81ff. I summarise
    Brown's argument in the following account.
21. For a summary of opinions on the four women, see Raymond E. Brown,
    The Birth of the Messiah, 'Why Bring on the Ladies?', pp. 71ff.
22. See Herbert Mortimer Luckock, *The Special Characteristics of the Four
    Gospels* (London: Longmans, 1900) p. 32: 'in this Gospel there is more
    frequent mention of money than in the others, and not only so, but more
    and rarer coins are introduced'. This would not be inappropriate, if the
    author really were the tax collector mentioned at 9:9. See also Edgar J.
    Goodspeed, *Matthew, Apostle and Evangelist* (Philadelphia: John C.
    Winston, 1959) p. 133.

23.   Eduard Schweizer, *The Good News According to Matthew*, p. 467. David
       Hill, *New Century Bible. The Gospel of Matthew* (London: Oliphants,
       1972) p. 326, says of the parable of the virgins that 'Not everyone is
       equally convinced about the entire absence of allegory ...'. R. V. G.
       Tasker, *The Gospel According to St. Matthew* (London: Tyndale Press,
       1961) p. 234, confirms one commonly accepted interpretation: 'Saving
       grace, it is here taught, is a personal possession and untransferable.
       When the final day of salvation comes none can deliver his brother.'
24.   William A. Beardslee, 'Uses of the Proverb in the Synoptic Gospels',
       Interpretation 24 (1970) pp. 61–76, suggests that the proverbial sayings
       are intensified by hyperbole. This point is developed in relation to the
       parables by Paul Ricoeur, in *Paul Ricoeur on Biblical Hermeneutics*, ed.
       John Dominic Grossan, *Semeia* 4 (1975), pp. 32 *et passim*. See also
       Bernard Harrison, 'Parable and Transcendence', ed. Michael Wadsworth,
       Ways of Reading the Bible (Sussex: Harvester Press, 1981) pp. 190ff., on
       the subversive element of the parables, and Paul S. Minear, *Matthew. The
       Teacher's Gospel* (London: Darton, Longman & Todd, 1982) p. 181: 'The
       parable places a premium upon *unconscious* goodness.... The parable
       discloses the self-deception that lurks so easily behind charity.'
25.   Hans Georg Gadamer, 'Aesthetics and Hermeneutics' in *Philosophical
       Hermeneutics*, trans. David E. Linge (University of California Press, 1976)
       p. 97. I summarise Gadamer's argument in this paragraph.
26.   James P. Martin, 'The Church in Matthew', ed. James Luther Mays,
       Interpreting the Gospels (Philadelphia: Fortress Press, 1973) p. 101:
       'Simplistic solutions which set all Jews against all Gentiles in deciding on
       the nature of the Matthean church are out.' Yet in footnote 14, Martin
       shows how some scholars have argued for Matthew's reprobation of
       Israel.
27.   Harold Bloom, *The Anxiety of Influence. A Theory of Poetry* (New York:
       Oxford University Press, 1973). Bloom's notion of 'clinamen' as a
       perennial feature of poetry has some resemblance to what I am describing
       as 'upheaval'. See p. 14: 'I take the word from Lucretius, where it means a
       "swerve" of the atoms so as to make change possible in the universe. A
       poet swerves away from his precursor.... This appears as a corrective
       movement in his own poem, which implies that the precursor poem went
       accurately up to a certain point, but then should have swerved, precisely
       in the direction that the new poem moves.'
28.   See Lloyd Gaston, 'The Messiah of Israel as Teacher of the Gentiles: the
       Setting of Matthew's Christology', ed. James Luther Mays, *Interpreting
       the Gospels*, pp. 78–96. Gaston makes explicit a concern which other
       commentators too frequently ignore: 'But when the Matthean picture of
       that "evil and adulterous generation" is projected unto actual Jews of any
       age, the consequences are absolutely disastrous' (p. 95). He concludes
       that 'this aspect of Matthew cannot be harmonised but must be rejected'
       (p. 95), and calls for a distinction between apostolic and sub-apostolic
       elements in the New Testament. See also, Douglas R. A. Hare, *The Theme
       of Jewish Persecution of Christians in the Gospel According to St.
       Matthew*, Society for New Testament Studies Monograph Series, 6
       (Cambridge University Press, 1967); Sjef van Tilborg, *The Jewish Leaders*

in Matthew (Leiden: E. J. Brill, 1972).

29.   For instance, Justin Martyr, *Apology*, I, 46.

CHAPTER 4: LUKE-ACTS: THE IRONIC TRAVELLERS

1.   See Frank Kermode, *The Sense of an Ending: Studies in the Theory of Fiction* (New York: Oxford University Press, 1967). Wolfgang Iser, *The Act of Reading: A Theory of Aesthetic Response* (Baltimore: Johns Hopkins University Press, 1978) stresses the reader's contribution to the process of interpretation. See p. 19: 'an interpreter can no longer claim to teach the reader the meaning of the text, for without a subjective contribution and a context there is no such thing'.

2.   Second Isaiah was written about 540 BC; Plato lived from c. 427–348 BC.

3.   Thorleif Boman, *Hebrew Thought Compared with Greek*, trans. Jules L. Moreau from the 2nd German edn, 1954 (New York: Norton, 1970). Some of Boman's interpretations have been questioned by James Barr, *The Semantics of Biblical Language* (London: Routledge & Kegan Paul, 1960), but Walter J. Ong, *The Presence of the Word. Some Prologomena for Cultural and Religious History* (New Haven: Yale University Press, 1967) pp. 3–4, counters Barr with the observation that Boman's main 'contrast itself remains clear enough'.

4.   Erich Auerbach, *Mimesis*, trans. Willard Trask (New York: Doubleday, 1957). I summarise Auerbach here, especially pp. 1ff. Gabriel Josipovici, 'The Bible: Dialogue and Distance', ed. Michael Wadsworth, *Ways of Reading the Bible* (Sussex: Harvester Press, 1981) p. 142, sees the stress on background, crisis and tension as reflecting Auerbach's German Protestantism. Josipovici maintains that the biblical narrative moves 'without fuss', trusting 'that all will be well'. It is the reader who wants to fill the gaps in the story: we want to know what Abraham feels, and why God is doing this. Still, I feel Auerbach is correct to stress the historical moment of choice.

5.   See *Republic* 508a ff., 514a ff., and *Timaeus* 37d ff., *et passim*.

6.   Thorleif Boman, *Hebrew Thought Compared with Greek*, pp. 125ff., 134.

7.   For a concise outline, see Norman Perrin and Dennis C. Duling. *The New Testament. An Introduction* (New York: Harcourt Brace Jovanovich, 2nd edn, 1982) pp. 293ff.

8.   See especially Charles H. Talbert, *Literary Patterns, Theological Themes, and the Genre of Luke-Acts* (Missoula, Montana: Society for Biblical Literature and Scholars Press, 1974).

9.   Salvation history is an important concept in Lucan studies. H. Conzelmann, *The Theology of St. Luke*, trans. Geoffrey Buswell (London: Faber, 1960), uses the term 'Heilgeschichte', translated as 'redemptive history', but Perrin, *The New Testament: an Introduction*, p. 301, among other critics, prefers 'salvation history'. Conzelmann's key work stresses Luke's delay of the parousia, and divides salvation history into three periods: Israel, Jesus, and the Church. Ernst Haenchen, *The Acts of the Apostles: a Commentary*, trans. from the 14th German edn (1965) by

Bernard Noble and Gerald Shinn, revised by R. McL. Wilson (Philadelphia: Westminster Press, 1971), also a ground-breaking work, is in the general spirit of Conzelmann, and interprets Acts as recording developments between the period of Jesus and the period of the church. Both Conzelmann and Haenchen have been revised by more recent scholars, but their work is basic. For an account of more recent opinion, see I. Howard Marshall, *Luke: Historian and Theologian* (Exeter: Paternoster Press, 1979; 1st edn 1970) pp. 77ff.

10. Vernon K. Robbins, 'By Land and by Sea: the We-Passages and Ancient Sea Voyages', ed. Charles H. Talbert, *Perspectives in Luke-Acts* (Edinburgh: T. & T. Clark, 1978) pp. 215–42. I summarise Robbins, pp. 215–6.

11. See Alfred Plummer, *The Gospel According to S. Luke* (Edinburgh: T. & T. Clark, 3rd edn, 1900) p. 263: 'A Hebraism.... It implies fixedness of purpose, especially in the prospect of difficulty or danger.'

12. K. L. Schmidt, *Der Rahmann der Geschichte Jesu* (Berlin: 1919) p. 269, translated in Conzelmann, *The Theology of St. Luke*, p. 61, and cited by Donald R. Miesner, 'The Missionary Journeys Narrative: Patterns and Implications', ed. Charles H. Talbert, *Perspectives in Luke-Acts*, p. 200. See also Arland J. Hultgren, 'Interpreting the Gospel of Luke', ed. James Luther Mays, *Interpreting the Gospels* (Philadelphia: Fortress Press, 1981) p. 190: 'there is no real progress towards Jerusalem'.

13. Norval Geldenhuys, *Commentary on the Gospel of Luke* (London: Marshall, Morgan & Scott, 1950) p. 291: 'This is in many respects the most important part of the third Gospel because the major portion of its contents does not occur in the three other Gospels.'

14. For instance, W. M. Ramsay, *The Bearing of Recent Discovery on the Trustworthiness of the New Testament* (London: Hodder & Stoughton, 1915), and A. N. Sherwin-White, *Roman Society and Roman Law in the New Testament* (Oxford: Oxford University Press, 1963), indicate that Luke is reliable on matters of geography and politics. Ward Gasque, *A History of the Criticism of the Acts of the Apostles* (Tübingen: J. C. B. Mohr, 1975) p. 138, concludes: 'indeed it may almost be said, *all* scholars who have studied Ramsay's work closely – have agreed that his major thesis has been proven'.

15. Luke had some contact with Johannine tradition, though it is not clear that he knew John's gospel. See C. H. Dodd, *Historical Tradition in the Fourth Gospel* (Cambridge University Press, 1963) p. 263, argues that 'behind the Fourth Gospel lies an ancient tradition independent of the other gospels', though Dodd also holds that it is impossible to disprove John had some knowledge of the synoptics. C. B. Caird, *The Gospel of St. Luke* (London: Adam & Charles Black, 1968. First published, Penguin Books, 1963) p. 139.

16. See Carroll Stuhlmueller, 'The Gospel According to Luke', ed. Raymond E. Brown *et al.*, *The Jerome Biblical Commentary*, II, 142, for an outline of such patterns.

17. Kenneth Bailey, *Poet and Peasant: a Literary-Cultural Approach to the Parables in Luke* (Grand Rapids: William Eerdmans, 1976) pp. 80–2. The diagram is reproduced in Donald R. Miesner, 'The Missionary Journeys

Narrative: Patterns and Implications', ed. Charles H. Talbert, *Perspectives in Luke-Acts*, p. 200.

18. See Vernon K. Robbins, 'By Land and by Sea', pp. 240–1, and John Drury, *Tradition and Design in Luke's Gospel: a Study in Early Christian Historiography* (London: Darton, Longman & Todd, 1976) pp. 96ff., 'The Great Omission and the Gospel's Axis': 'The "time of the gentiles" (Lk. 21:24) is not yet. Here is the reason, weighty because integral to his historical scheme, for Luke's Great Omission. . . . Gentile excursions are, very precisely, another story' (p. 98).

19. On extravagance and hyperbole in the parables, see note 24 of the previous chapter.

20. For uses of *dei* ('must'), see 2:49; 4:43; 9:22; 13:33; 17:25; 19:5; 22:37; 24:7, 26, 44. See also I. Howard Marshall, *Luke: Historian and Theologian*, pp. 106ff., for an account of critical assessments of predetermination and election in Luke.

21. This perennial concern is dealt with, in one way or another, by numerous critics. John Drury, *Tradition and Design in Luke's Gospel*, chapter I, 'Introduction – The Well of the Past', pp. 1–14, is especially suggestive. J. C. O'Neill, *The Theology of Acts in its Historical Setting* (London: SPCK, 2nd edn, 1970) p. 178, sees the church discovering its independent destiny through the journey narrative. William C. Robinson, Jr, 'The Theological Context for Interpreting Luke's Travel Narrative', *Journal of Biblical Literature* 79 (1960) pp. 20–31, argues that the journey narrative serves Luke's teaching on authenticated witness.

22. See Edward Schillebeeckx, *Jesus. An Experiment in Christology*, trans. Hubert Hoskins from the Dutch edn of 1974 (London: Collins, Fount Paperbacks, 1983) pp. 298ff., who points out that the consensus of the gospels suggests that Jesus' preaching in Galilee was a failure, and in light of that he concentrated on a small group of disciples and on venturing to Jerusalem where he must have expected rejection. How much he guessed at, or foresaw, the frightful consequences of that rejection and his subsequent treatment at the hands of the Romans remains uncertain.

23. See for instance Leon Morris, *The Gospel According to St. Luke* (London: Inter-Varsity Press, 1974) p. 286: the 'others' are the gentiles, an unthinkable thing for Jesus' listeners, which is why they say 'God forbid' (20:16).

24. Raymond E. Brown, *The Birth of the Messiah: a Commentary on the Infancy Narratives in Matthew and Luke* (New York: Doubleday, 1977) pp. 84, 242 et passim.

25. W. D. Davies, *The Gospel and the Land. Early Christianity and Jewish Territorial Doctrine* (University of California Press, 1974) p. 260.

26. See Eric Franklin, *Christ the Lord: a Study of the Purpose and Theology of Luke-Acts* (London: SPCK, 1975) p. 102; Carroll Stuhlmueller, 'The Gospel According to Luke', ed. Raymond E. Brown et al., *The Jerome Biblical Commentary*, II, 153: 'Gradually the notion of Temple becomes identified with Jesus himself.'

27. See for instance 1:41, 14; 2:21; 4:4, 32; 5:1, 5; 7:22; 8:11; 9:48, 49; 10:39; 11:27; 19:38; 20:26; 21:17, 33; 22:61, 71; 24:6, 8, 19, 44.

28.   On the vexed question of the kingdom within (whether an inner spiritual reality, within our power, or in the midst of us), see Eduard Schweizer, *The Good News According to Luke*, trans. David E. Green (London: SPCK, 1984) pp. 272ff. Schweizer concludes, p. 276: 'The whole discussion emphasises that we cannot picture what is to come in spatial or temporal terms. It therefore uses a variety of images intended to set people in motion and shape their present lives. . . . In fact the Kingdom of God chooses to relate to us by coming into our midst. Therefore we cannot assign the kingdom to its proper place because in Jesus' work it shapes the entire present.'

29.   Robert Graves, *King Jesus* (London: Cassell, 1946). I summarise the argument as the novel presents it. Edward Schillebeeckx, *Jesus*, pp. 299, 301, suggests that Jesus might have thought he would die by the sword like John the Baptist before him, Herod having the *ius gladii*, the right to execute by the sword.

30.   Martin Dibelius, *A Fresh Approach to the New Testament and Early Christian Literature* (New York: Charles Scribner's Sons, 1936) p. 263. For an account of Dibelius' contribution to the criticism of Acts, his influence on Ernst Haenchen, and on a generally sceptical attitude to Luke's reliability as a historian, see Ward Gasque, *A History of the Critisicm of the Acts of the Apostles*, Chapter IX, 'The Influence of Dibelius', pp. 201ff.

31.   Donald R. Miesner, 'The Missionary Journeys Narrative: Patterns and Implications', ed. Talbert, *Perspectives in Luke-Acts*, pp. 203ff.

32.   Vernon K. Robbins, 'By Land and by Sea', ed. Talbert, *Perspectives in Luke-Acts*, p. 235.

33.   See Ward Gasque, *A History of the Criticism of the Acts of the Apostles*, p. 160, on over-zealous critics who 'have treated the Book of Acts with a severity, indeed, with something akin to maliciousness with which no historian treats other historical documents'.

34.   Charles H. Talbert, *Literary Patterns, Theological Themes, and the Genre of Luke-Acts*.

35.   Debate on the fictional portrait of Paul in Acts is complex. Three useful articles have been edited by Leander E. Keck and J. Louis Martyn, *Studies in Luke-Acts* (Philadelphia: Fortress Press, 1980). These are: W. C. Van Unnik, 'Luke-Acts, a Storm Centre in Contemporary Scholarship', pp. 26ff., outlining the uncharacteristic quality of the Acts speeches attributed to Paul; Eduard Schweizer, 'Concerning the Speeches in Acts', pp. 208ff., dealing with Peter's speeches as well as Paul's; Erwin R. Goodenough, 'The Perspectives of Acts', pp. 51ff., suggesting that Paul's being a disciple of Gamaliel and a Roman citizen are likely to be Lucan fictions. Also, F. F. Bruce, *The Acts of the Apostles: Commentary on the Book of Acts* (London: Marshall, Morgan & Scott, 1954) p. 126, notices that Luke's usually fine Greek becomes unaccountably obscure when the apostles speak, thus suggesting that the author is not concerned about style. I. Howard Marshall, *Luke: Historian and Theologian*, p. 75, concludes that 'The general outline of Paul's career in Acts fits in well with what is disclosed in his letters', and 'The view that Paul's theology is inaccurately presented in Acts is a palpable exaggeration, provided we

do not ask too much of Luke and do not demand of him a verbatim report of Paul's words.'
36. I draw here on Norman Perrin, *The New Testament: an Introduction*, pp. 301ff.; I. Howard Marshall, *Luke: Historian and Theologian*, 'Ancient Historians', pp. 54ff.; John Drury, *Tradition and Design in Luke's Gospel*, pp. 5ff., for these fairly standard observations about the deliberately universalising elements of ancient historiography.
37. Donald R. Miesner, 'The Missionary Journeys Narrative: Patterns and Implications', ed. Talbert, *Perspectives in Luke-Acts*, p. 213.
38. See B. Gärtner, *The Areopagus Speech and Natural Revelation* (Uppsala: Acta Seminarii, no. 21, 1955); H. Conzelmann, 'The Address of Paul on the Areopagus', ed. Leander E. Keck and J. Louis Martyn, *Studies in Luke-Acts*, pp. 217–30; Martin Dibelius, *Studies in Acts of the Apostles*, pp. 186–91, 'Literary Allusions in the Speeches in Acts'.
39. Ernst Haenchen, *The Acts of the Apostles*, pp. 518–28, notes several parallels.
40. For examples of the first kind, see F. J. Foakes Jackson and Kirsopp Lake, *The Beginnings of Christianity*, 5 vols. (London: Macmillan, 1920–33), vol. II, *Prolegomena II, Criticism* (1922) p. 158: 'Few students doubt that the origin of the "we" sections is the actual diary of a composition of Paul. But to what extent this diary went, and the relation of the diarist to the compiler of Acts is disputed.' See also Carroll Stuhlmueller, 'The Gospel According to Luke', ed. Raymond E. Brown *et al.*, *The Jerome Biblical Commentary*, II, 198. The second kind of interpretation has been most fully developed by Vernon K. Robbins, 'By Land and by Sea'. For the third theory see Martin Dibelius, *Studies in the Acts of the Apostles*, ed. Heinrich Greeven, trans. Mary Ling (London: SCM, 1956) pp. 104ff., who finds traces of an itinerary document: 'Everywhere it seems that there underlies the account of the journeys an itinerary or stations where Paul stopped. . . . Such an itinerary seems to have formed the framework for the central part of Acts.' Against Haenchen's theory that Luke invented much and had few historical data, I. Howard Marshall, *Luke: Historian and Theologian*, pp. 67–8, points to the 'we sections': 'It seems beyond question that some kind of itinerary or itineraries lies behind these sections, even if the limits and contents of such sources cannot be closely defined.'
41. I summarise Robbins' article, 'By Land and by Sea'.
42. I. Howard Marshall, *Luke: Historian and Theologian*, p. 158.
43. See Johannes Munck, *The Anchor Bible. The Acts of the Apostles*, revised by F. Albright and C. S. Mann (New York: Doubleday, 1967) p. 122; H. Metzger, *St. Paul's Journeys to the Greek Orient*, ed. A. Parrot, Studies in Biblical Archaeology, 4 (London: 1955) pp. 25, 34.
44. C. S. C. Williams, *A Commentary on the Acts of the Apostles* (London: Adam & Charles Black, 1957) p. 160: 'Perhaps Paul fell ill with malaria, as Ramsay suggested, and for a cure sought the high ground of the mainland . . .'.
45. F. J. Foakes-Jackson, *The Acts of the Apostles*, p. 150.
46. Helen Gardner, *The Business of Criticism*, p. 122.
47. W. D. Davies, *The Gospel and the Land*, p. 253.

48.   Ibid., pp. 279–80: the frequent identification of Rome with the 'end of the earth' is uncritical.

CHAPTER 5: JOHN: SEEING AND BELIEVING

1.   Edward Schillebeeckx, *Christ: the Experience of Jesus as Lord*, trans. John Bowden (New York: Crossroad, 1983) p. 335. See also John Painter, *John. Witness and Theologian* (London: SPCK, 1975) p. 77: 'The emphasis in John on believing is clear. In twenty-one chapters we have almost half the uses in the New Testament and more than three times the total number of uses in the Synoptics.'

2.   See Alison A. Trites, *The New Testament Concept of Witness* (Cambridge University Press, 1977) ch. 8, 'The Concept of Witness in the Fourth Gospel', p. 78: 'The Fourth Gospel ... is of particular importance for it presents a sustained use of juridical metaphor', and George Johnston, *The Spirit-Paraclete in the Gospel of John* (Cambridge University Press, 1970) p. 155.

3.   For John's use of the verb 'to believe' see C. H. Dodd, *The Interpretation of the Fourth Gospel* (Cambridge University Press, 1968) pp. 179ff. Dodd discusses the moral and intellectual senses, and the connection between faith and vision (the detection of God's glory), and the unusual use of the verb with *eis*, which re-enforces the personal nature of belief. R. H. Strachan, *The Fourth Evangelist: Dramatist or Historian?* (London: Hodder & Stoughton, 1925) p. 93: 'We shall, therefore, be prepared to find that "faith" or "belief" is a dominant idea in the Fourth Gospel. One point, however, is deserving of notice. The noun "faith" (*pistis*), as has often been observed, is never used in the Gospel. The verb "to believe" alone is found. That can only indicate that the Evangelist conceives of faith as dynamic, and not as static; as a relationship between God and man, through Jesus Christ, which is either tragically conspicuous by its absence, or grows and deepens with increasing knowledge of Jesus Christ, the great object of faith.'

4.   The modern tendency is to emphasise the Jewish background to the gospel, and to play down the Greek. See Robert Kysar, 'Community and Gospel: Vectors in Fourth Gospel Criticism', ed. James Luther Mays, *Interpreting the Gospels* (Philadelphia: Fortress Press, 1981) pp. 266ff., and 274; and Robert Kysar, *The Fourth Evangelist and His Gospel. An Examination of Contemporary Scholarship* (Minneapolis, Minn.: Augsburg Publishing House, 1975) chapter III, 'The Johannine Dualism', pp. 215–21, and esp. p. 221: 'It is, therefore, to be judged more likely for a number of reasons that the redemptive content of the symbolism of the positive pole and the corrupting content of the symbolism of the negative pole should be emphasised.'

5.   John Donne, *The Divine Poems*, ed. Helen Gardner (Oxford: Clarendon Press, 1952) p. 11.

6.   See Lucio P. Rustolo, 'The Trinitarian Framework of Donne's Holy Sonnet XIV', *Journal of the History of Ideas* 27 (1966) pp. 445–6.

7. See David K. Cornelius, 'Donne's "Holy-Sonnet XIV" ', *Explicator* 24, no. 3 (1965) Item 25.

8. John uses several words for seeing, and just as seeing can be physical or spiritual, so can hearing. See C. H. Dodd, *The Fourth Gospel*, pp. 167ff., and Edward Schillebeeckx, *Christ*, pp. 309, 380.

9. C. K. Barrett, *The Gospel According to John* (Philadelphia: Westminster Press, 1978) pp. 76ff.

10. Norman Perrin and Dennis C. Duling, *The New Testament. An Introduction* (New York: Harcourt, Brace, Jovanovich, 1982) p. 336.

11. The complex textual problems indicated here are beyond the scope of this chapter, but are dealt with by most of the major commentators. On the church situation, see for instance C. K. Barrett, *The Gospel According to St. John*, pp. 100ff.; R. H. Lightfoot, *St. John's Gospel: a Commentary*, pp. 4ff.; Rudolf Schnackenburg, *The Gospel According to St. John*, 3 vols (New York: Crossroad, 1982) I, 75ff.; Raymond E. Brown, *The Anchor Bible: the Gospel According to John*, 2 vols (New York: Doubleday, 1966) I, lxvii ff. On the textual traditions and interpolations see C. K. Barrett, *The Gospel According to St. John*, pp. 21ff., and especially p. 22: 'I take it that if the gospel makes sense as it stands it can generally be assumed that this is the sense it was intended to make. That it may seem to me to make better sense when rearranged I do not regard as adequate reason for abandoning an order which undoubtedly runs back into the second century – the order, indeed, in which the book was published.' See also Rudolf Bultmann, *The Gospel of John: a Commentary*, trans. G. R. Beasley-Murray (Oxford: Basil Blackwell, 1971) pp. 3ff.; W. Marxsen, *Introduction to the New Testament*, trans. G. Buswell (Oxford: Basil Blackwell, 1968) pp. 252ff.; Rudolf Schnackenburg, *The Gospel According to St. John*, I, 59ff. For a summary account of the sources, see Robert Kysar, *The Fourth Evangelist and His Gospel: an Examination of Contemporary Scholarship* (Minneapolis: Augsburg Publishing House, 1975) pp. 13ff. For an assessment of Bultmann's influential theory and reconstruction of the Fourth Gospel, see Dwight Moody Smith, Jr, *The Composition and Order of the Fourth Gospel. Bultmann's Literary Theory* (New Haven, Conn.: Yale University Press, 1965).

12. Paul S. Minear, 'The Audience of the Fourth Evangelist', ed. James Luther Mays, *Interpreting the Gospels*, p. 258, note 22.

13. In the following paragraph I summarise Walter Ong, *The Presence of the Word. Some Prolegomena for Cultural and Religious History* (New Haven, Conn.: Yale University Press, 1967) pp. 128–9, 166 *et passim*, and *Interfaces of the Word. Studies in the Evolution of Consciousness and Culture* (Ithaca: Cornell University Press, 1977) esp. pp. 139ff.

14. C. H. Dodd, *The Interpretation of the Fourth Gospel*, pp. 151ff., cites Bultmann and re-affirms his point.

15. I summarise Walter Ong, *The Presence of the Word*, and refer here especially to pp. 189 and 45ff.

16. Paul S. Minear, 'The Audience of the Fourth Evangelist', ed. James Luther Mays, *Interpreting the Gospels*, p. 255.

17. C. H. Dodd, *The Interpretation of the Fourth Gospel*, p. 383.

18. Commentators are undecided about what Nathanael might have been

doing under the fig tree. See Brown, *The Gospel According to St. John*, pp. 83, 87. Rudolf Bultmann, in *The Gospel of John: a Commentary*, p. 104, note 6, concludes: 'perhaps it is enough to point out that the Rabbis favoured a place under a tree for study and teaching'.

19.   Ong, *The Presence of the Word*, p. 138.

20.   See for instance Brown, *The Gospel According to John*, I, 337, and the bibliography on p. 338; Lightfoot, *St. John's Gospel: a Commentary*, p. 347; C. K. Barrett, *The Gospel According to St. John*, 2nd edn, p. 592, who summarises several of the main opinions and concludes: 'In fact it is fruitless to ask what Jesus wrote on the ground.' An interesting interpretation is that Jesus was being tested in the same manner as in the incident about paying tribute to Caesar (Matt. 22:15–22): if he disagrees about stoning the woman, he is against the Mosaic law; if he agrees, he is against the Roman law. T. W. Manson suggests that, following Roman legal practice, Jesus first writes the sentence and then reads it, and that his judgement is a careful evasion. See 'The Pericope *de Adulteria* (John 7, 53–8, 11)', *Zeitschrift für die neutestamentliche Wissenschaft* 44 (1952–53) pp. 255–6. I am not concerned here with the debate on whether or not the story really belongs in the Fourth Gospel. For a summary of the textual tradition, see Edwyn Clement Hoskyns, *The Fourth Gospel*, ed. Francis Noel Davey, 2 vols (London: Faber, 1940) II, 673ff.

21.   See Bruce Vawter, 'The Gospel According to John', ed. Raymond E. Brown *et al.*, *The Jerome Biblical Commentary*, II, 423.

22.   See Edward Schillebeeckx, *Christ*, p. 311.

23.   G. Wilson Knight, *The Christian Renaissance* (London: Methuen, 1962) p. 147. See also John Painter, *John. Witness and Theologian*, pp. 50ff.

24.   Rudolf Schnackenburg, *The Gospel According to St. John*, I, 363–4, on the mixture of incident and symbol in the Nicodemus story.

25.   See Rudolf Schnackenburg, *The Gospel According to St. John*, I, 419ff., for an example of the general idea that 'the presence of a deeper symbolism always arises in John from the fact that the narrative also includes theological themes which are intrinsically connected with it' (421). See also J. Bligh, 'Jesus in Samaria', *Heythrop Journal* 3 (1962) pp. 329–46. Raymond E. Brown, *The Gospel According to John*, divides the scene into two sections (I, 176ff.), and sees in the story of the Samaritan woman 'the drama of a soul struggling to rise from the things of this world to belief in Jesus. Not only the Samaritan woman but every man must come to recognise who it is that speaks when Jesus speaks....' (I, 178).

26.   There is no scholarly consensus on relationships between John and the synoptics, though the claim that John knew any of the synoptics directly (as distinct from knowledge transmitted orally and by tradition) is held by a minority, among them C. K. Barrett, *The Gospel According to St. John*, pp. 42ff. See Robert Kysar, 'Vectors in Fourth Gospel Criticism', ed. James Luther Mays, *Interpreting the Gospels*, pp. 269–70; Robert Tomson Fortna, *The Gospel of Signs. A Reconstruction of the Narrative Source Underlying the Fourth Gospel*, Society for New Testament Studies Monograph Series 11 (Cambridge University Press, 1970) p. 226.

27.   A. Feuillet, 'La signification théologique du second miracle de Cana (Jo.

IV, 46–54)', *Recherches de sciences religieuses* 48 (1960) pp. 62–75, argues that this periscope is not the last section of what preceded, but the beginning of a new section, thereby establishing two Cana-Jerusalem incidents. As Raymond E. Brown (citing Feuillet) points out (*The Gospel According to John*, I, 198), it could fulfill both functions.

28. Rudolf Schnackenburg, *The Gospel According to St. John*, I, 469ff., deals with this issue, and draws a careful comparison with the centurion of Matt. 8:5–13, and Lk. 7:1–10. See also C. K. Barrett, *The Gospel According to St. John*, pp. 244ff., who concludes that it is reasonable to see chapters 2, 3, and 4 as a unit. Raymond E. Brown, *The Gospel According to John*, I, 194, discusses the editorial problem in relation to the 'signs source' theory.

29. C. H. Dodd, *The Interpretation of the Fourth Gospel*, p. 318: 'The word itself is significant: it is thrice repeated . . .'.

30. See Raymond E. Brown, *The Gospel According to John*, I, 196.

31. See for instance E. F. Scott, *The Fourth Gospel: Its Purpose and Theology* (Edinburgh: T. & T. Clark, 2nd edn, 1908) pp. 21–2: 'It even seems probable that the structure of the Gospel as a whole is determined by these two numbers, three and seven.'

32. See T. Francis Glasson, *Moses in the Fourth Gospel*, Studies in Biblical Theology 40 (London: SCM, 1963), and Edward Schillebeeckx, *Christ*, pp. 314ff.

33. Raymond E. Brown, *The Gospel According to John*, II, 995.

34. Literally, the imperative *me mou aptou* means 'stop touching me' (Raymond E. Brown, *The Gospel According to John*, II, 992). Rudolf Schnackenburg, *The Gospel According to St. John*, III, 318, says: 'the negative present imperative can also mean, Do not hold on to me any longer, let me go'. See also Rudolf Bultmann, *The Gospel of John: a Commentary*, trans. G. R. Beasley-Murray (Oxford: Basil Blackwell, 1971) p. 687: 'she thinks that the old relationship has been renewed, and in her joy she wants to embrace him – as a friend would do to a friend who has come back again'.

35. I summarise Walter Ong, *The Presence of the Word*, pp. 169ff.

36. See John Painter, *John. Witness and Theologian*, pp. 50ff (on glory in humiliation), and p. 56 (on the cross as enthronement); R. H. Lightfoot, *St. John's Gospel. A Commentary*, p. 316: 'The Lord is king indeed; the cross is the manner of his exaltation and glorification'; J. Terence Forestell, *The Word of the Cross: Salvation as Revelation in the Fourth Gospel* (Rome: Biblical Institute Press, 1974) p. 73: 'The fourth gospel views the cross as the visible sign of the exaltation and glorification of the Son of Man in the presence of God . . . the elevation of Jesus on the cross is the visible sign of this triumph.'

CHAPTER 6: PAUL TO THE CORINTHIANS

1. T. S. Eliot, *Collected Poems* (London: Faber & Faber, 1936) pp. 107–8.
2. Lancelot Andrewes' sermon is as follows: 'A cold coming we had of it at

this time of the year, just the worst time of the year to take a journey, and specially a long journey in. The ways deep, the weather sharp, the days short, the sun farthest off, *in salstitio brumali*, "the very dead of winter".'

3. See 1 Cor. 1:27: 'but God chose what is foolish in the world to shame the wise'.

4. See Calvin J. Roetzel, *The Letters of Paul. Conversations in Context* (Atlanta: John Knox Press, 2nd edn 1982) pp. 6ff.

5. On various traditional elements in the Pauline letters, see Roetzel, *The Letters*, pp. 41ff.; Beda Rigaux, *The Letters of St. Paul. Modern Studies*, ed. and trans. Stephen Yonick (Chicago: Franciscan Herald Press, 1968) pp. 115ff. On the Cynic-Stoic *diatribe*, a form of argument which answers questions uttered by imagined objectors, see Joseph A. Fitzmyer, 'Pauline Theology', ed. Raymond E. Brown *et al.*, *The Jerome Biblical Commentary*, 2 vols (New Jersey: Prentice-Hall, 1968) II, 803. On the epistolary form (salutation, thanksgiving, body, paranesis or ethical exhortation, conclusion), see Roetzel, *The Letters*, pp. 29ff., and William Doty, *Letters in Primitive Christianity* (Philadelphia: Fortress Press, 1973).

6. See Norman Perrin and Dennis C. Duling, *The New Testament: an Introduction* (New York: Harcourt, Brace, Jovanovich, 2nd edn 1982) p. 197: 'the centre is "the Christ event", that is, Jesus' death on the cross and his resurrection from the dead. For Paul, the cross-resurrection opens up the whole meaning of the divine plan and purpose'. It is surprising how little of Jesus' life is recorded in Paul. There is dispute about which letters are genuine. The list offered by Perrin (p. 128) is as follows: 1 Thessalonians, 1 Corinthians, 2 Corinthians, Philippians, Philemon, Galatians, and Romans.

7. See Rudolf Schnackenburg, *New Testament Theology Today*, trans. David Askew (London: Geoffrey Chapman, 1963) pp. 88–9: it is important 'to arrive at a proper understanding of his expectation of an imminent Parousia (and we cannot reasonably deny that he does expect this)'. Still, 'it is just as important not to reduce Paul's real "eschatological" attitude to what he says in I Thess. 5.1–11'. See also Hubert Richards, *St. Paul and His Epistles. A New Introduction* (London: Darton, Longman & Todd, 1979) p. 36: 'he saw the end coming as the climax of a struggle which had already reached its final stages. . . . No one in his senses would deny that if Paul were writing to Salonika today he would need to express himself rather differently. . . . When he wrote to the Corinthians only five or six years later, he had already changed his tune and assumed that both he and they would already be dead'. Albert Schweitzer, *The Mysticism of Paul the Apostle*, trans. William Montgomery (New York: Henry Holt, 1931), presents Paul as an eschatological mystic who expected an imminent messianic kingdom. For an assessment of the weakness in Schweitzer's influential argument, see W. D. Davies, *Paul and Rabbinic Judaism. Some Elements in Pauline Theology* (London: SPCK, 1948) pp. 288ff. Davies argues that the ascription to the apostle of belief in a temporary messianic kingdom is erroneous, and Paul's eschatology 'was determined not by any traditional scheme but by that significance which Paul had been led to give Jesus'.

8. See Hans Joachim Schoeps, *Paul: the Theology of the Apostle in the Light*

of Jewish Religious History, trans. Harold Knight (Philadelphia: Westminster Press, 1961) *passim*; Martin Buber, *Two Types of Faith*, trans. Norman P. Goldhawk (London: Routledge & Kegan Paul, 1951) pp. 46–50; 80ff.; 91ff.; E. P. Sanders, *Paul, the Law, and the Jewish People* (Philadelphia: Fortress Press, 1963) esp. pp. 143ff. Sanders warns against over-simple readings of Paul's treatment of the law. 'I have come to the conclusion that there is no single unity which adequately accounts for every statement about the law' (147). In particular, Paul is uninterested in the interior attitude with which the law is approached (146), and his treatment of the law is unsystematic. See also W. D. Davies, *Jewish and Pauline Studies* (London: SPCK, 1984) p. 108: 'There is no one Pauline attitude to the Law', yet Paul's teaching on *agape* 'achieved an immense and penetrating simplification' of the relationship between law and religion (120).

9. See George Bernard Shaw, *Androcles and the Lion* (London: The Bodley Head, 1972), The Bodley Head Shaw, vol. IV, pp. 546ff., 'Preface on the Prospectus of Christianity'. Shaw thinks that Paul's views on sin and sex make him 'the eternal enemy of Woman'. Robin Scroggs, 'Paul: Chauvinist or Liberationist?', *The Christian Century* 89 (1972) pp. 307–9; 'Paul and the Eschatological Woman', *Journal of the American Academy of Religion* 40 (1972) pp. 283–303; 'Paul and the Eschatological Woman: Revisited', *Journal of the Academy of Religion* 42 (1974) pp. 532–7, makes a case for Paul's liberalism. For a counterstatement, see Elaine Pagels, 'Paul and Women: a Response to Recent Discussion', *Journal of the American Academy of Religion* 42 (1974) pp. 538–49.

10. Daniel Patte, *Paul's Faith and the Power of the Gospel* (Philadelphia: Fortress Press, 1983), offers a structuralist reading of Paul's epistles similar to mine at this point, and based on the semiotic theories of A. J. Greimas. Patte emphasises the exploratory nature of faith, and the development of clusters of conviction. He maintains that Paul emphasises the importance of avoiding absolute claims for human knowledge and authority (see pp. 311, 322 for applications of this view to the Corinthian letters). It is consistent with the modern developments in literary theory which I have outlined in chapter 1, that semiotics should be the ground on which a New Testament scholar's approach to Paul is of special relevance to a literary critic. See also Wayne A. Meeks, 'The Christian Proteus' in *The Writings of St. Paul*, ed. Wayne A. Meeks (New York: Norton, 1972) p. 435: 'Paul has become the foe of all authoritative systems', and p. 442: 'Perhaps, indeed, Paul's chief value in the ethical realm lies precisely in showing up the dangers of systems.'

11. Adolf Deissmann, *Light from the Ancient East*, trans. Lionel Strachan (New York: Harper, 1923) p. 234.

12. For these opinions, see W. Marxsen, *Introduction to the New Testament: an Approach to its Problems*, trans. G. Buswell (Oxford: Blackwell, 1968) p. 24; Norman Perrin, *The New Testament: an Introduction* (New York: Harcourt, Brace, Jovanovich, 1974) p. 97; Bo Reicke, *The Anchor Bible: the Epistles of James, Peter and Jude* (Garden City, New York: Doubleday, 1964) pp. xxx–xxxiii; Ralph P. Martin, 'Approaches to New Testament Exegesis' in *New Testament Interpretation*, ed. I. Howard Marshall

(Grand Rapids, Michigan: William B. Eerdmans, 1977) p. 232; William G. Doty, 'The Classification of Epistolary Literature', *Catholic Biblical Quarterly* 31 (1969) p. 198.

13. *Alice in Wonderland*, ed. Donald J. Gray (New York: Norton, 1971) p. 272.

14. I draw here on Daniel Patte, *Paul's Faith and the Power of the Gospel*, pp. 298ff., and Robert Jewett, *Paul's Anthropological Terms: a Study of Their Use in Conflict Settings* (Leiden: E. J. Brill, 1971) pp. 23ff. See also Beda Rigaux, *Letters of St. Paul*, pp. 108ff.

15. See Jewett, *Paul's Anthropological Terms*, pp. 24ff.

16. Many of these problems in turn need to be reconstructed by us. See for instance G. Lüdemann, *Paulus, der Heidenapostel*, 2 vols (Göttingen: Vandenhoeck & Ruprecht, 1982); W. Schmithals, *Gnosticism in Corinth*, trans. John E. Steely (Nashville: Abingdon Press, 1971); Jewett, *Paul's Anthropological Terms*, pp. 26ff.; John Coolidge Hurd, Jr, *The Origin of I Corinthians* (London: SPCK, 1965).

17. T. S. Eliot, 'The Metaphysical Poets', p. 289.

18. Friedrich Nietzsche has given the central expression to this idea. See *The Antichrist. An Attempted Criticism of Christianity*, trans. Anthony M. Ludovizi, *The Complete Works of Friedrich Nietzsche*, ed. Oscar Levy (London: J. N. Foulis, 1909–11) XVI, 178ff. See also Geza Vermes, *Jesus the Jew* (London: Collins, 1973). This book presents Jesus as a simple, pious peasant who would have been repelled by the theological claims made in his name.

19. For an account of interpretations of this episode, see Hans Conzelmann, *I Corinthians: a Commentary on the First Epistle to the Corinthians*, trans. James W. Leitch (Philadelphia: Fortress Press, 1975) pp. 258ff.

20. The various discussions of Paul's mysticism are closely connected to what is meant by being 'in' Christ. See J. B. Nielson, *In Christ. The Significance of the Phrase 'In Christ' in the Writings of St. Paul* (Kansas City: Beacon Hill Press, 1960); E. Schweizer, 'Dying and Rising with Christ', *New Testament Studies* 14 (1967–68) pp. 1–14; Alfred Wikenhauser, *Pauline Mysticism. Christ in the Mystical Teaching of St. Paul*, trans. Joseph Cunningham (London: Nelson, 1960) esp. pp. 21ff., 'In Christ', and 50ff., 'The Meaning of the Phrase "In Christ" '; Adolf Deissmann, *Paul: a Study in Social and Religious History*, trans. William E. Wilson (New York: Hodder & Stoughton, 1926) pp. 135ff.; Albert Schweitzer, *The Mysticism of Paul the Apostle*, trans. William Montgomery (New York: Henry Holt, 1931).

21. I draw here on Rudolf Bultmann's influential teaching about Paul in *Theology of the New Testament*, 2 vols, trans. Kendrick Grobel (London: SCM, 1952) I, 190 ff. Bultmann stresses the anthropological side of Paul, describing faith as the choice of an authentic existence whereby we are freed from anxiety and self-seeking, and the futile search for security through our own achievements. Bultmann's existential emphasis reduces to vanishing point the historical significance of Paul's writing. Full attention to Paul's metaphors, I suggest, preserves a balance between historical identity and modern relevance.

22. See Robert Jewett, *Paul's Anthropological Terms*, pp. 49ff., 453ff. on which I also depend for the above examples.

23. Ibid., pp. 27ff.; Hans Conzelmann, *I Corinthians*, pp. 33ff.
24. The main contrast is between direct and indirect knowledge, though the figure of the mirror has occasioned much debate. See Norbert Hugède, *La métaphore du miroir dans les Epîtres de saint Paul aux Corinthiens* (Paris: Delachaux et Niestlé, 1957); Hans Conzelmann, *I Corinthians*, pp. 226ff.; James Moffatt, *The First Epistle to the Corinthians* (London: Hodder & Stoughton, 1938) p. 201, points out that there were some semi-transparent windows at this time, but the allusion is to a metal mirror, which the Corinthians made of polished bronze. Mirrors were also used in divination.
25. The phenomenon itself is not described, but can be associated, for instance, with the inspired babblings of the medium interpreted by the priests at Delphi. Yet, as Conzelmann points out, *I Corinthians*, p. 234: 'Unlike the Greek theory, Paul's opinion is not that what is said in tongues is unintelligible to the speaker himself. But like the Greeks, he is of the opinion that it can be translated into human language.' See also Frank W. Beare, 'Speaking with Tongues: a Critical Survey of the New Testament Evidence', *Journal of Biblical Literature* 83 (1964) pp. 229–46; Ralph P. Martin, *The Spirit and the Congregation: Studies in I Corinthians 12–15* (Grand Rapids, Michigan: William B. Eerdmans, 1984), examines Paul's attitude in detail. According to Martin, the ruling axiom is that worship should build up the entire congregation, and 'exclusive personalism' is seen as dangerous. Se also M. E. Thrall, *I and II Corinthians* (Cambridge University Press, 1965) p. 99, on Paul's suspicion of glossalalia even in private.
26. See Alfred Plummer, *A Critical and Exegetical Commentary on the Second Epistle of Paul to the Corinthians* (Edinburgh: T. & T. Clark, 1905) p. 340: ' "I *know* a man in Christ who fourteen years ago was caught up". Not "I *knew* (AV.) such a person fourteen years ago." St. Paul knows him intimately at the time of writing, but not until v. 7 does he show that he is speaking of himself.'
27. See Jewett, *Paul's Anthropological Terms*, pp. 447ff.; Fitzmyer, 'Pauline Theology', *The Jerome Biblical Commentary*, II, 801, 816, deals with Paul offering us 'vivid metaphors' which resist translation into theory.

CHAPTER 7: HEBREWS: BLOOD ON THE BOUNDARY

1. See Norman Perrin, *The New Testament: an Introduction*, p. 227.
2. These points are discussed in the main commentaries. See, for instance, *Peake's Commentary on the Bible*, *The Jerome Biblical Commentary*, Reginald R. Fuller, 'The Letter to the Hebrews', ed. Gerhard Krodel, *Hebrews-James-1 and 2 Peter-Jude-Revelation* (Philadelphia: Fortress Press, 1977), W. Marxsen, *Introduction to the New Testament*, trans. G. Buswell (Oxford: Basil Blackwell, 1968) pp. 217ff., F. F. Bruce, *Commentary on the Epistle to the Hebrews* (London: Marshall, Morgan & Scott, 1965), Ronald Williamson, *The Epistle to the Hebrews* (London: Epworth Press, 1964).

3. See Frank Kermode, *The Genesis of Secrecy: on the Interpretation of Narrative* (Cambridge, Mass.: Harvard University Press, 1979) pp. x ff. Raymond E. Brown, *The Birth of the Messiah* (New York: Doubleday, 1977), 'Appendix VIII: Midrash as a Literary Genre', pp. 557ff., raises the question of how creatively interpretive midrash is, and concludes that we ought not to identify midrash with fiction.

4. See Edward Schillebeeckx, *Christ: the Experience of Jesus as Lord*, trans. John Bowden (New York: Crossroad, 1983) p. 247.

5. This point is made about the cross by Paul Tillich, *The Dynamics of Faith* (New York: Harper, 1958) pp. 97, 42ff.

6. C. Spicq, *L'Epître aux Hébreux*, 2 vols (Paris: 1952); J. B. Carpzov, *Sacrae exercitationes in S. Paulli Epistolam ad Hebraeos ex Philone Alexandrino* (Amsterdam: 1750).

7. Ronald Williamson, *Philo and the Epistle to the Hebrews* (Leiden: E. J. Brill, 1970). Page numbers are cited in the text.

8. Ibid., pp. 565–6.

9. See for instance G. W. MacRae, 'Heavenly Temple and Eschatology in the Letter to the Hebrews', *Semeia* 12 (1978) pp. 179–99, argues that Hebrews combines a futurist eschatology with a realised eschatology through combining a Hellenistic idea of the temple with an apocalyptic one whereby the complete temple is present in heaven. For an interpretation of Hebrews as a creative poetic vision combining mythology and visionary insight, see P. S. Minear, 'An Early Christian Theopoetic?', *Semeia* 12 (1978) pp. 201–14.

10. See especially David Peterson, *Hebrews and Perfection: an Examination of the Concept of Perfection in the "Epistle to the Hebrews"* (Cambridge University Press, 1982).

11. See Reginald R. Fuller, 'The Letter to the Hebrews', pp. 15–16 for a summary of this debate; Graham Hughes, *Hebrews and Hermeneutics: the Epistle to the Hebrews as a New Testament Example of Biblical Interpretation* (Cambridge University Press, 1979) pp. 41ff.

12. Myles M. Bourke, 'The Epistle to the Hebrews', *The Jerome Biblical Commentary*, II, 395.

13. See Edward Schillebeeckx, *Christ*, p. 241.

14. See Graham Hughes, *Hebrews and Hermeneutics*, 'The Word of God in history necessarily takes the form of a promise', pp. 40ff.

CHAPTER 8: REVELATION: THE TWO-EDGED SWORD

1. D. H. Lawrence, *Apocalypse: and the Writings on Revelation*, ed. Mara Kalnis (Cambridge University Press, 1980) p. 67.

2. C. G. Jung, *Answer to Job*, trans. R. F. C. Hull (New York: Meridian Books, 1960) pp. 142–3.

3. Amos N. Wilder, 'The Rhetoric of Ancient and Modern Apocalyptic', *Interpretation* 25 (1971) pp. 441–2.

4. John Sweet, *Revelation* (London: SCM Press, 1979) p. 50. See also Anthony Tyrrell Hanson, *The Wrath of the Lamb* (London: SPCK, 1957),

and Martin Hengel, *Victory Over Violence*, trans. David E. Green (London: SPCK, 1975).

5. Austin Farrer, *A Rebirth of Images: the Making of St. John's Apocalypse* (Gloucester, Mass.: Peter Smith, 1970) p. 17.

6. Norman Perrin and Dennis C. Duling, *The New Testament: an Introduction* (New York: Harcourt, Brace, Jovanovich, 2nd edn 1982) p. 73: 'The Christian church began as an apocalyptic sectarian movement within ancient Judaism.' See also pp. 81, 89. See also Christopher Rowland, *The Open Heaven. A Study of Apocalyptic in Judaism and Early Christianity* (London: SPCK, 1982) esp. pp. 349ff., and W. A. Beardslee, 'New Testament Apocalyptic in Recent Interpretation', *Interpretation* 25 (1971) pp. 419ff.

7. J. Christiaan Beker, *Paul the Apostle: the Triumph of God in Life and Thought* (Philadelphia: Fortress Press, 1980) pp. 135–7. Beker summarises the schemes of Philip Vielhauer, 'Introduction to Apocalypses and Related Subjects', in E. Hennecke, *New Testament Apocrypha*, ed. W. Schneemelcher, 2 vols (Philadelphia: Westminster Press, 1963–65) vol. 2, pp. 581–607, and Klaus Koch, *The Rediscovery of Apocalyptic: a Polemical Work on a Neglected Area of Biblical Studies and Its Damaging Effects on Theology and Philosophy*, trans. Margaret Kohl (London: SCM, 1972) pp. 18–35. For other recent discussions, see Christopher Rowland, *The Open Heaven*, esp. pp. 7ff., 'What is Apocalyptic?' and J. J. Collins (ed.), *Apocalypse: the Morphology of a Genre*, *Semeia* 14 (1979).

8. Commentaries are the best guide. Besides *Peake's Commentary on the Bible* and *The Jerome Biblical Commentary*, see for instance John Sweet, *Revelation*; J. Massynberde Ford, *The Anchor Bible: Revelation* (New York: Doubleday, 1975); G. R. Beasley-Murray, *The Book of Revelation*, The New Century Bible Commentary (London: Marshall, Morgan & Scott, 1974); L. Morris, *Revelation* (London: Tyndale Press, 1969); G. B. Caird, *The Revelation of St. John the Divine*, New Testament Commentaries (London: A. & C. Black, 1966).

9. Klaus Koch, *The Rediscovery of Apocalyptic*, p. 26: 'The book of Revelation seems a unique exception. This *pseudonymity* is a much discussed but not convincingly explained phenomenon.' Also, St. John regards his role as prophetic (22:7). See Christopher Rowland, *The Open Heaven*, p. 351: 'The identification of a typical apocalypse, both in form and content, with the prophetic word of John of Patmos is an indication that we are dealing here with two related types of religious experience.'

10. Austin Farrer, *A Rebirth of Images*, p. 36. Subsequent references to this book are cited in the text.

11. M.-E. Boismard, *L'Apocalypse* (Paris: Cert, 1956).

12. John Wick Bowman, 'The Revelation of John: Its Dramatic Structure and Message', *Interpretation* 9 (1955) pp. 440ff.

13. André Feuillet, *The Apocalypse*, trans. Thomas E. Crane (New York: Alba House, 1965) pp. 54–62.

14. C. E. Douglas, *The Mystery of the Kingdom: an Attempt to Interpret the Revelation of S. John the Divine by the Method of Literary Criticism* (London: The Faith Press, 1915) pp. 7ff.

15.   John Sweet, *Revelation*, pp. 52–4 sets this out in summary form.

16.   In the section now following, I am indebted to a number of sources in
      some rather broad ways which defy detailed documentation. Austin
      Farrer's theories of 'interpolated visions' and cancelled conclusions are
      carefully worked through his text, and seem to me to describe John's
      technique very well, though I do not follow Farrer all the way. William A.
      Beardslee, *Literary Criticism of the New Testament* (Philadelphia:
      Fortress Press, 1970) p. 59ff., sees Revelation as combining 'a cyclic sense
      of repetition with a powerful thrust forward', punctuated by 'interludes',
      or anticipations of the perfection to come; Ibon T. Beckwith, *The
      Apocalypse of John* (Michigan: Baker Book House, 1979) pp. 216ff. *et
      passim*, notices the deliberate interruptions of orderly sequences and
      insertions of passages anticipating the end; John Sweet, *Revelation*,
      stresses the warnings against complacency, and detects various
      rhetorical devices for reminding us of its dangers. My notes acknowledge
      specific indebtedness to these authors, among others, but their general
      picture of how Revelation keeps us guessing by strategies of disruption
      and anticipation pervades my own account.

17.   See Farrer, *A Rebirth of Images*, pp. 40, 53.

18.   On the 'little scroll' and the prophetic call, see Ibon T. Beckwith, *The
      Apocalypse of John* (Michigan: Baker Book House, 1979, first published
      1919) p. 575; George Eldon Ladd, *A Commentary on the Revelation of St.
      John* (Michigan: William B. Eerdmans, 1972) p. 146, says that eating the
      little scroll is assimilating the prophetic message. On the metaphoric
      eating and measuring, see Farrer, *A Rebirth of Images*, pp. 43–4.

19.   The mysterious two witnesses suggest Moses and Elijah, who were to
      return as forerunners of the Messiah (Dt. 18:15; Mal. 3:22–4); also, at
      least two witnesses were necessary for valid testimony (Dt. 19:15), as the
      Gospel of John reminds us (8:17). See T. F. Glasson, *The Revelation of
      John* (Cambridge University Press, 1965) p. 66. For theories associating
      the two witnesses with the two lampstands, the church and the martyrs,
      see the summary in G. R. Beasley-Murray, *The Book of Revelation*,
      pp. 177ff.

20.   See John Sweet, *Revelation*, p. 190.

21.   Farrer points this out in *A Rebirth of Images*, pp. 54ff., and draws
      attention to the long drawn-out appendix to the brief vials section,
      balancing it with the other sevenfold sections.

22.   See John Sweet, *Revelation*, p. 249.

23.   See Edward Schillebeeckx, *Christ. The Experience of Jesus as Lord*,
      trans. John Bowden (New York: Crossroad, 1983) p. 455ff., for allusions
      to Psalm 90:4, where 1000 years is a day of creation, and to two early
      Jewish messianic conceptions of the final time of salvation, summarised
      below.

24.   The following summary draws broadly from the commentaries and
      studies mentioned in this chapter. Because the general principles are
      widely shared I do not document the sources in detail.

25.   Gematria, the ascription of numbers to letters, gives 666 for the Hebrew
      form of 'Neron Caesar'. The Latin form of the name, written 'Nero Caesar'
      (that is, without the Greek 'n'), gives 616. The best manuscript tradition

cites the number of the beast as 666, but some manuscripts have 616.

26. A. C. Charity, *Events and their Afterlife: the Dialectics of Christian Typology in the Bible and Dante* (Cambridge University Press, 1966). Page numbers are cited in the text.

27. The celestial woman's connections to Roman, Greek, Egyptian and Babylonian mythology are summarised by G. R. Beasley-Murray, *Revelation*, pp. 191–7. See also T. F. Glasson, *The Revelation of John* (Cambridge University Press, 1965) pp. 72ff., especially on the myth of Apollo and Leto; André Feuillet, *The Apocalypse*, trans. Thomas E. Crane (New York: Alba House, 1965) pp. 109ff.

28. This might also be a parody of the two witnesses, as Sweet says, *Revelation*, p. 125.

29. See C. G. Jung, *Answer to Job*, p. 168 *et passim*, on the fear of God. Jung also notices the impersonality and images of rigidity (p. 145), as does Amos Wilder, 'The Rhetoric of Ancient and Modern Apocalyptic', pp. 441ff.

30. See Anthony Tyrrell Hanson, *The Wrath of the Lamb* (London: SPCK, 1957) esp. pp. 159ff.; Martin Hengel, *Victory Over Violence*, trans. David E. Green (London: SPCK, 1975).

31. This is suggested by A. T. Hanson, *The Wrath of the Lamb*, p. 167: *hromphaia* is used six times, and *machaira* three times in reference to the swords of men. 'We are forbidden therefore to take *hromphaia* in a literal sense. It refers to the judgement of the Messiah; as we shall see, this is the judgement of the Cross. John uses *hromphaia* not *machaira* by way of indicating that the Messiah's judgement is something different from the judgement of men.'

32. Ibid. Page numbers are cited in the text.

33. Martin Hengel, *Victory Over Violence*. Page numbers are indicated in the text.

34. Thomas F. Torrance, *The Apocalypse Today* (London: James Clarke, 1960) p. 130.

35. Adela Yarbro Collins, *Crisis and Catharsis: the Power of the Apocalypse* (Philadelphia: Westminster Press, 1984). Page numbers are cited in the text.

Index